THE COTR HANDBOOK

A Five-Step Process for Stronger Organizational Performance

By Steven Stryker and Don Philpott

Government Training Inc.™

Published by
Government Training Inc. ™
www.GovernmentTrainingInc.com

About the Publisher – Government Training Inc. ™

Government Training Inc. provides worldwide training, publishing and consulting to government agencies and contractors that support government in areas of business and financial management, acquisition and contracting, physical and cyber security and grant writing. Our management team and instructors are seasoned executives with demonstrated experience in areas of Federal, State, Local and DoD needs and mandates.

For more information on the company, its publications and professional training, go to www. GovernmentTrainingInc.com.

This book has drawn heavily on the authoritative materials published by the a wide range of federal agencies including the Federal Emergency Management Agency (FEMA), the Department of Homeland Security (DHS), the Government Accountability Office (GAO), the General Services Administration (GSA), and Headquarters, Department of the Army. These materials are in the public domain, but accreditation has been given both in the text and in the reference section if you need additional information.

The author and publisher have taken great care in the preparation of this handbook, but make no expressed or implied warranty of any kind and assume no responsibility for errors or omissions. No liability is assumed for incidental or consequential damages in connection with or arising out of the use of the information or recommendations contained herein.

CONTENTS

About the authors

Steven Stryker

Steven Stryker is a professional trainer and consultant. He provides custom-tailored, just-in-time training, facilitating and consulting services to enhance the successful performance of federal acquisitions, programs and projects. He also has supported the lifecycle process of program and project success. Mr. Stryker continues to meet the challenge of successful performance acquisition implementation in a "cradle to grave" process—as a primary achievement of OMB & agency Acquisition Policy. Based on previous efforts with the DHS, EPA, Treasury, HHS as well as DOL, DOI, DOT, GSA, NIH, HUD, Justice, Commerce, USDA, GPO, Army, Air Force & Navy as well as government-focused firms, the results have demonstrated a categorical improvement in more effectively fulfilling the client's requirements through saved time, money and reduced problems, while obtaining higher-quality performance and outputs.

Mr. Stryker is a Certified Trainer through DAU and FAI to meet the learning competencies of the FAC-COTR and FAC-P/PM professional development programs from the Office of Federal Procurement Policy.

Mr. Stryker has authored three books: Plan to Succeed: A Guide to Strategic Planning, Guide to Successful Consulting, and Principles and Practices of Professional Consulting.

Mr. Stryker is co-author of The COTR Handbook: Effective Catalyst For Stronger Organizational Performance to be published by Government Training Inc. in 2010.

Over the last three years, Mr. Stryker has been a requested speaker and presenter at a number of conferences and seminars on Performance Based topics (with a focus on enhancing performance application and accountability). The Conference sponsors include: The Performance Institute, The Government Contracting Institute, FOSE, Market Access, NCMA, Council for Excellence in Government and HHS.

Don Philpott

Don Philpott is editor of International Homeland Security, a quarterly journal for homeland security professionals, and has been writing, reporting and broadcasting on international events, trouble spots and major news stories for more than 40 years. For 20 years he was a senior correspondent with Press Association -Reuters, the wire service, and traveled the world on assignments including Northern Ireland, Lebanon, Israel, South Africa and Asia.

He writes for magazines and newspapers in the United States and Europe and is a contributor to radio and television programs on security and other issues. He is the author of more than 90 books on a wide range of subjects and has had more than 5,000 articles printed in publications around the world. His most recent books are Terror - Is America Safe?, The Wounded Warrior Handbook, The Workplace Violence Prevention Handbook, and Public School Emergency Preparedness and Crisis Management. He is a member of the National Press Club.

"For my son, Micah, who continues to show me that strong effort is best done with as much focus on who as on what!"

Steven C. Stryker, Co-Author

INTRODUCTION AND THE FIVE STEP PROCESS

A. Why the "need" for a COTR?

Federal contract spending on goods and services topped $360 billion in 2008 – $160 billion more than in 2000. So federal contracting is clearly an effective and efficient way to do the government's work, but there is always room for improvement.

"The billions of dollars that federal agencies spend annually to purchase products and services from contractors is a testament to the fact that the government finds contracting to be an appropriate and effective way to accomplish a significant part of its work."

A. 1. U.S. Merit Systems Protection Board

"While there may be disagreement over what is contracted and why, everyone can agree that contracts must be developed and managed well to ensure positive contract outcomes —deliverables that meet government requirements for quality, completeness, timeliness and cost."

Contracting — also called procurement or acquisition — is a significant and complex government activity involving government employees at all levels and from a number of different occupations. Contracting varies in complexity depending on a number of factors including the type of the contract and the agency procurement process, systems, and culture within which contracting is conducted. Achieving positive contract outcomes (in terms of timeliness, quality, completeness, and cost of deliverables) depends on the contracting rules and procedures used, how well government employees implement them, and ultimately on the actual performance of the contractor. (See Attachment One at the end of this book for a Glossary of Acquisition and Contract Terms.)

Contracting is the primary method federal government agencies use to purchase products or services from sources outside the agency. The primary set of regulations governing contracting is the Federal Acquisition Regulation (FAR). According to the FAR, the "vision for the Federal Acquisition System (FAS) is to deliver on a timely basis the best value product or service to the customer, while maintaining the public's trust and fulfilling public policy objectives."

Government agencies can contract for, purchase, or acquire products and services from private sector entities, other federal agencies, state or local government organizations, or other non-profit organizations, although it is perhaps more common to think of contracting as occurring primarily between the government and the private sector.

One of the key government players in ensuring the acquisition process is carried out well is the Contracting Officer's Technical Representative (COTR). COTRs sit in the center of a multi-pronged acquisition process, with stakeholders distributed across departmental lines, as well as within and outside the federal government. Several changes have occurred to present COTRs with a vibrant, challenging acquisition environment in which to contribute.

[Note: Agencies and departments have different acronyms to describe the Contracting Officer's Technical Representative (COTR). Other titles used are: Contracting Officer's Representative (COR), Government Technical Representative (GTR), Project Officer (PO) and Government Technical Evaluator (GTE). For purposes of this book, COTR is used throughout.]

Acquisition reforms, technology-driven changes in work processes and communication, competition for acquisition work, and the focus on leveraging acquisition to achieve mission-relevant outcomes are driving new ways of doing business in the federal government.

Historically, agencies and acquisition professionals have approached procurement and contracting from a process-based perspective. Legislation was then enacted that affected the nature of tasks performed by the acquisition workforce. The 1993 Government Performance and Results Act, (GPRA), the 1994 Federal Acquisition Streamlining Act (FASA), and the 1996 Clinger-Cohen Act, moved the government toward acquiring services and products against established performance measures and outcomes.

A.2. Recent Trends and Concerns

In recent years, the dollar value of contracting has increased and the types of contracts have changed. In addition, there have been changes in the number of federal employees who are involved in contracting.

The work of the government has changed over time as technology has become a critical part of its everyday work and as we have shifted from an industrial- to a knowledge-based economy. These changes have caused agencies to procure an increasingly complex and costly array of products and services from contractors.

Along with tremendous growth in the amount of contracting is an increase in the proportion of contracts being used to purchase more complex products and services, and

in the proportion of contracts for services. The government no longer contracts for just office supplies, facility support, and production of ships, planes and other major weapon systems. Now the government uses contractors to provide complex management consulting (such as technology support and financial system development), and highly complex research and development services (such as for new defense and security systems based on advanced and yet-to-be-developed technologies). Indeed, in some contracts, the government works in partnership with the contractor to develop cutting-edge solutions to rapidly developing problems.

Ensuring that the government meets the public's interests in achieving successful contract outcomes requires that agencies have enough federal employees with the right skills and competencies to design and oversee contracts. The federal employees who work on contracts constitute a critical part of the government workforce responsible for billions of dollars of government resources. It is important, therefore, to assess the degree to which these employees are being effectively and efficiently managed to carry out their contracting work.

Two groups of federal employees bear the primary responsibility for developing and managing contracts. One group consists of the contracting professionals (such as COs, contracting specialists, and purchasing agents) who are involved in the business aspects of contracting. They ensure that the government selects a contracting approach that is appropriate for a specific purchasing need, that the contracting process ensures sufficient fair and open competition, and that the process operates ethically and according to law and regulation. The other group of federal employees with a critical role in contracting consists of the program and technical employees who provide the technical expertise to ensure that contracts meet the requirements of the government. While COs handle the business aspects of contracting, COTRs develop the contract's technical requirements and determine if a contractor meets them. For example, the engineers and scientists who serve as COTRs develop and oversee the work of contractors working on major weapons, cleaning up nuclear sites, and applying environmental regulations.

Well-formulated contracting rules and procedures and superior COs alone are not sufficient to ensure that contracts meet the government's technical and programmatic needs. After all, the best managed contract from a business point of view won't be successful if it does not result in products and services that meet the government's needs. Indeed, the complexity of the contracting process and the variety and complexity of the products and services being purchased mean that it is unlikely and unreasonable that one person can possess the technical and contracting expertise to effectively design and oversee successful contracts.

COTRs and COs work — or will work — hand-in-hand to develop and manage contracts that meet federal requirements for quality, timeliness, completeness, and cost.

Most of the work done assessing the employees involved in contracting has been focused on COs and other employees working on the business aspects of contracting. Unfortunately, while contracting has become more costly and more complex, the number of COs available to work on contracts has remained essentially the same. In response to this situation, various approaches have been proposed to improve the ability of the acquisition workforce to handle this increasing contracting workload. These approaches have focused on the strategic management and skill development primarily of COs.

Surprisingly little attention has been paid to COTRs who provide the technical and program expertise for developing the technical aspects of contracts and for overseeing the technical work of the contractor. These employees are critical to ensuring positive contract outcomes, and the technical aspects of their contracting work have become increasingly complex. In addition, COTRs may have added pressure to take on more responsibility for managing contracts because there are relatively fewer COs available to work on current contracts.

A.3. The Current Position

Today, acquisition contributors are responsible for the entire business cycle, from using relevant marketplace knowledge to inform strategy and planning activities to managing contractor performance and maintaining useful business relationships into the future. Successful acquisitions now require a fresh, results-oriented view of the process with acquisition professionals serving as business advisors to their respective agency stakeholders. A key guiding principle for any acquisition contributor is to develop a sound business solution that links short-and long-term goals. The COTR's role bridges the acquisition and program communities.

This handbook looks at the complex duties performed by COTRs and explains how best to carry them out in order to achieve a stronger organizational performance. The easy-to-follow Five Step Process explains the environment in which the COTR operates, how the COTR and other team players are selected, key skill areas required and how these are applied throughout the contracting process. Finally, we discuss how the COTR's influence can be extended through developing a career model, continuous training and expanding this to broader applications across other organizational activities. Throughout the book, we give case studies, checklists, exercises and advice designed to prepare you for the tasks in hand, motivate you to succeed, and inspire you to adopt best practices in order to achieve even more positive outcomes.

Facilitating COTR Excellence

Two mechanisms exist to facilitate excellent COTR performance and successful adoption of the business leadership role during contract lifecycles and beyond.

Clarify COTR Responsibilities Upfront

One clear method that contributes to COTR effectiveness is a clear understanding of what is expected of COTRs and how COTRs are to work with COs and other program and acquisition contributors. These contributors will make a concerted effort to clearly communicate norms surrounding "what a COTR does in his/her work group" upon nomination. Furthermore, ongoing actions (i.e., demonstrated behaviors) and words (i.e., communicated attitudes) will reaffirm norms, rather than conflict with norms. It is acknowledged that COTR responsibilities can vary depending on the unit, work group, division or agency. Executive-level leaders, in partnership with COTR supervisors, must set solid expectations about the COTR role. Resources are wasted when individuals form their own assumptions about the role in the absence of expectations. Clear communication can reinforce a strong culture around contracting in any government agency.

Integrate COTR Duties into Performance Management

Another valuable mechanism to facilitate COTR excellence is the creation of clear relationships between performing COTR duties and an individual's performance appraisal. Additionally, substantial power and reinforcement can be employed when COTR responsibilities are rewarded on an informal basis. As the CO (or other supervisor), actions you take to include COTR duties in documented performance appraisals, as well as informally in on-the-job recognition and rewards, will help ensure the COTR position is viewed as a vital responsibility.

A.3.a. The Legal Framework

The framework includes the "guiding principles" and the policies and procedures contained in the Federal Acquisition Regulation (FAR), Part 11. These "guiding principles" are:

Satisfy the customer (agency program or program manager) in terms of cost, quality, and timeliness; for example:

☐ Maximize the use of commercial products and services

☐ Use contractors who have performed well in the past and have the current ability to perform

☐ Promote competition

☐ Minimize administrative operating costs

☐ Conduct business with integrity, openness, and fairness

☐ Fulfill public policy objectives

The policies and procedures in the FAR also include more specifics on carrying out these guiding principles by discussing the type of contract, the level of competition, the pricing

structure, and how to gather and assess proposals. They also include information about how to alter the terms of a contract; the requirements for accountability, authority, and limitations on the actions of government employees involved in contracting; and how to resolve disputes between contractors and the government. Recently, the Services Acquisition Reform Act of 2003 (SARA) formally defined acquisition to include requirements definition, measurement of contractor performance, and technical management direction, in addition to traditional contracting activities.

There are also specific standards of conduct, ethical guidelines, and integrity requirements established in the FAR to ensure that contracting is conducted fairly and openly, with no real (or apparent) conflict of interest, and in the interests of the government. These ethical requirements cover issues, such as the content and timing of information exchanges with contractors, employment offers or acceptances between government employees and the contractor (or contractor employees with the government), and bribes or gratuities to government personnel. All of these principles and practices are couched today in a Certification Program that any COTR must achieve. In essence, the program mandates initial training prior to performance of COTR duties and subsequent professional development to sustain and further his or her capabilities.

A.3.b. The Team

No one person has all of the necessary skills for successful contract management. It requires a team, with each member having specialized expertise and responsibilities. The COTR is a key member of this team. Delegated authorities to act on behalf of the CO include:

☐ Assisting the contractor interpret technical requirements

☐ Recommending changes in contract terms to the CO

☐ Monitoring and evaluating contractor performance

☐ Reviewing contractor invoices

☐ Recommending corrective actions

☐ Inspecting and accepting contract deliverables

The "acquisition team" consists of all participants in the acquisition process including government employees ranging from senior agency leaders to administrative and support employees. Key players:

Program managers know generally what is needed by their organization and why, and are responsible for certifying that there is a legitimate government need for the products or services to be covered by the contract. In addition, program managers authorize the program funds to pay for the item. For example, the director of a research center can determine a need for new testing equipment and provide the funds to pay for that equipment. Program managers are the customers and their needs drive the procurement process.

Procurement professionals, primarily COs, serve as the government's "agent" and are responsible for the business aspects of the contract and for ensuring adherence to procurement laws and the regulations contained in the FAR. In contracting, the "law of agency" refers to one party (the principal) who appoints another party (the agent) to enter into a business or contractual relationship with a third party (the contractor). The government is the principal, the CO the agent, and the contractor is the third party. The authorities of the CO, as well as the limits to that authority, are spelled out for the CO in a certificate of appointment, more commonly referred to as a "warrant." The CO usually works in the procurement office rather than the program office and provides the expertise on the business aspects of the contracting process. The FAR provides criteria for the selection of a CO based on the complexity and dollar value of the acquisitions (contracts) to be assigned and the candidate's experience, training, education, business acumen, judgment, character, and reputation. He or she is responsible for ensuring performance of all necessary contracting actions, compliance with the terms of the contract, and safeguarding the interests of the United States in its contractual relationships. Legally, it is the CO, as the government's agent, who is responsible for ensuring the integrity of the contracting process. The CO must retain certain contracting responsibilities and tasks, but can delegate certain other contracting responsibilities and tasks to others. For example, COs may, but rarely do, possess sufficient expertise in the functional area of the contract to manage or oversee the contract's technical aspects. Therefore, it is common for the CO to delegate the technical oversight and/or administrative management aspects of the contracting process to the COTR. Delegation of technical responsibilities to the COTR is also important in small agencies where one or two COs cannot possess all of the technical expertise required to develop and oversee all of the agency's contracts. In reality, a small agency may have a need to purchase nearly as many different products and services as a large agency.

The COTRs usually work in the program office — the functional organization that needs a product or service provided by the contract. COTRs provide the technical and program expertise necessary to develop and manage the contract. Procurement policy specifically includes COTRs and other equivalent positions as part of the minimal definition of the acquisition workforce. COTRs are usually selected by or with the advice of the program office. In addition, COTRs only have authority to work on contracts to the degree they have been formally delegated such authority by the CO. While the FAR provides guidance and

criteria for the selection of COs, it provides no such guidance or criteria for the selection of COTRs. Therefore, the process for COTR selection (and assignment) occurs at the agency level. Agencies may select COTRs based on their expertise in a technical or functional area, experience, training, knowledge of contracting rules or procedures, the complexity or dollar value of the contract or other pertinent factors. (See Attachments Four and Five, http://www.governmenttraininginc.com/The-COTR-Handbook.asp)

The Contractors who provide the products and services to the government are also members of the acquisition team. Contractors endeavor to fulfill the contract by providing the deliverables stipulated and to make a profit in doing so. Poorly performing contractors will deliver less than optimal contract outcomes.

A.3.c. The Agency Role

Factors, such as how an agency is organized, how much contracting it does, and how complex are the items being purchased, affect the complexity of the agency's contracting activities. Agencies have considerable flexibility in adjusting their contracting function to best suit their organization and specific contracting needs. For example, small agencies that do little contracting may find it most effective and efficient to centralize the procurement function in one person within the office of administration. This one CO would then conduct procurement activities as requested by program managers throughout the agency. Depending on the level of technical complexity of the product or service being purchased, a technical person in the affected program area may be assigned as a COTR to participate in contract development and management.

In contrast, large agencies, or those that make many complex and costly purchases, may have a multi-person procurement office within their office of administration. Large agencies also may find it more effective and efficient to decentralize the procurement function along major program or bureau designations. Large agencies may also use "integrated project teams" (IPTs) composed of a number of professionals from the procurement, program, technical, finance, supply, and accounting fields who share responsibility for developing and managing a particular contract. The CO usually leads this IPT, and the COTR will ultimately ensure that the requirements are met.

A.3.d. Emphasis on Innovation

Agencies and their individual employees who are involved in contracting have considerable flexibility to make decisions that have a huge potential impact on a contract's outcomes. According to the FAR, each agency — or involved agency employee — will assume that any policy, procedure, strategy, or practice that is in the best interest of the government

and not prohibited by law, executive order, or regulation that is otherwise consistent with law, is permitted under the FAR, Part 20. Rather than assume that an action is forbidden if it is not specifically authorized, agencies and procurement personnel will assume they can take any action that is not specifically prohibited, as long as it does not violate the law. For example, an agency may use a new or unique approach to purchasing a particular product or service as long as law does not prohibit the action. They do not have to refrain from using a new approach just because the approach has not been specifically described or authorized in the FAR. Because of the wide latitude of discretion given by the FAR, the judgments made by procurement employees can make the difference between a successful contract and one that does not meet the requirements of the government.

A.4. The Contracting Process and the Role of COTRs

Contracting is usually carried out in three stages — contract planning, contract formation, and contract management. The contract planning stage begins when a program manager or executive (the contract customer) decides that the government needs a product and/or a service and ends with determining the terms and conditions of the solicitation (the notice to contractors to apply for a government contract). The contract formation stage begins with the formal solicitation for offers or bids and ends with a signed contract awarded to the contractor with the best proposal. The contract management stage begins with the initiation of work on the contract and ends with contract closeout or termination.

Contract Planning
- Determine need
- Analyze requirement
- Determine extent of competition
- Source selection planning
- Solicitation terms and conditions

Contract Formation
- Solicitation of offers
- Bid evaluation or proposal evaluation
- Contract award

Contract Management

- ◆ Initiation of work and contract administration
- ◆ Inspection and quality assurance
- ◆ Contractor HR management, payment and accounting
- ◆ Modification and special terms
- ◆ Contract closeout or termination

COTRs may be Designated as Follows:

Level 1 - This level is for contracts of relatively low complexity and low contract management risk. Indicators for Level 1 are total estimated dollar values between $100,000 and

$1,000,000 and fixed-price contract type or straightforward cost-type contracts with relatively uncomplicated performance monitoring features. (See Attachment Two, http://www.governmenttraininginc. com/The-COTR-Handbook.asp, for a discussion of the types of contracts.)

Level 2 - This level is for contracts of moderate to high complexity and contract management risk. Indicators are total estimated dollar values greater than $1,000,000 and less than $10,000,000, fixed-price or cost-type contracts, particularly those that have award fee, incentive fee, or other complex contract performance controls to monitor and administer.

Level 3 - This level is for contracts of moderate to high complexity and contract management risk. Indicators are total estimated dollar values greater than $10,000,000 or for major systems contracts. For major systems contracts, the COTR shall ensure that clear lines of authority and responsibility are established with the program manager.

A.5. Regulatory Aspects of Managing

Agencies need to fulfill the regulatory aspects of managing COTRs to include formal delegation of authority, improved COTR training, and strategic management of the COTR workforce. Agencies also need to improve the day-to-day management of COTRs. These day-to-day issues include improving COTR selection and assignment, ensuring COTRs begin early in the contracting process, ensuring COTRs perform critical pre-award technical contracting tasks, ensuring COTRs have enough time to do their contract management work, rating COTRs on the performance of their contracting work, and considering the other federal employees who affect the COTR's contracting work. Fulfilling the regulatory requirements for managing COTRs more effectively, day-to-day are significantly related to more positive contract outcomes. Taking these steps will help ensure that the over $360 billion spent on contracting achieves effective and efficient results for the taxpayer.

A.6. Contract Administration and its Impacts on COTRs

Contract administration involves those activities performed by government officials after a contract has been awarded to determine how well the government and the contractor performed to meet the requirements of the contract. It encompasses all dealings between the government and the contractor from the time the contract is awarded until the work has been completed and accepted or the contract terminated, payment has been made, and disputes have been resolved. As such, contract administration constitutes that primary part of the procurement process that ensures the government gets what it paid for.

In contract administration, the focus is on obtaining supplies and services, of requisite quality, on time, and within budget. While the legal requirements of the contract are determinative of the proper course of action of government officials in administering a contract, the exercise of skill and judgment is often required in order to protect effectively the public interest.

The specific nature and extent of contract administration varies from contract to contract. It can range from the minimum acceptance of a delivery and payment to the contractor to extensive involvement by program, audit and procurement officials throughout the contract term. Factors influencing the degree of contract administration include the nature of the work, the type of contract, and the experience and commitment of the personnel involved. Contract administration starts with developing clear, concise performance-based statements of work (SOWs) to the extent possible and preparing a contract administration plan that cost-effectively measures the contractor's performance and provides documentation to pay accordingly.

The government is becoming increasingly aware of the importance of proper contract administration in ensuring the maximum return on our contract dollars. The COTR plays a critical role in affecting the outcome of the contract administration process. The technical administration of government contracts is an essential activity. It is absolutely essential that those entrusted with the duty to ensure that the government gets all that it has bargained for must be competent in the practices of contract administration and aware of and faithful to the contents and limits of their delegation of authority from the CO. The COTR functions as the "eyes and ears" of the CO, monitoring technical performance and reporting any potential or actual problems to the CO. It is imperative that the COTR stays in close communication with the CO, relaying any information that may affect contractual commitments and requirements.

The COTR's contract administration duties can be simple or complex and time-consuming, depending on the type of contract, contractor performance, and the nature of

the work. Reducing the use of cost-reimbursement contracts and relying more on fixed-price, performance-based contracts will allow the COTR to work smarter in carrying out contract administration. The primary objective of the contract administration process is to establish best practices that agencies can use to improve contract administration to ensure responsiveness to customers and best value to taxpayers. Improving contract administration practices will help to achieve excellence in contractor performance so that the government receives goods and services on time, and within budget.

Distinction between Acquisition and Assistance

Acquisition encompasses the processes the government employs to obtain supplies or services through contracts or similar instruments, such as purchase orders and basic ordering agreements. The acquisition process almost always results in a contract. This flows from an offer made by a bidder or offeror and an acceptance of that offer by a CO on behalf of the government.

Assistance describes the process by which the government transfers money, property, services, or anything of value to recipients to accomplish a public purpose of support or stimulation authorized by federal statute. The instruments used to carry out the assistance process are grants and cooperative agreements. These instruments usually result from an application being made by a recipient and an acceptance being put into effect by a grants officer on behalf of the government.

In general, the acquisition process is used when the purpose of the proposed instrument to be executed is "the acquisition by purchase, lease, or barter of supplies or services for the direct benefit or use of the federal government." This quotation comes from the Federal Grant and Cooperative Agreement Act of 1977 (PL 95-224), whose purpose is to ensure that government contracts and grants are used appropriately.

B. Current organizational performance challenges

B.1. Weaknesses

Several weaknesses have been identified in contract administration practices used by civilian agencies. The principal problem is that contracting officials often allocate more time to awarding contracts rather than administering existing contracts. This often leads to problems in contractor performance, cost overruns, and delays in receiving goods and services. Several other deficiencies have been noted, such as unclear roles and responsibilities of the COTR, excessive backlog in contract closeout and incurred costs audits, improperly trained officials performing contract oversight, unclear statements of work that hinder contractor performance, and inadequate guidance on voucher processing and contract closeout. These weaknesses were identified in reports issued by the Office of Management and Budget, namely, the "Report on Civilian Agencies Contracting Practices" (1992), the "Report on Service Contracting Practices" (1993), and the "Interagency Report on Civilian Agency Contract Administration" (1993).

B.2. Development of COTRs

To address these weaknesses, the FAC-COTR Certification Requirements have been developed to outline the basis for COTR professional development. Training is certainly a major part of this activity. COTRs with at least moderate training in several contracting areas, as well as in their technical area and in general competencies, experienced better contract outcomes. Most formal training (or on-the-job training) covers more than one topic or competency. Therefore, it is practical to think that moderately increasing the amount of training in selected groups of topics could be an effective and efficient approach to COTR training. Agencies will select the topics by assessing the competencies of their COTRs (and by asking the COTRs for their own perceptions of their training needs) to ensure that training is provided in the most appropriate topic areas.

To achieve a particular contract outcome, such as reduced contract cost or improved quality, an agency may choose to focus its training on those contract topics most related to the areas needing improvement. However, given that many training areas have an impact on at least one contract outcome, agencies may also opt to use established courses on contracting that cover a wide range of areas. If using established courses has generally been successful in the past, there is no need to develop specialized courses unless there is a particularly compelling issue (e.g., contract quality or cost) to resolve. Knowing more about how training can affect contract outcomes is helpful to ensuring that COTR training is effective and efficient.

Technical training is related to better contract outcomes, making it critical that agencies ensure that their COTRs are able to keep abreast of changes in their technical area of expertise, especially in the use of software and equipment used in the performance of their duties. A recent study found that most COTRs think that computer-based training (CBT) is ineffective. Most effective is on-the-job training followed by classroom training whether agency or vendor-provided.

COTRs seem to find that training in which they can interact with their colleagues or other participants in the contracting process is more useful than CBT or self-paced learning. Contracting professionals need to discuss and exchange ideas/solutions with a live person, hopefully well qualified, in order to return to the office and be more effective as a result of the knowledge gained in class.

Also, the recent Office of Management and Budget (OMB) FAC-COTR policy requires agencies to identify and strategically manage their COTRs to ensure that they have enough employees with the right skills to effectively develop and manage the technical aspects of

contracts. In addition, GAO advises agencies to conduct strategic human capital planning that includes integration of acquisition workforce data.

COTRs comprise a critical workforce for the government generally, and especially for agencies that rely on contracts to perform or support a significant portion of their mission. As a critical workforce, COTRs will specifically be included in agencies' strategic human capital plans. These human capital plans will cover issues, such as how many COTRs agencies need now and in the future, and what competencies those COTRs will have. Agencies also need to know who their current COTRs are, where they are located, and what competencies they currently have. Agencies also need to be able to compare what they need and what they have, and develop plans to alleviate any shortcomings in COTR numbers and competencies, particularly since one-third of COTRs will soon be eligible to retire. Finally, even though few government employees are hired with the job title of COTR, the performance of these "other duties as assigned" need to be included in the periodic personnel evaluations.

The Office of Federal Procurement Policy (OFPP) Act required that agencies track COTRs and COTR training. It is difficult, if not impossible, to strategically manage a workforce without this information. Some agencies have developed automated systems to track COTR training and some have systems that tracked where COTRs worked. Many other agencies do not have readily accessible data systems for tracking who their COTRs are, what training they have, and where they work. Some agencies said that identifying and locating their COTRs would require going through, by hand, paper files on every current contract. Agencies must overcome the fundamental problem of identifying and locating their COTRs if they are to effectively manage them as a critical workforce.

B.3. COTRs Involvement in Acquisition Lifecycle

Various day-to-day managerial actions can ensure that COTRs have the structure and management support they need from their agencies. COTRs who believed that they were selected and assigned by their agencies based on their functional/technical expertise and their knowledge of contracting also reported better contract outcomes. However, many agencies do not have specific guidance or criteria for selecting COTRs. Because of the importance of COTR work, it is advisable for agencies to establish more formal criteria for COTR selection rather than leave this process to chance. In addition, our data indicate that when COTRs begin their involvement on a particular contract early in the contracting process, they report better contract outcomes than if they begin their work after the contract was awarded. When COTRs are involved early in the process, they are better able to ensure that the contract clearly sets out the technical requirements. This helps the COTR manage the contract once it is awarded.

When our COTRs were involved in both the pre-award and post-award technical tasks of the contract, they reported better contract outcomes. In addition, when COTRs perceived they had enough time for their contracting work, they reported better outcomes. Interestingly, spending a larger proportion of their time working on contracts did not lead directly to reports of improved contract outcomes. It was the COTRs' perception of having enough time that was the issue. This means that agencies need to communicate with COTRs about their time needs and then help COTRs balance their contracting and non-contracting work to ensure COTRs can devote sufficient time to their contracts. COTRs who report that their agencies rate them on the performance of their COTR duties also reported better contract outcomes. In addition, COTRs' interactions with COs, agency managers at all levels, and with other federal employees working on contracts affect how well they can do their jobs. We found that when COTRs had positive perceptions of these groups — i.e., perceptions that these groups were competent, ethical, and supportive of the COTR — COTRs also reported better contracting outcomes.

Agencies have the primary responsibility for ensuring that COTRs are managed well. And, within agencies, several groups of people share responsibility for managing COTRs. These groups include COs, COTR supervisors, program or line managers, senior agency leaders, agency procurement managers, and agency human resources (HR) managers. COTRs can also take certain actions to help themselves perform their contracting work more effectively. In addition, government-wide policymakers have an important role in determining effective policies and establishing government-wide systems that are more efficient than agency specific ones.

Summary and MSPB Recommendations

When COTRs are formally delegated their authority to perform contracting work by the CO, they report better contract outcomes. When COTRs have sufficient (initial and repeated) training in contracting, technical, and general competencies presented in the right way, contract outcomes are better. Agencies must manage COTRs strategically to ensure they have enough COTRs with the right skills to handle their current and future contracting needs. These regulatory requirements exist for a reason, and agencies will treat them as more than pro forma requirements. To that end, since there is only one COTR delegated per contract, it also makes sense that no COTR be managing more than a small number of contracts at any one time.

Contract outcomes are more positive when agencies:

♦ Formally delegate authority to the COTR

♦ Ensure that COTRs get the right training at the right time in the right way

♦ Manage COTRs strategically by identifying, locating, and tracking COTRs and their competencies

♦ Contract outcomes are better when agencies:

- Select/assign COTRs based on established criteria including their technical expertise and knowledge of contracting
- Ensure that COTRs start work on a contract early in the contracting process
- Ensure that COTRs more frequently perform contracting tasks related to the technical aspects of the contract
- Ensure that COTRs have enough time for their contracting-related work
- Rate COTRs on the performance of their contracting duties
- Consider the other federal employees who affect the COTRs contracting work

C. What COTRs can do to strengthen achieving these challenges

COTRs, agencies, and government-wide policymakers can all take steps to improve the ability of COTRs to do their jobs effectively. While COTR management is fundamentally an agency responsibility, there are actions that COTRs themselves can take to improve their own ability to manage contracts better. In addition, there are actions that policymakers can take to help agencies manage COTRs better, thus helping ensure a more effective government-wide COTR workforce.

Responsibilities of the COTR vary with the type of contract and complexity of the acquisition. Each contract must be treated on an individual basis, because it may place responsibilities on the COTR unique to that contract. Normally, a COTR has the responsibility/authority to monitor all aspects of the day-to-day administration of a contract except issues that deal with "time and money." Formally said, a COTR does not have the authority to make any commitments or changes that affect price, quality, quantity, delivery, or other terms and conditions of the contract. Specifically, they cannot do any of the following: make any agreement with the contractor requiring the obligation of public funds (they cannot sign any contract, including delivery orders, purchase orders, or modify a contract, or in any way obligate payment of funds by the government); encourage the contractor by words, actions, or a failure to act to undertake new work or an extension of existing work beyond the contract period; interfere with the contractor's management prerogative by "supervising" contractor employees or otherwise directing their work efforts; authorize a contractor to obtain property for use under a contract; allow government property accountable under one contract to be used in the performance of another contract; issue instructions to the contractor to start or stop work; order or accept goods or services not expressly required by the contract; and discuss acquisition plans or provide any advance information that might give one contractor an advantage over another contractor in forthcoming procurements.

While the COTR limitations can be simply stated in a letter, in the real world assuring that the COTR does not exceed the authority granted is much more complex. In the course of performing COTR responsibilities, situations may result in an implied change to the contract which, in turn, may impact the delivery schedule, funds, or other areas outside the authority of the COTR. The following example illustrates that COTRs may exceed the scope of their authority by inaction or improper action.

Example: An individual is designated as COTR on a contract for the installation of equipment. The equipment is scheduled for delivery the next month. The COTR sets up a COTR file and places the file in the filing cabinet after noting the scheduled installation date on the calendar. The installation day arrives, and the contractor, as promised, arrives with the equipment. However, it cannot be installed because the COTR did not ensure that the government had done its part by installing an electrical outlet and raised floors. By inaction, the COTR has allowed a potential claim to be made for government-caused delay.

The importance of maintaining complete and orderly files cannot be overemphasized, and it is critical to transfer of responsibility if the COTR is changed during the term of the contract. As a matter of practice, the COTR holding discussions or conducting business with contractors shall prepare Memoranda for Record (MFRs) of meetings, trips, and telephone conversations relating to the contract. Each MFR, other similar records, and correspondence relating to the contract shall cite the contract number. A copy of all actions or correspondence shall be furnished to the CO and all other interested parties having a need to know.

Documents that may contain contractor proprietary data or other business-sensitive information will not be released outside the government without approval of the CO. Duplicate copies of file documents shall be destroyed as soon as they have served their purpose, but in no event shall such documents be retained for longer than one year after acceptance of the final deliverable under the contract. Records pertinent to unsettled claims for or against the United States, open investigations, cases under litigation, or similar matters shall be preserved until final clearance or settlement of the matters even though retention of these records may exceed a period longer than six years and three months after final payment.

D. Overview of ways and means to increase COTRs' success

☐ Maintain an arms-length relationship with the contractor.

☐ Keep the CO fully informed of any technical or contractual difficulties encountered during performance.

☐ Assure the CO that the contractor's performance meets the technical requirements, terms, and conditions of the contract.

☐ Inform the contractor of failures to comply with the technical requirements of the contract.

☐ Coordinate site entry for contractor personnel as needed.

☐ Ensure that any government-furnished property is available when needed and is being accounted for by the appropriate property personnel.

☐ Ensure that all required items, documentation, data, and/or reports are submitted as required by the contract.

☐ Evaluate proposals and participate in negotiations for contract modifications and claims, as requested by the CO.

☐ Review vouchers for cost-reimbursement type work and recommend approval/disapproval to the CO.

☐ Review and process invoices and vouchers in a timely manner in accordance with the Prompt Payment Act.

☐ Document decisions made and actions taken as the COTR.

☐ Maintain adequate records to sufficiently describe the performance of duties as COTR during contract performance.

☐ Provide the CO with a copy of any correspondence sent to the contractor.

☐ Conduct site visits at the location(s) where the work is being performed.

☐ Verify that required Dept. of Labor and Equal Employment Opportunity documents are posted in view of employees.

☐ Perform final inspection and acceptance of all work required under the contract.

The subsequent modules seek to expand and inter-relate the various aspects of a "COTR lifecycle." Each builds on the previous one to provide a clearer, practical understanding and capability to "walk the walk" well in carrying forth COTR responsibilities. They are:

Step One – Challenges to being a Successful COTR

Step Two – Getting the COTR Onboard

Step Three – Key Skill Areas

Step Four – COTR Applications

Step Five - Increasing Viable COTR Influence Implications

Key Agency Responsibilities for COTRs

Every day, agency supervisors and managers make decisions about COTRs that affect the ability of COTRs to do their work in developing and overseeing successful contracts. Agency procurement managers and HR managers also affect these decisions through the agency-wide policies they establish. The quality of all of these management decisions at all levels affects the ability of COTRs to do their contracting work, and in turn, affects the outcomes of the contract.

There are three important regulatory requirements for managing COTRs that affect the ability of COTRs to do their job effectively. First, since COTRs are considered acquisition personnel, agencies are required to train them to conduct their contracting duties. Second, according to the FAR, the CO must formally delegate contracting authority (for a contract) as responsibilities the COTR is to carry out. Third, agencies are required to strategically manage their COTR workforce to ensure they have enough COTRs with the right skills to manage their contracts now and in the future.

COTRs are required to have a formal delegation of authority from the CO before they can perform any contracting duties. This formal delegation, usually in the form of a letter or memorandum, assigns a COTR to a specific contract, states what the COTR can and must do, and what the COTR cannot do in relation to the contract. The delegation letter helps protect the agency and the COTR from adverse effects of acting beyond the scope of his or her authority, or acting without authority.

Step One – Challenges to being a Successful COTR

A. Situations that give rise to the COTR function

A COTR comes into play in the government when the acquisition process is used to stimulate competition, enter into contracts and buy needed items. The COTR's influence is to ensure that the technical portions of the acquisition lifecycle are carried out well as described below:

A. 1. Competition

Federal law defines acquisition methods and processes. Although these methods and processes differ substantially, they have in common the goal of enhancing competition in contracting. Full and open competition in federal contracting is the norm. Deviations from the norm are possible but often require careful justification and high-level approval. Maximum competition is usually desirable from a public policy perspective. It is also desirable because, if properly administered, competition in contracting will result in the timely delivery to the government of quality supplies and services at a reasonable cost. Acquisition can be looked at in two dimensions. One dimension describes the acquisition methods in terms of degree of competition. The other describes the different process activities involved in implementing a particular method.

A.2. Contract

A contract can be defined as an agreement between two or more parties consisting of a promise, or mutual promises, for breach of which the law gives a remedy, or the performance of which the law in some way recognizes as a duty. Unlike most social exchanges of promises, a contract establishes a binding legal relationship that obligates parties to keep their promises. In nearly all government contracts, one party is a "seller" obligated by the contract to provide supplies or services. The other party is the government, which, as the "buyer," is obligated to pay for those supplies or services. In government contracting, the bid or proposal is the offer. It is made by an offeror seeking to enter into a contract with the government. An Invitation for Bid (IFB) or a Request for Proposal (RFP) is not an offer. Rather these are

called solicitations and are used to communicate government requirements to prospective contractors and to solicit bids or proposals. There are other requirements for the formation of contracts. A contract must have a lawful purpose. It cannot violate a statute, for example. Contracts must be entered into by competent parties. They must be mentally and legally competent for the contract to be valid.

Contracts must have certainty of terms and conditions to be enforceable. Since courts have to rely on the meaning of the language of a contract to enforce it, this language must be clear and certain. SOWs, for example, must communicate clear requirements. Although non-government contracts may sometimes be oral, government contracts (including modifications) are always in writing. When the government, after bid opening or proposal evaluation and negotiation, chooses one bidder/offeror to contract with, it performs the act of acceptance. The consideration in government contracts is usually payment by the government and delivery of supplies or services by the contractor.

A.3. What is being purchased?

☐ Contracts are used when the agency needs to acquire supplies and such services as:

☐ Evaluation (including research of an evaluative nature) of the performance of government programs, projects, or grants initiated by the funding agency for its direct benefit

☐ Technical assistance rendered to the government or on behalf of the government to any third party, including recipients of grants and cooperative agreements

☐ Surveys, studies, and research that will provide information the government will use for its direct activities or will disseminate to the public

☐ Consulting services or professional services of all kinds, if provided to the government or to a third party on the government's behalf

☐ Training projects where the government selects the individuals or group to be trained or specifies the curriculum content (fellowship awards are excepted)

☐ Planning for government use

☐ Production of publications or audiovisual materials for the conduct of direct operations of the government

☐ Design or development of items for government use or pursuant to agency definition or specifications

☐ Generation of management information or other data for government use

☐ Research and development

☐ Conferences conducted on behalf of the government

The COTR best serves the government need when it is a requirement that "emerges" through a series of functional activities that the contractor executes during the course of the contract. This performance situation then needs periodic government monitoring and surveillance to ensure that the requirements are being met.

Elements of Every Contract

- Legal Capacity to Contract
- Offer — A bid or proposal by a competent offeror that a contract be entered into.
- Acceptance — The offeree's assent to the offer and communication of that assent to the offeror.
- Lawful Purpose
- Consideration — Something of value in the eyes of the law exchanged by the parties to bind the agreement.
- In Accordance with Law and Regulation

A.4. Partnering

As the following exhibits show, the success of a contractual effort is only as good as the building and sustaining of an effective relationship with the contractor. It is a seminal success factor that the stronger the mutual communication, the greater the degree for success. Although "Partnering" is not a formal contract clause, it can be the catalyst toward ensuring that "when the going gets tough," both parties will work out the differences.

Myths	Realities
Additional legal requirement	Accomplished through informal procedure consistent with the contract
Imposes. irrelevant behavioral conditions for contract performance	Establishes business/working relationships between the government and the contractor
Even though Partnering is not suppose to, it favors one party over another'	Both sides are to initially input equal intention to improve communication, teamwork, and cooperation thereafter
Partnering suppose to provide --Message-to contractor "incentive" for stronger performance	Message to government & contractor: can effectively interact while maintaining arms length relationship
Partnering is part of current "acquisition streamlining"	Partnering been used successfully for over 15 years to reduce cost, schedule, litigation and interpersonal problems

Myths	Realities
If have Partnering in place, then will have lasting performance difference	Metric which indicates Partnering success is "change in attitude" toward mutual interaction and trust to meet the government's requirement
To work, Partnering is primarily done through team interface	Both teams and individuals can be proactive to directly address a concern
Partnering causes increased administration and oversight	When the going gets tough, both sides work it out- at your level- through open dialogue in respecting each other's position & working through differences
Partnering means more responsibility and more effort	Partnering means knowing and using effective communication and problem solving to ensure responsibilities carried out better in handling future issues

Partnering—Principles And Practices

Principles	Practices
Government & contractor are teaming to accomplish SOW purpose	Define effective partnering roles & responsibilities
Mutual benefits	Stronger contractor baseline performance & better government monitoring
Evolving trust	Partners together actively anticipate problems, resolve them & prevent recurrence
Effective communication	Understand each other:s expectations and sustain consensus on SOW Objectives
Effective management involvement	Each side committed to internal improvements needed to strengthen partner relationship
Handling conflict and measuring success	Use ADR and ensure periodic performance evaluations occur'
Establishing a harmonious working environment	Acknowledge differing perspectives as means toward innovation
Be ethical--in behavior	Be ethical—in performance

B. Various organizational responses to this need

COs have an important stewardship role in the acquisition process. They act as the United States' agents for the acquisition of supplies and services. They are responsible to ensure that contractors live up to their contracted obligations. COTRs must ensure that they do nothing

to infringe upon unique CO responsibilities. They may be given certain limited authority to act on behalf of the COs, particularly in providing technical direction to the contractor.

Just as the government requires agents to act on its behalf, so does the other party to the contract, the contractor. Agents will almost always be used by the contractor — necessarily so if the contractor is a corporation — to enter into and carry out the contract with the government. One important difference is that only a person with actual authority (by statute, regulation, or contract terms) may bind the government. An agent with apparent, as well as actual, authority may bind the contractor. Nevertheless, contractors usually try to limit and specify those who are their agents authorized to act on their behalf.

> Head of agency (also called agency head) means the secretary, attorney general, administrator, governor, chairperson, or other chief official of an executive agency, unless otherwise indicated, including any deputy or assistant chief official of an executive agency.

B.1. Small Business Concerns

An important governmental policy is to place a fair proportion of its acquisitions with small business, small disadvantaged business, and women-owned small business concerns. It is government policy to ensure that such concerns also will have the maximum practicable opportunity to participate as subcontractors in the contracts awarded by any executive agency, consistent with efficient contract performance. A small business concern is any organization including its affiliates that is independently owned and operated, not dominant in the field of operation in which it is bidding on government contracts, and qualified as a small business under the criteria established by the Small Business Administration.

Within each agency, the functional management responsibilities for the agency's small business, small disadvantaged business, and women-owned small business concerns are delegated to the Director of Small and Disadvantaged Business Utilization (OSDBU) in the Office of the Secretary. Each agency division has appointed a small business specialist (SBS) who is responsible for ensuring that the programs are implemented within their divisions. They locate capable small business, small disadvantaged business, and women-owned small business sources for current and future acquisitions. The SBS also must ensure that contracting and technical staff are knowledgeable about these program requirements and that they take all reasonable action to increase small business participation. Although the primary responsibility for implementing these policies rests with the CO, COTRs will be knowledgeable about these programs and will take steps to include these businesses in their acquisitions.

B.2. Competition

By statute (10 USC 2304 and 41 USC 253) and Regulation (FAR Part 6), "full and open" competition is required with certain limited exceptions, and COs shall promote and provide for full and open competition in soliciting offers and awarding government contracts. "Full and open competition" means that all responsible sources are permitted to compete (FAR 2.101). This policy is based on two blocks. Full and open competition will:

☐ Result in the "best value" for the government

☐ Allow all contractors to compete, thus maximizing the confidence of the governed — contractors and taxpayers — in the fairness and cost-effectiveness of the federal acquisition system

☐ Therefore, the CO always begins the acquisition process with the assumption that it will be accomplished via full and open competition. Full and open competition is divided into two categories:

☐ Full and open competition (without qualification)

☐ Full and open competition after exclusions of sources resulting from:

☐ Exclusion to establish or maintain an alternative source

☐ Set-asides for small business

Specific set-asides for socially and economically disadvantaged firms, 8(a) eligible contractors (established by the SBA), HUBZone small business competitions (small businesses located in certain geographic areas (HUBZones), Veteran-owned small businesses, Service-disabled, Veteran-owned small businesses or Women-owned small businesses

Observe that "full and open competition" after exclusion of sources for any of the above-stated reasons departs from that which is generally thought of as full and open competition (i.e., "everybody") because sources are excluded. Thus, for example, a regulatory "full and open competition" small business set-aside excludes offerors that are not small businesses (i.e., large businesses and non-profits).

The practical difference between regulatory and generic full and open competition becomes apparent considering that FAR 19.501(d) requires the CO to set aside acquisitions for small business participation only unless he or she determines (and documents) that:

☐ Only one offer is likely to be received if set aside

☐ The award will not be made at a fair market price if set aside

☐ In many cases, the CO is unable to make this determination. Thus, many regulatory "full and open competition" acquisitions are set aside for small business participation only, contrary to the generic idea that full and open means every organization can offer. COs may provide for fulfillment of the full and open competition requirement by using "competitive procedures" (FAR 6.101) for the acquisition including:

☐ Sealed bids

☐ Competitive proposals

☐ Combinations of competitive procedures

☐ Other competitive procedures including:

☐ Selection of architect-engineer contractors in accordance with the Brooks Act (40 USC 541)

☐ Certain competitive research and development via a public "Broad Agency Announcement" or soliciting all contractor offers and a peer review

☐ Use of GSA multiple award schedules

☐ Other Than Full and Open Competition

Both Congress and the implementing FAR, however, recognize that in some acquisitions, it may not be possible or practical to have full and open competition. Rather, there will have to be "Other Than Full and Open Competition." Such situations are, however, a fallback choice and are an exception to the usual requirement for full and open competition. As such, generally, they require a robust "Justification for Other Than Full and Open Competition (JOFOC). The JOFOC, signed by the CO or higher authority, if the acquisition is over $500,000, must demonstrate that the acquisition that it supports fits clearly into the description of one of the seven statutory/regulation exceptions that permit other than full and open competition. These seven exceptions are:

☐ Only one responsible source and no other supplies or services will satisfy agency requirements;

☐ The agency's need is of such an unusual and compelling urgency that the government would be seriously injured unless the agency is permitted to limit the number of sources solicited;

☐ Industrial mobilization; engineering, developmental, or research capability; or expert services;

☐ An international agreement or treaty between the United States and a foreign government or international organization;

☐ A federal statute authorizes or requires acquisition through certain sources (e.g., Federal Prison Industries, Qualified Nonprofit Agencies for the Blind or other Severely Disabled, Small Business Act, Section 8(a) non-competitive, HUBZone non-competitive, the Robert T. Stafford Disaster Relief and Emergency Assistance Act);

☐ Disclosure of the agency's needs would compromise the national security unless the number of solicited sources is limited;

☐ An agency head determines that it is not in the public interest to have full and open competition — this determination must be made by the secretary, who must notify Congress 30 days before contract award.

As a practical matter, this list of exceptions shrinks to three:

Only one responsible source and no other supplies or services will satisfy agency requirements;

The agency's need is of such an unusual and compelling urgency that the government would be seriously injured unless the agency is permitted to limit the number of sources solicited; and

A federal statute authorizes or requires acquisition through certain sources (e.g., Federal Prison Industries, Qualified Nonprofit Agencies for the Blind or other Severely Disabled, Small Business Act, Section 8(a) non-competitive, HUBZone non-competitive, the Robert T. Stafford Disaster Relief and Emergency Assistance Act) for all but a few buys.

☐ Specific grounds for exception justifications that are not acceptable are (FAR 6.301(c)):

☐ A lack of advance planning by the requiring office;

☐ Concerns related to the funds available, e.g., funds will expire before award can be made.

The strong policy for maximizing the competition requires that, even when full and open competition has been limited by application of an appropriate exception, as, for example, by an unusual and compelling urgency, the CO must solicit as many firms as is practical in the particular circumstances.

B.3. Processing Requirements

In processing requirements, we consider the level of competition somewhat in reverse order. The CO will first check the requirement against mandatory sources of supply, such as UNICOR and the Blind and Severely Handicapped agencies (NIB/NISH). If a mandatory source is not applicable, the requirement will then be examined for the appropriateness of

set-asides or whether a sole source situation or an urgent and compelling need circumstance exists. If such a condition exists and can be properly justified, the procurement will be made using other than full and open competition. FAR 6.302 cites all of the circumstances under which other than full and open competition may be utilized and discusses the justifications required for their use. If anything other than full and open competition cannot be properly justified, the acquisition will be processed using some form of full and open competition.

C. Non-personal and personal services factors

The fundamental tenet herein is that any contractor/COTR interaction is based on a full and complete rendering of the contract requirements. Further, the working relationship between a contractor and the COTR is at "arms length" to sustain that each party will carry out their respective functions to benefit the agency program or project. Therefore, the COTR/contractor relationship is one built on and sustained by professional interaction. (Some of these factors include parenthetical explanations or qualifications that indicate the type of judgment that you will exercise.)

C.1. The Nature of the Work

To what extent the government can obtain civil servants to do the job, or whether the contractor has specialized knowledge or equipment that might be useful in a doubtful case (but it will not in itself create doubt about services that are otherwise clearly non-personal).

To what extent the services represent the discharge of a governmental function that calls for the exercise of personal judgment and discretion on behalf of the government. (This factor, if present in a sufficient degree, may alone render the services personal in nature.)

To what extent the requirement for services to be performed under the order is continuing rather than short-term or intermittent. (This factor is one that might be useful in a doubtful case, but it will not in itself create doubt about services that are otherwise clearly non-personal.)

C.2. Other Factors

Whether the services can properly be defined as an end product.

Whether the contractor undertakes a specific task or project that is definable either at the inception of the order or at some point during performance, or whether the work is defined on a day-to-day basis. (However, this does not preclude use of requirements or other indefinite delivery-type contracts, provided the nature of the work is specifically described in the contract, and orders are formally issued to the contractor rather than to individual employees.)

Whether payment will be for results accomplished or solely according to time worked. (This is a factor that might be useful in a doubtful case but will not in itself create doubt about services that are otherwise clearly non-personal.)

To what extent the government is to furnish the office or working space, facilities, equipment and supplies necessary for performance. (This is a factor that might be useful in a doubtful case but which will not in itself create doubt about services that are otherwise clearly non-personal.)

D. Personnel concerns in administration of the contract

☐ To what extent the contractor employees are used interchangeably with government personnel to perform the same functions.

☐ To what extent the contractor employees are integrated into the government's organizational structure.

☐ To what extent any of the elements above are present in the administration of the order, regardless of whether they are provided for by the terms of the contract.

Definition of "Personally" and "Substantially"

The regulations often refer to federal employees who are "participating personally and substantially." FAR 3.104-1 defines "participating personally and substantially" as:

Active and significant involvement of an official in any of the following activities directly related to that procurement:

(i)   Drafting, reviewing, or approving the specification or statement of work for the procurement

(ii) Preparing or developing the solicitation

(iii) Evaluating bids or proposals, or selecting a source

(iv) Negotiating price or terms and conditions of the contract.

(v)   Reviewing and approving the award of the contract.

When there is a question of whether an individual is "participating personally and substantially," the activities of the individual will be analyzed by the CO to determine whether there is both personal and substantial involvement in procurement.

D.1. Appearance of Impartiality

There may be circumstances other than conflicting financial interests in which an employee will not perform official duties in order to avoid an appearance of loss of impartiality. Employees will obtain specific authorization before participating in certain

government matters where their impartiality is likely to be questioned. These matters include those:

Involving specific parties, such as contracts, grants or investigations, that are likely to affect the financial interests of members of employees' households; or

In which persons with whom employees have specific relationships are parties or represent parties. This will include, for example, matters involving employers of spouses or minor children, or anyone with whom employees have or seek a business or financial relationship.

Executive Order 11222 extends this policy somewhat in providing that "an employee need not have a financial interest that actually conflicts with his or her duties to violate the prohibition of Executive Order 11222. Any financial interest that could reasonably be viewed as an interest that might compromise the employee's integrity, whether or not this is in fact true, is subject to this prohibition."

Generally, employees who will have a conflict of interest, as described above, must disqualify themselves from participating in the acquisition process. However, this discussion of conflict of interest is only a general treatment of a fairly complex subject. Government employees who are required to participate in a particular procurement that may present them with a conflict of interest will refer to the applicable sections of their agency's Standards of Conduct for full details. Consult your deputy ethics counselor for the procedures by which employees may be authorized to participate in such matters when it serves the agency's interests.

D.2. Disclosing/Obtaining Procurement Information

No person or other entity may disclose contractor bid or proposal information to any person other than one authorized in accordance with applicable agency regulations or procedures by the head of the agency or designee, or the CO, to receive such information. FAR 2.101 defines "Source selection information" as any of the following information that is prepared for use by an agency for the purpose of evaluating a bid or proposal to enter into an agency procurement contract, if that information has not been previously made available to the public or disclosed publicly:

(1) Bid prices submitted in response to an agency invitation for bids, or lists of those bid prices before bid opening

(2) Proposed costs or prices submitted in response to an agency solicitation, or lists of those proposed costs prices

(3) Source selection plans

(4) Technical evaluation plans

(5) Technical evaluations of proposals

(6) Cost or price evaluations of proposals

(7) Competitive range determinations that identify proposals that have a reasonable chance of being selected award of a contract

(8) Rankings of bids, proposals, or competitors

(9) Reports and evaluations of source selection panels, boards, or advisory councils

(10) Other information marked as "Source Selection Information — See FAR 2.101 and 3.104" based on a case-by-case determination by the head of the agency or the CO, that its disclosure would jeopardize integrity or successful completion of the federal agency procurement to which the information relates.

D.3. Soliciting or Discussing Employment

Government officers and employees are prohibited from participating personally and substantially in any particular matter that would affect the financial interests of any person with whom the employee is seeking employment. An employee who engages in negotiations or is otherwise seeking employment with an offeror or who has an arrangement concerning future employment with an offeror must disqualify himself or herself. (FAR 3.104-2(b)(2)). Further, if an agency official, participating personally and substantially in federal agency procurement for a contract in excess of the simplified acquisition threshold, contacts or is contacted by a person who is an offeror in that federal agency procurement regarding possible non-federal employment for that official, the official must:

(i) Promptly report the contact in writing to the official's supervisor and to the agency ethics official; and

(ii) Either reject the possibility of non-federal employment or disqualify himself or herself from further personal and substantial participation in that federal agency procurement (see 3.104-5) until such time as the agency authorizes the official to resume participation in that procurement, in accordance with the requirements of 18 USC 208 and applicable agency regulations, because:

(A) The person is no longer an offeror in that federal agency procurement; or

(B) All discussions with the offeror regarding possible non-federal employment have terminated without an agreement or arrangement for employment.

Post-Employment Restrictions
   FAR 3.104-3(d) states:

A former official of a federal agency may not accept compensation from a contractor that has been awarded a competitive or sole source contract, as an employee, officer, director, or consultant of the contractor within a period of one year after such former official:

(i)   Served, at the time of selection of the contractor or the award of a contract to that contractor, as the procuring CO, the source selection authority, a member of a source selection evaluation board, or the chief of a financial or technical evaluation team in a procurement in which that contractor was selected for award of a contract in excess of $10,000,000;

(ii) Served as the program manager, deputy program manager, or administrative CO for a contract in excess of $10,000,000 awarded to that contractor; or

(iii) Personally made for the federal agency a decision to —

(A) Award a contract, subcontract, modification of a contract or subcontract, or a task order or delivery order in excess of $10,000,000 to that contractor;

(B) Establish overhead or other rates applicable to a contract or contracts for that contractor that are valued in excess of $10,000,000;

(C) Approve issuance of a contract payment or payments in excess of $10,000,000 to that contractor; or

(D) Pay or settle a claim in excess of $10,000,000 with that contractor.

Post-employment restrictions prohibit certain activities by former government employees, including representation of a contractor before the government in relation to any contract or other particular matter involving specific parties on which the former employee participated personally and substantially while employed by the government (FAR 104-2(h)(3)). Questions related to individual post-employment situations will be directed to the appropriate agency ethics official.

D.4. Sexual Harassment

Sexual harassment is defined as deliberate, unsolicited verbal comments, gestures, or physical contact of a sexual nature that are unwelcome. The regulations specifically prohibit this conduct in relationships between department personnel who take or recommend action on a grant or contract and the grantee or contractor.

E. What has gone well and means to improve

Despite the necessity and importance of formal delegation, many COTRs report that they are never formally delegated in writing. The degree to which agencies are failing to formally delegate authority to COTRs means that COTRs may not be clear on what they are to do and not do on the contract.

Formal delegation is positively related to better contract outcomes. COTRs who worked only on fixed-price — conceivably less complex — contracts were no more or less likely to be formally delegated their authority than were those who worked on contracts with more complex pricing arrangements. However, COTRs who reported working on longer and more costly — conceivably more complex — contracts reported that they were more frequently provided formal delegation of their contracting authority. COTRs who are always formally delegated the authority to perform contract work are also more likely to be appointed as COTRs early in the contracting process, perform a variety of pre- and post-award contract tasks more frequently, and report more contract training. Formal delegation may actually work to improve contract outcomes through increasing these day-to-day activities. Alternatively, formal delegation could simply be one of many contract management practices in agencies with effective and accountable contract management cultures. Regardless of the mechanism through which delegation relates to outcomes — on its own, or as a surrogate marker for other aspects of COTR management — it is clear that formal delegation is consistently related to more positive contract outcomes. Therefore, it is important that agencies view formal delegation of authority as more than a pro-forma requirement. Formal delegation of authority is required, and is one of the more definitive and straightforward steps an agency can take to promote the effectiveness and efficiency of the COTR workforce.

NOTE: Such delegation also strengthens the COTR's awareness and sensitivity to the major topics previously discussed: Partnering, Competition, and Non-personal services builds the bridge to effective nomination and selection of COTRs discussed next.

Step Two – Getting the **COTR** Onboard

Agencies make specific decisions about the COTRs' involvement in contracts that can affect how well COTRs are able to do their contracting work. For example, key agency representatives, such as COTR supervisors, program managers, and COs, make a variety of decisions every day that effect how COTRs are able to do their work. These professionals select which COTRs are involved in a particular contract, determine when COTRs are first involved in a particular contract, assign the specific tasks that COTRs must do on a particular contract, determine how much time COTRs are able to work on their contracting duties, rate COTRs on the performance of their contracting work, and manage the COTRs' interactions with the other federal employees who do contracting work.

COTRs are to become involved in the contract early in the contracting process; preferably, at the point the agency is contemplating obtaining a particular good or service through a contract. When COTRs are involved early in the process, they can help ensure that the technical aspects of contract development are done correctly. Well-developed contracts are easier to manage and are more likely to result in better outcomes. COTRs who performed certain pre-award tasks more frequently also reported better contract outcomes in at least one of the four outcome areas.

Agencies, and in particular CO, will assign tasks to the COTR that are critical for ensuring positive contract outcomes. In particular, these tasks will include those involving the technical aspects of the contracting process, such as establishing requirements, defining contract objectives and incentives, developing or applying proposal review criteria, and participating in the contractor selection process. These tasks require the COTRs expertise and are important for ensuring a well-developed contract, which in turn is important for effective contract oversight leading to better contract outcomes. The technical oversight provided by COTRs after a contract is awarded is critical to ensuring the contract produces results that meet the government's technical requirements.

As with the assigning of pre-award tasks, agencies will assign COTRs the post-award tasks that most effectively use the COTRs' expertise. While COTRs may not need to perform all of the possible post-award tasks for each contract, they need be assigned those that are most related to the technical aspects of the contract. These tasks include evaluating contractor

performance, providing technical guidance to the contractor, reviewing and accepting deliverables, determining that work is within the scope of the contract, monitoring the day-to-day work of the contractor, suggesting contract modifications, and conducting program reviews.

A. Discovering and designating the need for a COTR

A COTR is typically nominated by the product/service team lead or other management official from the requiring organization. The CO designates the COTR by written memorandum outlining specific authorities and responsibilities. Before formally designating the nominated COTR, the CO may conduct a pre-appointment interview to determine if the nominee has the required training, technical knowledge, and skill to perform the delegated duties. A training plan for the COTR may result from this pre-appointment interview.

When possible, the COTR will be identified well before contract award. His or her technical expertise may be needed during planning and source selection stages of the procurement process. By helping with planning, solicitation, and evaluation activities, the COTR gains an in-depth understanding of the contract and is better equipped and motivated to oversee the contract after award.

The COTR is nominated in writing by the requirement's generating organization; designated in writing in the contract schedule; and notified by letter signed by the CO and in turn acknowledged by the COTR signing and returning a copy of the notification/ designation letter. This letter will be tailored specifically for each contract. Large dollar or complex contracts require increased monitoring. Factors, such as the contract type, the item or service being procured, and the COTRs level of experience, influence the degree of involvement needed for effective contract administration. The designation letter will reflect this. The designation does not change or supersede the established line of authority and/ or responsibility of an organization. Changes in designation of the COTR will be made by modification to the contract, as the need arises. If the COTR changes a new designation letter must be completed. Individual offices may designate a COTR by other titles in accordance with local practices, e.g., Project Manager, Project Officer, etc. An Alternate COTR (ACOTR) will also be designated to fill in for the primary COTR. Due to the scope or technical complexity of some contracts, "sub-COTRs" are necessary, they will be included in the letter of appointment of the COTR, and will be the responsibility of, and responsive to, the COTR.

While some agencies may be selecting COTRs based on reasonable criteria, other agencies may need to focus more overtly on both the COTRs technical and contracting skills and experiences. In addition, our interactions with agencies revealed that some agencies have established criteria for selecting COTRs while other agencies have no criteria.

Given the level of responsibility COTRs have in overseeing contracts, it may be advisable for agencies (and for government-wide policymakers) to consider establishing criteria for selecting COTRs. The new Certification Requirements are enabling a more "common framework" for ensuring stronger COTR contract management. Some of the criteria listed in the FAR for selecting COs, such as contracting experience and training, can be useful for COTRs. Additional criteria for selecting and assigning COTRs will include the required expertise in particular functional or program areas, and perhaps other factors, such as work location.

A.1. COTR Nomination

(See Attachment Four http://www.governmenttraininginc.com/The-COTR-Handbook.asp for a Sample Nomination Letter)

Program/Requiring Offices are responsible for proactive planning to ensure qualified individuals are available for COTR appointment. Program/requiring offices are also responsible for nominating only technically competent and qualified individuals to be COTRs.

Only COs have the authority to appoint a COTR to assist in performing specific technical and administrative functions in support of a government contract. COTR appointments are made at the outset of the acquisition process if possible to enable the COTR to participate in developing the contract specification/work statement and other pre-award activities that will affect the COTR's post-award responsibilities. Contracting offices will maintain a list of COTRs to use in providing relevant information related to contracting matters, best practices, and training opportunities.

Nominating officials are responsible for:

☐ Nominating an individual to be appointed as a COTR if deemed necessary for contract performance by either the program/requiring office or the CO;

☐ Ensuring that the person nominated has completed or will complete COTR training and certification requirements prior to contract award or within six months of appointment;

☐ Certifying prior to appointment that the individual possesses technical expertise consistent with the duties to be assigned;

☐ Issuing a nominating memorandum to the CO prior to performance by the nominee in contract execution duties. The COTR nominee must have the requisite security

clearance and sufficient time available to perform the COTR duties. It is necessary for offices to nominate individuals as primary and alternate COTRs in the event the primary COTR is unavailable for an extended period. Each individual nominated for appointment must be technically and professionally competent, free of conflicts of interest, and qualified to serve as a COTR. The nomination letter shall contain:

a. The nominee's technical qualifications and experience;

b. The recommended technical functions and duties to be performed; Duties assigned shall be applicable to the contract, line item, or order;

c. If the nominee will be serving as alternate COTR, the nomination letter shall so state whether the individual's performance rating elements include the COTR function (if not, an explanation of why not); and:

Provide timely notice to the appointing CO as to when the COTR must be replaced or the appointment terminated, such as, if a conflict of interest develops or the COTR is transferred;

Ensure that any changes to those duties recommended in the nomination letter are discussed and agreed to by the CO prior to issuing the appointment letter.

Nomination

The requiring activity submits the nomination to the CO. The nominee's supervisor must certify the nomination before its submittal to the CO. Nomination packages will demonstrate through training and relevant experience that the nominee possesses:

Knowledge of the government contracting process;

♦ Understanding of pertinent contract clauses, such as changes, payments, government-furnished property, inspection and acceptance, and termination;

♦ Familiarity with pertinent concepts, such as contracting authority, contract incentives, fixed-price versus cost-reimbursable contracts, excusable versus non-excusable delays in contract performance, options, and Task Order contracts;

♦ The ability to analyze, interpret, evaluate, and document factors involved in contract administration; and

♦ Sufficient time and resources to accomplish these duties, given the contracts nominee is currently managing and other workload commitments.

The nomination package will identify:

The contracts for which nominee has performed COTR duties;

Relevant education and training, including nominee's:

♦ On-the-job training experience, describing each work assignment and the instruction provided and including dates for each assignment;

- ◆ Mandatory COTR training, providing completion date and mode of instruction; and
- ◆ Equivalent training, providing information about the course to enable the CO to determine its acceptability as an equivalent.

The nominee's security clearance or other specified requirements, if needed.

Each requiring activity will have an overall nominating official, normally the head of the requiring activity, to ensure that all nominees will have the experience, training, and ability appropriate to the importance and complexity of the contracts they will manage.

A.2. Appointment Responsibilities

1. COs are responsible for:

Formally designating (appointing) a COTR in a contract when:

a. Technical direction is to be provided to clarify, define or give specific direction within the Performance Work Statement, such as engineering services or research and development contracts; or

b. Task/delivery ordering is used under an indefinite delivery type or equivalent type contract; or

c. The contract requires unusual monitoring and surveillance efforts beyond what the CO is able to provide.

Verifying the date when the COTR completed training and certification requirements;

If concurring with a nomination, making the appointment through issuance of a separate appointment letter. Appointments may be made for the total contract or at the delivery/task order level or other appropriate sub-level as determined by the CO. The appointment memorandum must be a complete and stand-alone document, therefore, either repeat or enclose the nomination letter responsibilities and limitations. COs may add, delete, revise or elaborate on the COTR responsibilities contained in the nomination letter as necessary. The sample is not all inclusive and will be tailored to the appointment. At a minimum, the memorandum shall contain the following:

d. The contract/line item/order number to which the COTR is being appointed;

e. The period covered by the appointment;

f. A statement that COTR duties are not re-delegable;

g. A statement that the COTR may be personally liable for unauthorized acts; and

h. A statement that the COTR's signature on the appointment letter certifies the information as correct to the best of his or her knowledge.

Ensuring that a single individual is technically responsible for technical performance monitoring for the entire contract. This monitoring can include: (a) administrative functions, (b) surveillance functions, (c) accounting functions and (c) change process functions. However, to ensure any of these functions are carried out well, effective communication and relationship building with the contractor counterparts and other contract stakeholders is essential;

Personally and clearly briefing COTRs on the functions to be performed and the limitations of authority being delegated;

Withholding or terminating appointments when there is reason to believe the appointment would not be in the best interest of the government. When appointments are withheld or terminated, the CO will immediately notify the nominating official of the reason(s) (i.e. contract is completed, retirement, transferred to another agency, conflict of interest, inadequate training or experience);

Annually meet with and review the COTR files and COTR adherence to appointed duties;

Providing a copy of the contract, any modifications, and any additional guidance as needed to the COTR;

Providing a copy of the COTR appointment/termination letter to the contractor.

Appointment of a COTR (see Attachment Five, http://www.governmenttraininginc.com/ The-COTR-Handbook.asp, for a Sample Letter)

The following conditions apply:

The individual must:

- Be a government employee, unless otherwise authorized in agency regulations; and
- Have training and experience commensurate with the COTR responsibilities in accordance with department/agency guidelines.

The designation must be in writing, with a copy furnished to the contractor and the contract administration office, stating:

- The extent of the COTR's authority to act on behalf of the CO;
- Any limitations on the COTR's authority;
- The period covered by the delegation;
- That the authority cannot be redelegated; and
- That the COTR may be personally liable for unauthorized acts.

The COTR may not receive the authority to:

Perform functions that have been delegated to a contract administration office under FAR 42.202(a); or

Make any commitments or changes that would affect the price, quality, quantity, delivery, or other terms and conditions of the contract.

The COTR must maintain a file for each assigned contract. The file must include, as a minimum:

- A copy of the CO's letter of designation and any other documentation describing the COTR's duties and responsibilities; and

- Documentation for all actions performed under the delegation of authority.

COs normally only appoint one COTR for each contract. In some cases, particularly in large or complex acquisitions, the CO may appoint other technical personnel to assist the COTR in carrying out performance monitoring responsibilities. They also must be appropriately trained and receive appointment letters. In addition, the CO may designate an alternate COTR (ACOTR) with authority to assume the responsibilities and functions assigned to the COTR, if the COTR is absent due to leave, illness, or official business. The CO must make this designation in writing, subject to the same requirements as the primary COTR. The ACOTR will maintain an active role throughout the life of the contract.

When appointing a COTR, the CO must:

Insert the clause about the COTR, in the solicitation and contract;

Prepare the appointment letter(s) in compliance with the requirements in the agency acquisition regulations and/or guidance;

Determine that the nominee has the requisite job experience and accomplished the required training;

Assess the nominee's technical and administrative competence to ensure his or her ability to perform the COTR duties in an effective and responsible manner;

Provide orientation, instructions, and training specific to the instant acquisition;

Ensure that all COTR appointment letters are properly signed by the appointee and returned in a timely manner; and

Maintain records in the official contract file for each COTR, including:

- The nomination package;

- Signed letters of appointment; and

- Other pertinent documents relating to the COTR's qualifications and actions.

B. COTR profile

Once a decision is made to acquire products or services through the contracting process, a partnership is created between the COTR and the CO. This partnership is essential to establishing and achieving contract objectives because these two officials are responsible for ensuring that the contracting process is successful. COs and COTRs have both separate and mutual responsibilities, with lead responsibility shifting from one to the other during the various stages of the contracting process. During the pre-solicitation phase, the COTR has the lead and the CO operates in an advisory capacity. However, as this phase ends and the solicitation and award phase begins, the lead responsibility shifts to the CO with the COTR

acting largely as an advisor. During post-award administration, the COTR assumes lead responsibility for technical monitoring, and the CO for legal, administrative aspects. COs sign contracts on behalf of the government and bear the legal responsibility for each contract. They alone can enter into, terminate, or change a contractual commitment on behalf of the government. COTRs support the CO in these administrative endeavors. As a team, they must ensure that program requirements are clearly defined and that the contract is designed to meet them. Together, they are responsible for ensuring that competitive sources are solicited, evaluated, and selected; and that the price the government pays for the goods and services it acquires is reasonable. They must establish quality standards and delivery requirements, and make sure that these are met. While the contract is in force, COTRs monitor compliance with all contract terms and conditions, and must report any deviation to the CO.

B.1. Role of the CO and COTR

The CO is the legal agent of the government, responsible for integrity of the contracting process. The CO safeguards the government's interests, ensures all necessary contracting actions are performed, and oversees compliance with contract terms and conditions. Only a CO may enter into, change, or terminate a contract, order, agreement, lease, or other transaction on behalf of the government. The CO signs and has legal responsibility for obligating documents. A CO's authority, and any limits to that authority, is stated in a certificate of appointment, commonly referred to as a "warrant." Although the CO must retain certain contracting responsibilities, he or she may delegate some responsibilities. For example, a CO may not have expertise to oversee the technical aspects of contractor performance, and may delegate this function to a COTR.

A COTR is the CO's technical "eyes and ears" in all facets of contract management. A contractor has responsibility for delivering quality, timely supplies or services required by a contract; the COTR observes, interfaces, documents, and reports on the contractor's technical performance. COTRs help during procurement planning and source selection phases of the contracting process. When required, they work with the CO, program officials, and other functional specialists to analyze the marketplace, define requirements, identify potential vendors, establish source evaluation criteria, and participate in source evaluation and selection.

C. Responsibilities of the COTR

Subject to program policy and operational procedures, individuals designated by the CO as COTRs are assigned specific responsibilities. These responsibilities are tailored to the specific contract and contract administration situation. They can include the following:

☐ Assist the CO in developing the contract specification of work statement to promote full and open competitive procurement actions.

☐ Reviewing all proposed procurement actions for consideration for 8(a) or small business set-aside or other socioeconomic program goals.

☐ Coordinating with the program office all actions relating to funding and changes in scope of work.

☐ Assist in the technical evaluation of prospective contractors when applicable.

☐ Act as the government technical representative for contract administration.

☐ Supervise all technical and clerical personnel assigned to assist the COTR in his or her duties.

☐ Assist the CO conducting the post-award orientation conference.

☐ Represent the government in conferences with the contractor and prepare memorandums for the record of pertinent facts.

☐ Confer with representatives of the requesting office and other user groups on performance matters.

☐ Maintain a filing system.

☐ Monitor the contractor's performance of the technical requirements of the contract to ensure that performance is strictly within the scope of the contract.

☐ Confirm in writing all significant technical instructions to the contractor.

☐ Ensure prompt review of draft reports and provide approval to the contractor so that the distribution of the reports can be made within the specified completion date of the contract, and ensure prompt inspection and acceptance or rejection of other deliverable items.

☐ Inform the CO when a contractor is known to be behind schedule, with the reasons therefore, and coordinating with the CO corrective actions necessary to restore the contract schedule.

☐ Furnish to the CO a copy of government-contractor conference reports and correspondence, and coordinating with the CO on the content of any contractually significant correspondence addressed to the contractor, in order to prevent possible misunderstanding or the creation of a condition that may be the basis of a later claim. Normally, correspondence addressed to the contractor will be signed by the CO.

☐ Request the CO to authorize government-furnished property and, when requested by the CO, furnish disposition advice on government-furnished property or contractor-acquired property.

☐ Evaluate the contractor's request for travel.

☐ Monitor financial management controls.

☐ Review the contractor's invoices to ensure that they reflect accurately the work completed in accordance with the requirements of the contract and certifying acceptance.

☐ Furnish the CO a notice of satisfactory or unsatisfactory completion; of delivery or performance of a contract, purchase order, delivery order, or any modification thereto.

☐ Report promptly and directly to the CO or Inspector General, any suspected procurement frauds, bribery, conflicts of interest, and other improper conduct.

☐ Review and submit recommendations to the CO on subcontracts with respect to their relationship with the prime contracts.

Ensure that the contractor has a current facility security clearance, if applicable, as well as clearances for personnel actually engaged in contract performance to have access to security information as soon as it is determined that access to such information will be required. Examples of clearances are most commonly found in access to Information Technology (IT) systems and contractor-owned software. Such a determination will be made in the beginning phase of the procurement process. It will be noted, however, that there are absolutely no exceptions authorized for the release of security information to contractors who do not possess a security clearance.

Recommend to the CO approval/disapproval of the contractor's requests for public release of information regarding work being performed under the contract.

☐ Notify the CO of inventions by the contractor during the performance of the contract.

☐ Assist with contract closeout including an Overall Performance Evaluation.

☐ Ensure that changes in the work or services, and resulting effects on delivery schedule, are formally negotiated and implemented by written supplemental agreement or change order issued by the CO before the contractor proceeds with the changes.

When required, furnish the CO a formal request for termination and other duties specific to the particular nature of the effort and/or the contract.

C.1. Limit of Authority

The COTR must fully understand the limits of his or her authority. Although the CO may delegate certain responsibilities to a COTR, authority to legally bind the government remains with the CO. A COTR cannot change any requirement that affects price, delivery, quality, quantity, or other contract terms. COTRs must be particularly careful that their words or actions do not commit the government to any condition not specified in the contract. Unauthorized commitments are serious acts of misconduct; anyone without proper authority committing the government is accountable and may be subject to disciplinary action.

What the COTR is Prohibited from Doing

☐ Primarily, the major prohibition in performing COTR duties is "obligating the government." The COTR is expressly prohibited from performing or being responsible for the following:

☐ Making commitments or promises oral or written to any contractor relating to the award of a contract;

☐ In competitive requirements, writing contract language around the product or capacity of one source, without disclosing such information to the CO and Competition Advocate;

☐ Soliciting proposals;

☐ Discussing procurement plans or any other advance information that might provide preferential treatment to one firm over another when a solicitation is issued for a competitive procurement;

☐ Directing the contractor to begin work prior to contract award date;

☐ Giving guidance to a contractor, either orally or in writing, which might be interpreted as change in scope or terms of the contract;

☐ Issuing oral or written instructions to a contractor to start or stop work;

☐ Approving items of cost not specifically authorized by the contract;

☐ Authorizing delivery or disposition of government-furnished property;

☐ Modifying any of the stated terms of the contract;

☐ Signing change orders or supplemental agreements;

☐ Negotiating;

☐ Taking any action with respect to termination, except to notify the CO that the action is desired.

If such actions do occur, the CO can replace the COTR among other consequences. (See Attachment Six, http://www.governmenttraininginc.com/The-COTR-Handbook.asp.)

D. Finding and approving the COTR and the other team members

An effective contracting process requires appropriate rules and procedures and enough highly skilled employees who can effectively implement those rules and procedures. Considerable effort in the last several years has focused on improving and streamlining contracting rules and procedures. This has resulted in more modern, flexible systems including new, innovative methods of contracting to meet the more complex needs of government. While these new systems provide significant advantages, they also create additional challenges for those who must implement them. The new procedures and systems provide more flexibility and thus require more expertise and personal judgment on the part of the federal employees using them. The employees who are required to effectively implement this flexibility must be especially well selected, trained, and managed. Otherwise, even with the most effective rules and procedures, the desired contract outcomes will not be realized.

Contract Administration Team

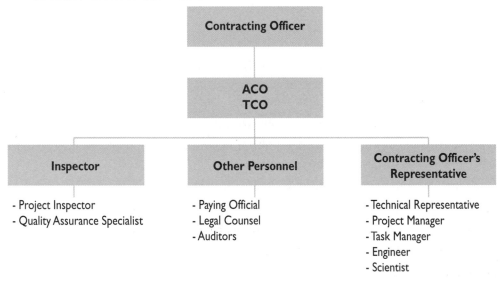

Successful programs depend on stakeholders working cooperatively. Stakeholders include people from the requiring organization, program office, contracting office, other functional areas, and the contractor. Solid stakeholder relationships, based on open communication and

focused on customer's need, keep a program on target. The COTR plays a unique "linking-pin" function among stakeholders, providing both technical and management expertise. The COTR works with the CO, financial representatives, work-package managers, program office representatives, and contractor personnel to achieve the program's objectives.

High-quality contracts are produced when the COTR collaborates with other technical representatives, has a good rapport with the CO, remains unbiased, and concentrates on ensuring the best contracting arrangement for the agency. COTRs can leverage their unique role, seeing from three perspectives - procurement, technical, and contractor - to solve problems and avoid squabbling associated with competing objectives. Cooperation between the COTR and CO is crucial. Together they ensure program requirements are clearly defined, the contract is properly structured to satisfy those requirements, the best contractor is selected, and quality products or services are delivered.

It is also important for a COTR to build an effective relationship with the contractor. Vendors have a commitment to support program outcomes required by the contract. With a team approach, contractors can provide vital information and assistance to solve problems, improve performance, and reduce costs.

Transactions involving taxpayer dollars require the highest degree of public trust and standards of conduct. COTRs must conduct themselves in a manner that instills public confidence. They must carry out their duties consistent with law, regulation, policy, order, and the agency's mission. COTRs must maintain a level of behavior and performance that will promote efficiency of the federal service and conform to ethical principles. The general rule is COTRs must strictly avoid any actual or apparent conflict of interest in their contractor relationships. As with any issue involving conduct, the appearance of misconduct may be damaging even if there is no actual misconduct. Always keep in mind that a COTR's behavior is being watched, and any appearance of unethical behavior is as damaging as the actual deed. The COTR will consult their cognizant legal counsel and CO about any questions or issues pertaining to standards of conduct.

D.1. Importance of Teamwork

The CO relies on the advice and support of many specialists from the technical, financial, legal, safety, security, small business and other disciplines that can make up the acquisition team. In a contract for services, the COTR is one of the most important and serves as the technical overseer of performance on behalf of the CO.

Throughout the acquisition process, the contracting office, which consists of the CO and may include contracting specialists and contract administrators, must work closely with

the requiring activity, or functional office. Certain tasks fall under the responsibility of the contracting office, with the assistance of the functional office. For other tasks, the contracting office provides assistance to the functional office. The following table shows the allocation of responsibility.

Action	Functional Office	Contracting Office
Market Research	Responsible	Assist
Prepare SOW/PWS	Responsible	Assist
Prepare QASP	Responsible	Assist
Prepare SDS	Responsible	Assist
Prepare GFP List	Responsible	Assist
Develop Sources	Assist	Responsible
Prepare Solicitation	Assist	Responsible
Conduct Pre-bid Conference	Assist	Responsible
Evaluate Proposals	Assist	Responsible
Award Contract	Assist	Responsible
Contract Surveillance	Responsible	Assist
Request Modifications	Responsible	Assist
Make Modifications	Assist	Responsible
Conduct Progress Meetings	Assist	Responsible
Inspection/Acceptance	Responsible	Assist
Evaluate Contractor's Performance	Responsible	Assist

Quality Assurance Specialist:

An example of additional technical support personnel for the contract management "team" is the Quality Assurance Specialist (QAS). The QASs are the officials with the responsibility for day-to-day monitoring of the contractor's technical performance. Each QAS is responsible to work with the COTR in terms of daily monitoring, assessing, recording and reporting on the technical performance of the contractor. They have the primary responsibility for completing the Individual Event Reports (ERs) and reporting their findings to the CO.

1. The QA personnel are required to be familiar with numerous documents and operating procedures as follows:

a) The SOW

b) The Government's Quality Assurance Plan

c) The Government's Award Fee Determination Plan

d) The Contractor's Technical Proposal

e) The Contractor's Quality Control Procedures

f) The Contractor's Preventive Maintenance Procedures

2. The areas of the contractor's performance that the QASs monitor, are those defined in the various chapters of the SOW. These may include, but are not limited to:

a) All Integration Services

b) Software Development

c) Administrative Support Services

d) Maintenance effort, work control and scheduling, recording and reporting, man-hour accounting and material reconciliation

3. It is extremely important for the QA personnel to establish and maintain open lines of communication with the contractor's senior staff, as well as government staff due to the daily contact required for monitoring functions. Equally important, the QASs must keep abreast of all current policies and procedures, and the changes thereto. Changes need to be disseminated to all concerned so as to provide current contract information.

4. Complaints and malfunctions received by the QASs will be immediately reported to the contractor and reconciled at regularly scheduled meetings. The QASs, CO, and project manager must work together as a team to satisfy complaints, correct malfunctions and, in general, ensure that required work is accomplished in an efficient manner. The daily interaction dictates the level of intensity for any area of concern with contract operations. There will be no hesitation to call special meetings to discuss and immediately resolve serious problems. Less serious problems will be discussed and resolved at regularly scheduled weekly and monthly meetings.

E. Common source selection modes

There are three contracting methods: sealed bidding, contracting by negotiation, and simplified acquisitions. With any of these modes, the key inputs and actions that a subsequently designated COTR can provide and do are the ones designated in the previous table.

E.1. Sealed Bidding (FAR Part 14)

Sealed bidding is a method of contracting that employs competitive bids, public opening of bids, and awards. An Invitation for Bid (IFB) is prepared describing the government's requirements clearly, accurately, and completely. These IFBs are then publicized in sufficient time to enable prospective bidders to prepare and submit bids. The bids are publicly opened at a predetermined time and place. The amount of each bid is publicly announced.

The government evaluates each bid but holds no discussion with the bidders. An award is made to the responsible and responsive bidder, whose bid is most advantageous to the government, considering only price and price-related factors. A "responsive" bidder is one whose bid conforms to the terms and conditions of the solicitation. Statute and regulations give preference to sealed bidding over other competitive proposals. COs shall solicit sealed bids if:

- Time permits the solicitation, submission, and evaluation of sealed bids.

- Award will be made on the basis of price and other price-related factors.

It is not necessary to conduct discussions with the responding bidders about their bids.

There is a reasonable expectation of receiving more than one sealed bid.

If any one or more of these conditions is lacking, the CO can contract by negotiation. Sealed bidding is used when the requirements are so clearly specified that the government can be sure that prospective bidders will understand and be able to prepare a responsive bid. Further, price must be the factor that determines who "wins" the contract among equally responsive and responsible bidders.

Sealed bidding is the most economical and efficient method of procurement; most prospective bidders view sealed bidding as the fairest of methods. On the other hand, sealed bidding is the least flexible method of procurement. Sealed bidding commits the government to a predetermined solution (in the form of hard and fast specifications) to its needs; there is no allowance for trade-offs between price and non-price evaluation factors.

Only firm fixed-price contract or fixed-price contract with economic price adjustment clauses can be used in the sealed bidding process. Sealed bids are most often used to acquire supplies and equipment that can be clearly specified and described and to acquire services that are equally clean-cut. Examples of supplies are nearly endless. They include commercial items, food, medical and scientific equipment, fuel, industrial chemicals, machinery, electrical and electronic equipment components, and hundreds of other categories. Services that can be acquired through sealed bids include, but are not limited to, transportation, photographic services, provision of lodging and subsistence, certain repair and maintenance services, and housekeeping services.

Two-step sealed bidding is a combination of competitive procedures designed to attain the benefits of sealed bidding when adequate specifications are not available. An objective is

to permit the development of a sufficiently descriptive and not unduly restrictive statement of the government's requirements, including an adequate technical data package, so that subsequent acquisitions may be made by conventional sealed bidding. This method is especially useful in acquisitions requiring technical proposals, particularly those for complex items. It is conducted in two steps:

Step one consists of the request for, submission, evaluation, and (if necessary) discussion of a technical proposal. No pricing is involved. The objective is to determine the acceptability of the supplies or services offered. As used in this context, the word "technical" has a broad connotation and includes, among other things, the engineering approach, special manufacturing processes, and special testing techniques. It is the proper step for clarification of questions relating to technical requirements. Conformity to the technical requirements is resolved in this step.

Step two involves the submission of sealed priced bids by those who submitted acceptable technical proposals in step one. Bids submitted in step two are evaluated and the awards made in accordance with FAR Subparts 14.3 and 14.4.

E.2. Contracting by Negotiation (FAR Part 15)

Program or project personnel have more involvement in the negotiated method of procurement than in the sealed bidding method. If one of the four conditions for sealed bidding is absent, the government uses this process. Because of the nature of the various missions of the department, it is not always possible to develop a set of totally unambiguous specifications such as are required for sealed bids. In addition, given the nature of these requirements, award may have to be made on the basis of factors in addition to price or cost. These factors often relate to the proposed technical approach, and quality of the staff. In addition, the requirements and the specifications for such acquisitions often result in offers that must be clarified through discussion after they are submitted.

Contracting by negotiation includes several steps. After the requirement is determined and the acquisition is planned according to departmental requirements, the CO must disseminate information on the proposed contract actions as follows:

For proposed contract actions to exceed $25,000, by synopsizing (summarizing) in FEDBIZOPPS;

For proposed contract actions expected to exceed $10,000, but not expected to exceed $25,000, by displaying in a public place, or by any appropriate, agency internal electronic means.

E.2.a. Request for Proposals

A Request for Proposals (RFP) is prepared and transmitted to a number of sources, many of whom comprise an established list of offerors and many of whom responded to the Fedbizopps synopsis. Offerors then prepare and submit proposals in response to the RFP. These proposals consist of a technical proposal and a business or cost proposal. Technical proposals are evaluated against a set of technical evaluation factors and subfactors that were included in the RFP. Cost or price proposals also are evaluated to determine whether the proposed costs or prices are reasonable, and to determine the offerors' understanding of the work and their ability to perform the contract.

E.2.b. Competitive Range

The CO next determines which proposals are in the competitive range for the purpose of conducting written or oral discussions. The determination is made on the basis of cost or price and technical factors and past performance information. Proposals are included in the competitive range when they are evaluated as most highly rated unless the range is further reduced for purposes of efficient competition.

E.2.c. Written or Oral Discussion

The next step is the conduct of oral or written discussions. Although this is not a mandatory step, it is a usual one. During these discussions, the government attempts to resolve uncertainties concerning the technical proposal and to provide the offeror with reasonable opportunity to revise its proposal as a result of bargaining on price, schedule, technical requirements, type of contract or other terms of a proposed contract.

E.2.d. Final Proposal Revision

After discussions are concluded, the CO may request proposal revisions that clarify and document understandings reached during negotiations. Requests for final proposal revisions must advise offerors that the final proposal revisions must be in writing and that the government intends to make award without obtaining further revisions.

E.2.e. Source Selection

The next step is evaluation of final proposal revisions and selection of the source to perform the contract. Selection is based on a comparative assessment of proposals against all source selection criteria in the solicitation. Any type of contract may be used in the contracting by negotiation process (see Attachment Two, http://www.governmenttraininginc.com/The-COTR-Handbook.asp). The foregoing steps constitute the negotiation process. This book discusses each step in more detail in Step Three.

E.3. Simplified Acquisitions (FAR Part 13)

The Federal Acquisition Streamlining Act (FASA), Public Law 103-355, was enacted on October 13, 1994. The Act created a threshold for the use of Simplified Acquisition Procedures (SAP). These exempt contracts and subcontracts at or below the Simplified Acquisition Threshold (SAT) from a variety of laws, provisions, and clauses.

The FAR also provides special authority to use SAPs for acquisition of commercial items exceeding the SAT but not greater than $5,000,000, including options. Awards can be made by using one of the following simplified procedures:

- ☐ Purchase orders;
- ☐ Government-wide Commercial Purchase Card/SmartPay Card;
- ☐ Blanket Purchase Agreements (BPAs);
- ☐ Imprest Funds or Third Party Drafts; and
- ☐ Test programs for certain commercial items.

The CO makes the decision to use SAPs but the PO, during the acquisition planning process, is required to give suggestions and conduct discussions with the acquisition staff concerning approaches to acquisition. There are some general principles relating to simplified acquisitions. First, except for micro-purchases of $2,500 or less, COs generally solicit oral or written quotations from three or more vendors to promote competition to the maximum extent practicable. Second, SAPs must be used in ways that encourage acquisition from small businesses. Except for micro-purchases of $2,500 or less, simplified acquisitions anticipated to exceed $2,500 but not $100,000 are reserved exclusively for small businesses, unless the CO finds that certain exceptional conditions exist. Third, acquisitions using SAPs will not be used to circumvent regular acquisition requirements. It is improper, for example, to break down into smaller acquisitions a requirement that will cost an aggregate of more than the SAT, merely to permit the use of SAPs.

E.3.a. Purchase Orders

Purchase orders are offers by the government to buy supplies or services upon specified terms and conditions, the aggregate amount of which does not exceed the SAT. The purchase order is unique in government acquisition in that it is an offer by the government. Bids and proposals are offers by the prospective contractor; a contract comes into being when the government accepts that offer. On the other hand, purchase orders are government offers that do not become part of a contract until the contractor indicates its acceptance by signing the purchase order document or beginning work or delivering the supplies or services. Quite

frequently in the department, contractors are not required to sign purchase orders. They exhibit the acceptance by beginning the work described in the purchase order.

Purchase orders sometimes follow the solicitation of quotations. While solicitations can be made orally, for complex or certain other acquisitions a Request for Quotation (RFQ) is issued by the department. An RFQ solicits information from a prospective contractor about its price, and sometimes its approach and capabilities. The response to an RFQ by one organization or individual is not an offer. Rather it is an informational response that has no legal standing.

E.3.b. Government-wide Commercial Purchase Card/SmartPay Card

The Government-wide Commercial Purchase Card/SmartPay Card is designed to look like a regular commercial credit card so that stores will recognize it as a normal credit card with normal payment mechanisms. Each purchase card is issued with certain limits and restrictions coded electronically onto the magnetic strip on the back. As a purchase cardholder, you are assigned two kinds of spending limits: a single-purchase limit and a monthly (cumulative) limit. The purchase card is the preferred means to purchase and pay for micro-purchases. Micro-purchases are not required to be set-aside for small business concerns, and they are not subject to the "Buy American Act."

E.3.c. Blanket Purchase Agreements (BPAs)

BPAs are an example of an agreement used for filling anticipated repetitive needs for supplies and services. A BPA, in effect, is a charge account with qualified sources of supply and services. It has an overall price limitation that cannot be exceeded by the aggregate of all purchases made under it, unless the limit is raised by the CO. Under a BPA, separate acquisitions are made according to detailed but simple procedures. No one purchase can exceed the SAT or $5,000,000 for acquisition of commercial items conducted under FAR Subpart 13.5.

E.3.d. Imprest Fund and Third Party Drafts

Imprest funds and third party drafts may be used to acquire and pay for supplies or services in accordance with agency policies and procedures. The imprest fund may be used when the transaction does not exceed $500. The third party draft may be used for transactions that do not exceed $2,500. The imprest fund limit may be adjusted by the agency head. Third party draft adjustments must be in accord with Treasury restrictions.

E.3.e. Expedited Purchasing

When the government buys commercial products or services (that are currently sold in the private sector marketplace also), the acquisition strategy (for buys of five million or less)

is to use Simplified Acquisition (to shorten the procurement lead-time) with Contracting by Negotiation (to allow for a more complete response from each offeror).

Whenever a contractor is selected, before an award is made the CO (or Ordering Officer) need determine that a prospective contractor is responsible; that is:

Has adequate financial resources to perform the contract, or the ability to obtain them;

Is able to comply with the required or proposed delivery or performance schedule, taking into consideration all existing commercial and governmental business commitments;

Has a satisfactory performance record; A prospective contractor shall not be determined responsible or non-responsible solely on the basis of a lack of relevant performance history, except when there is a special standard necessary for a particular or class of acquisitions;

Has a satisfactory record of integrity and business ethics including satisfactory compliance with the law including tax laws, labor and employment laws, environmental laws, antitrust laws, and consumer protection laws;

Has the necessary organization, experience, accounting and operational controls, and technical skills, or the ability to obtain them. This includes, as appropriate, such elements as production control procedures, property control systems, quality assurance measures, and safety programs applicable to materials to be produced or services to be performed by the prospective contractor and subcontractors;

Has the necessary production, construction, and technical equipment and facilities, or ability to obtain them;

Is otherwise qualified and eligible to receive an award under applicable laws and regulations.

F. Special topic: Services

The federal marketplace spends the overarching percentage of acquisition dollars on services.

A "services buy" means a contract that directly engages the time and effort of a contractor whose primary purpose is to perform an identifiable task rather than to furnish an end item of supply. A service contract may be either a non-personal or personal contract. It can also cover services performed by either professional or non-professional personnel whether on an individual or organizational basis. Some of the areas in which service contracts are found include the following:

☐ Maintenance, overhaul, repair, servicing, rehabilitation, salvage, modernization, or modification of supplies, systems, or equipment

☐ Routine recurring maintenance of real property

☐ Housekeeping and base services

☐ Advisory and assistance services

☐ Operation of government-owned equipment, facilities, and systems

☐ Communications services

☐ Architect-Engineering

☐ Transportation and related services

☐ Research and development

"Non-personal services contract" means a contract under which the personnel rendering the services are not subject either by the contract's terms or by the manner of its administration, to the supervision and control usually prevailing in relationships between the government and its employees.

"Personal services contract" means a contract that, by its expressed terms or as administered, make the contractor personnel appear to be government employees. In most cases, it is necessary to obtain the review of legal counsel since it is the contractual exception. Document the file with:

The opinion of legal counsel, if any;

A memorandum of the facts and rationale supporting the conclusion that the contract does not violate the prohibition requiring agencies not to award personal services contracts unless specifically authorized by statute; and,

Any further documentation that your agency may require.

F.1. Criteria for Recognizing Personal Services

Civil Service laws and regulations and the Classification Act establish requirements that must be met by the government in hiring its employees. In addition, these laws and regulations established personnel ceilings for each agency.

The purchasing agent is responsible for ensuring compliance with the policy against personal services purchases and must be aware of the sensitivity of the issue, and ensure that applicable statutory and regulatory procedures are followed. In doubtful cases, check with senior purchasing management personnel before proceeding.

When properly issued and administered, orders for non-personal services represent an approved resource for the accomplishment of your agency's programs. The FAR provides guidelines for characterizing particular services as "personal" or "non-personal." There are many factors involved, all of which are not of equal importance. The characterization of

services in a particular case cannot be made simply by counting factors, but can only be the result of a balancing of all the factors in accordance with their relative importance.

The following examples of personal versus non-personal services are provided to help clarify their differences. They are provided for illustrative purposes only. YOU WILL NOT use them as the basis for a determination in any specific case.

Personal Services -- Examples of personal services orders that may not be made include:

☐ Order for preparation of a staff-type report on the operation of a particular government office or installation, where no specialized skills are required and where the report would ordinarily be prepared by the regular officers or employees of the office or installation, even if there is to be no government supervision and even if payment is to be for an "end product" report;

☐ Order for the furnishing of persons to perform the various day-to-day functions of administration of orders for a government agency, even if there is no government supervision (this does not preclude the use of architect-engineers as "construction managers");

☐ Order with an accounting firm to come in and perform day-to-day accounting functions for the government.

Non-personal Services -- The following are examples of non-personal service orders that may be made:

☐ Order for an expert in a given area to review grant applications received and recommend which applications will be awarded the grant;

☐ Order for field engineering work requiring specialized equipment and trained personnel unavailable to the government but not involving the exercise of discretion on behalf of the government where the contractor performs work adequately described in the order, free of government supervision;

☐ Order with an individual for delivery of lectures without government supervision, at specific places, on specific dates, and on a specialized subject, even if payment is by the hour;

☐ Order for janitorial services, where the order provides for specific tasks to be performed in specific places, free of government direction, supervision, and control over the contractor's employees, at a fixed price for the work to be performed;

☐ Furnishing of equipment and personnel to plow a field, harvest a crop, or weed a plot when the job is done on a fixed-price basis;

Research and development order, providing a fixed price for a level of effort, as long as the work is performed by the contractor independently of government direction, supervision, and control.

Purchasing Provisions Concerning the Contractor's Employees

In considering the following, you will note that supervision and control of a contractor or his/her employees, if present in a sufficient degree, may alone render the services personal in nature, and thus not in the best interest of the government to procure:

To what extent the government specifies the qualifications of, or reserves the right to approve, individual contractor employees;

(It is permissible to some extent to specify in the order the technical and experience qualifications of these employees, if this is necessary to ensure satisfactory performance.)

To what extent the government reserves the right to assign tasks to and prepare work schedules for contractor employees during performance of the order;

(This does not preclude including work schedules for the contractor at the inception of the order, or the establishment of a time of performance for orders issued under a requirement or other indefinite delivery-type contract.)

To what extent the government retains the right (whether actually exercised or not) to supervise the work of the contractor employees, either directly or indirectly;

To what extent the government reserves the right to supervise or control the method in which the contractor performs the service, the number of people it will employ, the specific duties of individual employees, and similar details;

(However, it is always permissible to provide in the order that the contractor's employees must comply with regulations for the protection of life and property. Also, it is permissible to specify a recommended, or occasionally even a minimum, number of people the contractor must employ, if this is necessary to ensure performance.

In those events, it will be made clear in the order that this does not in any way minimize the contractor's obligation to use as many employees as are necessary for proper performance.)

To what extent the government will review performance by each individual contractor employee, as opposed to reviewing a final product on an overall basis after completion of the work;

To what extent the government retains the right to have contractor employees removed from the job for reasons other than misconduct or security.

F.2. Competition in Services

The statutes and regulations requiring competition are fully applicable to services orders. You must obtain competition to the maximum practicable extent, as you would do for any simplified acquisition. Also, any services contract issued must go through a local wage rate determination (see Attachment Three, http://www.governmenttraininginc.com/The-COTR-Handbook.asp).

F.3. Government Use of Private Sector Temporaries

In this era of "rightsizing," it is not uncommon for the government to use the services of private sector temporaries. Agencies may enter into contracts for the services of temporary help service firms. These contracts may be for brief or intermittent use of the skills of private sector temporaries. The services provided by temporary help firms may not be regarded or treated as personal services. They must not be used in lieu of regular recruitment under civil service laws or to displace federal employees. Purchase of these services must be in accordance with the authority, criteria, and conditions of 5 CFR Part 300, Subpart E, Use of Private Sector Temporaries, and your agency procedures.

The primary activity of the COTR during this phase is technical advice, and evaluation of offeror's proposals against evaluation criteria established during procurement planning. The results of this activity help determine which vendor's offer is the best value to the government for contract award purposes.

G. Contract management actions that prepare and motivate the COTR to succeed

Activities during contract administration ensure the contractor meets technical, quality, and quantity requirements within contractually established cost and time. Success depends on the contractor's performance and government's monitoring. COTRs perform technical monitoring and oversight during this phase.

Contract administration includes:

☐ Initiate Contract Administration

☐ Plan contract administration; and

☐ Conduct necessary post-award orientation.

☐ Administer Contract Changes

☐ Modify contract; and

☐ Exercise contract options.

☐ Administer Contract Performance

☐ Monitor contract performance;

☐ Use appropriate remedies to protect the government's rights; and

☐ Document contractor performance for future reference in source selection decisions.

☐ Administer Contract Financial Terms

☐ Monitor contract bonds or other forms of performance or payment security;

☐ Monitor contract financing, such as progress payments;

☐ Administer contractually specified price or fee adjustments based on market factors or contractor performance;

☐ Review invoices for payment; and

☐ Watch for possible fraud.

☐ Perform Other Contract Administration Duties

☐ Terminate the contract for convenience when appropriate;

☐ Terminate the contract for default or cause when appropriate; or

☐ Closeout the contract when it is complete.

G.1. Summary of COTR Duties

Duty	Duty Summary	Duty Standards
Duty 1 – Work Package	Develop a procurement request work package for transmittal to the CO to initiate procurement of a government requirement for a service or supply.	The COTR supplies sufficient documentation to support the procurement.
Duty 2 – Government Property	Recommend whether to provide government property.	The COTR correctly recommends the use of government property for the procurement and any justifications fully support the recommendation.
Duty 3 – Technical Assistance	Provide technical assistance when requested by the CO.	Technical assistance is sufficient to support actions taken by the CO; Assistance conforms to source selection procedures established for the procurement; Actions did not exceed delegated authority.
Duty 4 – COTR Work Plan	Prepare a COTR work plan and establish and maintain appropriate record-keeping files.	Work plan clearly defines assigned tasks; Assignments are workable; Concerns are identified; Milestones tasks are flagged; Records support actions taken.

Duty	Duty Summary	Duty Standards
Duty 5 — Post-award Orientation	Assist and participate in the post-award orientation.	The contractor is correctly informed of all post-award rights, duties, and milestones of both parties that affect performance; All potential issues that may affect substantial performance are identified and resolved; The resolution of each issue is fully documented; The CO is notified of any issues that were not resolved; The contractor is advised of procedures, including rebuttal rights, for documenting performance in the agency past performance file.
Duty 6 — Administer Government Property	Monitor the acquisition, control, and disposition of government property by government personnel and the contractor. Assess contractors for any loss, damage, or destruction of property.	Government property is transferred and monitored according to the terms of the contract; Any damage, loss, or destruction of government property is accurately documented and costs are assessed by the CO.
Duty 7 — Monitor Contractor Performance	Monitor contractor actions as authorized by the CO; document contractor performance.	All potential performance and delivery problems are reported to the CO; Any noncompliance with terms and conditions of the contract is identified and reported to the CO; Sufficient documentation of contractor performance exists to support payments under the contract; Technical analysis is sufficient to support CO's negotiations and decisions.
Duty 8 — Inspection and Acceptance	Inspect and accept contract deliverables; inform the CO when rejecting or accepting nonconformance.	Supplies or services tendered by contractors meet contract requirements. Nonconforming supplies or services are rejected or otherwise resolved.

Duty	Duty Summary	Duty Standards
Duty 9 – Document Performance	Document contractor performance in the past-performance file.	Past-performance documentation fairly characterizes contractor performance. Past-performance information is complete and sufficient for application in pre-award source selection.
Duty 10 – Payment	Recommend whether to authorize payment of an invoice in full, in part, or not at all.	Sufficient information is provided to the CO to support payment of an invoice in full, in part, or not at all.
Duty 11 – Closeout	Closeout contract files and submit to the CO.	The contractor and government have fulfilled their obligations in a timely manner. All outstanding contract administration issues are resolved and all records are correctly disposed.
Duty 12 – Contract Modifications	Identify a need to change the contract. Prepare a technical analysis to support a change to the contract.	A technical analysis addressing quality, quantity, price, and other factors impacting a contract modification is complete. Any documentation necessary to support actions by the CO to resolve a modification request is complete. CO will also resolve constructive changes.
Duty 13 – Contract Options	Recommend in writing whether an option will be exercised under the contract. Submit market research data to support a recommendation to exercise the option.	The option is exercised within the timeframe established in the contract. Relevant market research data is submitted to support the recommendation to exercise the option. The option represents the most advantageous offer available from the commercial market.
Duty 14 – Contract Delays	Notify the CO about a delay in the delivery or performance schedule under the contract.	Technical analysis is sufficient to support action taken by the CO to remedy a delay.

Duty	Duty Summary	Duty Standards
Duty 15 – Stop Work	Assist in administering stop-work orders.	The need for a stop-work order is determined and documented. A stop-work order is administered to avoid unnecessary costs. Government risk is minimized.
Duty 16 – Claims	Assist the CO to analyze a claim; recommend a settlement position; participate in the resolution process.	The validity of the claim is correctly determined. A proper and complete report is prepared that fully supports the CO. Government interests are protected while treating the contractor fairly and equitably within terms of the contract.
Duty 17 – Remedies	Provide sufficient evidence of a breach and suggest an appropriate contract remedy. Assist in evaluating contractor response.	An adequate, timely remedy notification is provided that supports the CO's decision. A remedy is suggested that best minimizes the impact of contractor performance problems on the requirement, schedule, and cost.
Duty 18 – Termination	Assist the CO in determining whether to terminate a contract.	Termination situations and procedures are recommended that support a termination for convenience or a termination for default (or cause) when necessary.

G.2. Documentation Requirements

Complete and orderly files are vital in administering the contract to ensure that the government meets its obligations in order to have a successful contract, particularly when disagreements or questions of interpretation arise. The COTR file will play a critical role in resolving a dispute before an administrative or legal review board. A good COTR file will facilitate the transfer of responsibility if the COTR is replaced during the contract. The program office will hold periodic status or progress meetings with the CO, the COTR, the contractor and other personnel as necessary (at least quarterly) to discuss problems, progress of the contract and contractor performance. COTRs must ensure that they receive copies of written minutes and other correspondence related to these meetings, including follow-up actions. COTRs must maintain records documenting all telephone calls, e-mails, and other

correspondence between the COTR, the contractor, the CO, and other personnel relating to contract performance. The COTR will maintain a log of any resulting actions.

G.2.a. COTR File

The COTR file is a part of the official contract file and must be maintained in accordance with the CO's instructions. The COTR file must be available for review by the CO, Inspector General, GAO, or other authorized officials. Good file practices include:

Maintain a separate current file for each contract.

As a matter of practice, prepare a "Memorandum for Record (MFR)" no later than one business day after a significant meeting or discussions with the contractor or the CO, including telephone conversations and trip reports.

Clearly index all documents and file by group, in chronological order in a suitable folder.

Forward to the CO any correspondence received from the contractor.

Send copies of all correspondence the COTR prepares to the CO.

Mark the contract number clearly on all documents sent to the CO.

Upon completion of the contract, forward the COTR file to the CO for retention in the official contract file.

Retain records that pertain to unsettled claims, open investigations, cases under litigation, or similar matters until final clearance or settlement, even if retention of these records exceeds the period required under FAR 4.8.

Destroy duplicate copies of file documents after they have served their purpose, but in no event retain them more than one year after closeout of the contract. Remember that e-mails are legal documents.

Some tips to remember in maintaining your contract file.

Include the contract number on each record and all correspondence relating to the contract.

In your computer files, create a separate folder for each contract to enable ready access to pertinent files.

Be sure that the CO and other interested parties receive copies of all significant correspondence.

Give the utmost care to safeguarding proprietary data, and classified and business-sensitive information.

Do not rely on your memory – document events on the day or next working day after they occur.

Keep a record of important telephone conversations.

Take good meeting notes, even for the informal meetings.

G.2.b. COTR File Contents

Include the following documents in the COTR file. The contents of each will vary according to the size and complexity of the contract.

COTR Nomination, Appointment and Termination Memos

☐ Names and position titles of individuals who are functioning as technical and administrative assistants

☐ Copy of signed/acknowledged COTR appointment and designation letters

☐ Any correspondence from the CO that amends the letter of appointment

☐ Other materials or information pertaining to actions taken in accordance with the designation letter

COTR Training

☐ Proof of completion of the COTR training or equivalent

☐ Copies of certificates/evidence of attendance for additional COTR related training (i.e., COTR refresher training, ethics training)

COTR Assessments by the CO

☐ COTR Performance Review by the CO (no less than annually)

☐ COTR File Review by the CO (no less than annually)

☐ Copies of any written notifications from the CO to the COTR's functional area supervisor

☐ Copies of the checklist used by the CO in conducting the COTR reviews

A copy of the contract, including all orders and contract modifications

The Notice of Award or Notice to Proceed

Minutes of the post-award conference and all meetings with the contractor

☐ Identify persons present, dates, matters discussed, and actions taken

A list of all applicable regulations

Approved and accepted plans that have been signed by the CO and/or functional area office

☐ Quality Assurance Surveillance Plan

☐ Quality Control Plan

☐ Transition Plan

☐ Strike Plan

☐ Contractor's approved work plan

☐ Contractor Quality Control Plan

☐ Any other approved or accepted plans

Installation security requirements and guides

☐ Names and Social Security numbers of all employees provided by the contractor for a post passes

☐ Security passes for building entry

☐ Contractor vehicles that require company identification

☐ Security clearances

☐ Other security requirements, as applicable

Correspondence relating to contract performance

☐ Records of meetings and briefings

☐ Synopses of telephone conversations with the contractor

☐ Documentation of onsite visit results

☐ Monthly certifications regarding personal services

☐ Data, reports, and other documentation furnished by the contractor, including COTR's analysis and action taken

☐ Approvals the COTR has given to the contractor (Note: these approvals may only be within the COTR's designated authority.)

☐ Copies of any approvals by the CO, IAW the Materials and Workmanship clause in construction contracts

☐ Interim and final technical reports or other products

☐ Documentation of acceptability/unacceptability of deliverables

☐ COTRs final assessment of contract or order performance

☐ Copies of any other data as may be required by the contract provisions

☐ Any labor reviews and progress schedules approved by the CO

Surveillance documentation

☐ Contract Monitoring and Surveillance Report

☐ COTR Schedule

☐ Customer Complaints

☐ Surveillance Activity Checklists

☐ Contract Discrepancy Report

☐ Progress schedules approved by the CO

☐ Progress reports submitted by the contractor

☐ Laboratory test reports (Note: in some construction contracts the technical specifications require laboratory tests for some materials used in the performance of the contract, including, samples, photographs, witness statements, and other factual data.)

☐ Records of unusually severe conditions that affected contract performance in accordance with the respective default clause, for example, weather conditions are particularly important for construction contracts and other contracts that call for performance outside

☐ Delinquency Reports

Other contractor reports

☐ Resumes due to contractor employee changes

☐ Past Performance Information Maintenance Systems (PPIMS) Evaluations

Concerning contract funding and payment

☐ Maintain a payment register/payment log that tracks all payments by the government to ensure that expenditures do not exceed money available

☐ Ensure that payment register balances in the COTR file match those in the contracting office file

☐ Maintain copies of all contractor invoices/receipt documents (DD Form 250s) processed with all supporting documents

☐ Follow-up with DFAS to ensure that submitted documents are in the proper format

Concerning any government-furnished property (GFP) and contractor-acquired property (CAP) under the contract

☐ Maintain an inventory list of all government-owned property

☐ Take an inventory of government-owned property on the contract at least annually

COTR Status Reports to the CO

H. Ethics in the acquisition lifecycle

Each year, the federal government spends billions of dollars on acquisitions. With this magnitude of spending, it is inevitable that public officials who participate in the acquisition process will come under close public scrutiny and may occasionally be subjected to situations that may lead to improprieties, abuse of office, fraud, or theft.

By virtue of their unique position and responsibilities regarding the acquisition process, POs are particularly susceptible to improper influences from those who seek to do business with the government. Therefore, COTRs will take particular care to familiarize themselves with both government-wide and departmental regulations governing standards of ethical conduct for government employees. This section briefly discusses those ethical conduct standards that are particularly relevant to COTRs. Government-wide standards are found at 5 CFR Part 2635.

Ethics is a means of motivating stronger professional actions to protect and sustain the government's interest. The following elements are seminal to achieving effective ethical behavior:

The Ethics Program sets the following fundamental ethical principles:

☐ Integrity: People with integrity are principled, honorable, and upright. They are consistent in their moral behavior and do not adopt an "end-justifies the means" philosophy.

☐ Honesty: Honest people are truthful, sincere, and candid. They do not mislead, act deviously, or misuse or disclose information learned in confidence.

☐ Fairness: Fair people show a commitment to justice, equal treatment, and tolerance. They are unbiased, open-minded, and where appropriate, willing to change their positions.

These principles are based on the two-fold standard in dealing with any government ethical situation: i) the act itself and/or ii) the appearance of the act.

H.1. Protect the Integrity of the Acquisition Process

The term "integrity of the acquisition process," in this instance, means allowing private sector firms to compete for the government's business on a scrupulously fair basis. The emphasis here is on the word "fair." Not only is fairness a prerequisite in government acquisition due to the government's unique position as representative of the American people, but fairness also helps ensure that the government will obtain its supplies and services at the best price available. Government personnel who are associated with the acquisition process have a responsibility to protect its integrity by maintaining fairness in the government's treatment of all vendors.

There are numerous points within the acquisition process where the potential to lose this fairness is high. For example:

☐ Pre-solicitation – Allowing a vendor or vendors access to information on a particular acquisition (especially the specification or work statement), before such information is available to the business community at large, may give the vendor(s) receiving the information an unfair advantage over others.

☐ Specifications – Intentionally writing an unnecessarily restrictive specification or work statement that would effectively exclude the products or services of a vendor and/or increase the prospects for award to another vendor is an obviously unfair practice. Not only does this give advantage to one or more vendors over others, it also restricts competition and makes it more likely that the government will ultimately pay a higher price.

☐ Confidentiality of proposals – From time to time, requests for information are received concerning proposals, before a contract is awarded. All information concerning the proposals, including their number and submitters' identities, must be held in strict confidence. Should this information become available to one or more offerors, it could put other offerors at a distinct disadvantage. Proprietary data remains confidential after award.

H.2. Conflicting Financial Interests

The government-wide Standards of Ethical Conduct (5 CFR Part 2635) deal with government employees' participation in matters affecting a personal financial interest. Basically, the standards prohibit an employee from participating "personally and substantially" as a government employee in a matter in which any of the following individuals or organizations has a financial interest:

The employee, the employee's spouse, the employee's minor child, or the employee's general partner;

An organization in which the employee serves as an officer, director, trustee, general partner, or employee; or

A person or organization with which the employee is negotiating for prospective employment or has an arrangement for prospective employment.

In acquisition matters, this means that a CO, COTR, proposal evaluator, source selection official, or any other government official having a financial interest in one or more offerors responding to a proposal would be prohibited from engaging in decisions, approvals, disapprovals, recommendations, and investigations; providing advice; or making any other significant effort regarding the acquisition process. This includes participating in drafting specifications or SOWs for acquisitions when the drafter expects a company in which he or she has a financial interest to submit a proposal. Generally, employees who will have a conflict of interest, as described above, must disqualify themselves from participating in the acquisition process.

H.3. Gifts and Gratuities

As a rule, no government employee may solicit or accept any gratuity, gift, favor, entertainment, loan, or anything of monetary value from anyone who:

Has or is seeking to obtain government business with the employee's agency,

Conducts activities that are regulated by the employee's agency, or

Has interests that may be substantially affected by the performance or nonperformance of the employee's official duties.

The terms "gratuity" and "gift" include nearly anything of monetary value (i.e., entertainment, hospitality, transportation, lodgings, meals, services, training, discount, loan or forbearance).

It does not include items that clearly are not gifts:

☐ Publicly available loans from banks and financial institutions;

☐ Discounts available to the general public;

☐ Anything paid for by the government, secured under government contract or accepted by the government under specific statutory authority;

☐ Training to facilitate use of its products provided by a vendor whose products are furnished under government contract.

It also does not include certain inconsequential items:

☐ Modest items of food and refreshments (each agency establishes its own definition of "modest");

☐ Plaques and certificates having no intrinsic value.

☐ There are several exceptions to the prohibitions against accepting gifts. For example, with some limitations, employees may accept:

☐ Unsolicited gifts with a market value of $20 or less per occasion, aggregating no more than $50 in a calendar year from any single source;

☐ Gifts motivated by a family relationship or personal friendship;

☐ Free attendance at certain widely-attended gatherings, such as conferences and receptions, when the cost of attendance is borne by the sponsor of the event; and

☐ Food, refreshments and entertainment at certain meetings or events while on duty in a foreign country.

H.4. Use of Official Information

The public interest requires that certain information in the possession of the government be kept confidential, and released only with general or specific authority under department or other regulations. Such information may involve the national security or be private, personal, or business information that has been furnished to the government in confidence. In addition, information in the possession of the government and not generally available may not be used for private gain.

The "Standards of Conduct" include a prohibition against engaging in financial transactions using nonpublic information, or allowing the improper use of nonpublic information to further private interests. Most of the prohibitions against use of official information are applicable to the regulations governing conflict of interest. Government employees are sometimes able to obtain information about an action the government is about to take or some other matter that is not generally known. Such a use of official information is clearly a violation of a public trust. Employees shall not, directly or indirectly, make use of official information not made available to the general public, for the purpose of furthering any private interest.

Actions the COTR must do

Be familiar with the requirements of the FAR 3.104, Procurement Integrity, and supplements concerning contractor employment.

☐ Treat contractors impartially.

☐ Avoid any situations involving conflicts of interest.

☐ Safeguard all procurement sensitive and proprietary information.

☐ Report any suspected violations to the CO and/or the ethics counselor.

☐ File required financial and employment disclosure reports.

☐ Attend yearly ethics and procurement integrity training.

If you are uncertain about any situation you encounter, contact your CO or ethics counselor.

Actions the COTR must not do

☐ Discuss acquisition plans or provide advance information that might give one contractor an advantage over other potential contractors in a forthcoming procurement.

☐ Discuss with the contractor or subcontractors any potential employment opportunities for yourself or your friends, associates, or family members.

☐ Engage in any personal business or professional activity that would cause a conflict of interest between the private interests of the COTR and the public interests of the United States.

☐ Use the COTR position to induce, coerce, or influence any person, including subordinates, to provide any benefits financial or otherwise, for yourself or others.

☐ Solicit or accept favors, gratuities, considerations, assistance, or entertainment offered to the COTR or family members from a contractor or subcontractor that is contemplating doing business with the government.

☐ Release to any individual, or any individual business concern or its representatives, any knowledge acquired in any way concerning proposed procurements by any procuring activity.

H.5. Summary of Practical Ethical Concerns

As a useful summary of "practical" ethical concerns effecting everyday interaction with the contractor, the following chart is provided:

Circumstance	Concern	Recommendation
Office or work areas are shared with contractor personnel.	Privacy is impaired and safeguarding material, data, and communications is difficult.	If offices or work areas must be shared, make sure government employ-employees are trained in ethics and understand their authorities under the contract.
Informal meetings and discussions are held between government and contractor employees.	Objectivity may be impaired. The results of informal meetings are often not documented.	Formalize meetings, take notes, record results and agreements, obtain contractor's agreement "on the record," and keep the CO advised.
Government employees rely on the contractor's records of meetings and discussions.	It is easy to alter the sense of a discussion or an agreement simply by the way it is recorded.	Keep your own [i.e., government) records of all meetings and agreements. Where feasible, obtain contractor agreement on content.
Government employees rely on memory to prompt actions or decisions.	Missed government commitments can mean unduly hindering contractor performance.	Keep adequate records, use to-do lists, etc. Do not rely on daily contact as a reminder.
Prolonged relationships create a "cooperative" atmosphere.	Contractors request consideration from the government with respect to accepting services that almost conform to contract requirements.	The government cannot give up what is paid for without legal consideration, even under the guise of "cooperation." Refer the matter to the CO.
Friendships and social relationships grow out of frequent association with contractor employees.	A conflict of interest could arise. Biased or inflated evaluations could result from favoritism or relaxed standards.	Do not deliberately socialize with contractor personnel (e.g., car pools, lunch, coffee breaks, after work). Rotate contractor performance evaluation assignments.

H.6. Exercise: Conflict of Interest

Determine whether each of the following scenarios constitutes an impermissible conflict of interest.

1. You are a member of a Technical Valuation Panel. You own a single share of stock in a widely held corporation (e.g., IBM) which has submitted a proposal for a major ADPE systems development project. Although the company stands to gain

substantially through the award of a contract, your own financial gain is speculative and, in any respect, insignificant.

2. You are a member of a Technical Evaluation Panel. Your spouse is an employee of one of the offerors -- however, not in the division which has submitted the proposal. In fact, the company establishes a separate profit center for each of its divisions. Thus, the gain or loss of one division does not affect the income statements of the others.

3. You are engaged in writing an SOW for a five-year ADP support services contract. During this period, you have also sent resumes and cover letters to 50 prospective employers, many of whom have regular dealings with your program and are expected to propose on the upcoming solicitation. Forty-five employers did not respond; however, five firms did send a cordial form letter stating that your resume will be retained for future reference.

4. You are conducting a site visit as a COTR. In casual conversation, you inform the contractor that you will be leaving the government in the next couple of months on an "early out" retirement basis. The contractor suggests that if and when you do leave you drop a resume in the mail. The contractor further states that it uses people in your prospective position all the time as consultants. Although it might be questionable to use you on the current contract without agency permission, there is plenty of other work around which is right up your alley.

5. You have received a proposed Key Personnel change. As the COTR, you have been asked to review and recommend approval to the CO. The proposed substitute is highly qualified for the position of Project Manager – the slot being vacated. He is also your former division director who left government last month. Before leaving, he had general oversight responsibilities and appointed staff to serve on the evaluation panel during the award of the subject contract.

Fill in your answers based on what you have learned so far, and review them again after you have read the following chapters to see whether you should amend your answers.

1.

2.

3.

4.

5.

I. What has gone well and means to improve

One of the most vital areas of COTR activity is performance evaluation — the contractor's and the COTR's. It is this activity that is the centerpiece of determining the success of the contractor, the success of the COTR's effort, and what can be done better going forward.

Contractor Performance Evaluation

Document Performance

To identify, classify, and record performance information, the COTR will:

Document performance information

Notify interested parties

Maintain evaluations

(See Attachment Ten for a Sample In-Process Evaluation Form, http://www.governmenttraininginc.com/The-COTR-Handbook.asp)

Document Performance Information

Evaluations are prepared when work under the contract is completed. The manner in which the evaluation is done is usually provided in the contract and may specify:

Which government officials evaluate and document performance

What is included in the documentation

The format for documenting the evaluation

Contracts that have not specified evaluation procedures will at least include information needed for use in future source selection. Interim evaluations will be prepared on contracts with periods of performance (including options) exceeding one year. Interim evaluations will be conducted at sufficient intervals to be useful to source-selection officials seeking current performance information about a contractor. Note: the Interim Evaluation is simply the composite of all the periodic evaluations the COTR does (using, as example, the form in Attachment Ten, http://www.governmenttraininginc.com/The-COTR-Handbook.asp).

Rate Performance

The contract will specify the manner in which contractor performance will be rated. The COTR will rate performance without bias. Examples of areas in which a COTR may evaluate and rate contractor performance include:

☐ Quality of Product or Service - compliance with contract requirements, accuracy of reports, technical excellence.

☐ Timeliness of Performance - compliance with milestones; reliable, responsive to technical direction; completed on time; no liquidated damages assessed.

☐ Cost Control - within budget; current, accurate, and complete billings; actual costs consistent with negotiated costs.

☐ Business Practices - effective management, effective small/small disadvantaged business subcontracting program; reasonable and cooperative behavior; flexible; effective contractor solutions; business-like concern for government interests.

☐ Customer Satisfaction - satisfaction of end users with contractor service.

☐ Key Personnel - how long key personnel stayed on the contract and how well they managed their portion of the contract.

☐ Quality Awards - Receipt of widely recognized quality awards or certifications.

Provide Appropriate Information to Contractor

The CO provides copies of the evaluation to the contractor for comment as soon as practicable after completion. If the contractor disagrees with the evaluation, the COTR may be asked to assist the CO in evaluating any contractor rebuttal.

Notify CO of Recurring Performance Problems

The types of information a COTR needs to include are:

☐ Description of the performance problem

☐ Discussion of mitigating or extenuating circumstance, if any

☐ File of related documents

Analysis of the impact contractor performance problems has had on overall cost and delays in obtaining needed supplies and services; and potential impact on mission accomplishment

Assist the CO Prepare Reports to Debarment and Suspension Official

If circumstances merit contractor debarment or suspension, the COTR provides any additional data requested by the debarment official, such as:

Potential impact of a debarment or suspension on the government's ability to meet its needs

Current mailing address for the contractor and any affiliates

Maintain Evaluations

Retain performance evaluations

Release performance information to other government officials

Destroy past performance records

Retain Performance Evaluations

The following will be filed in the contract file or past-performance database:

Evaluations

Any interim evaluations

Contractor response

Review comments (if any)

The documents will be marked "Source Selection Information" and will be readily accessible by contracting office personnel.

Release Past-performance Information to Other Government Officials

The past-performance evaluations are kept in a database at www.ppirs.gov. They may only be released to other government officials and the contractor whose performance is being evaluated. Disclosure of such information to anyone else could cause harm to both the government and the competitive position of the contractor. The contractor's statement and government review of any contractor rebuttals must be attached to the performance evaluation report and provided to source selection officials requesting a reference check.

Destroy Past-performance Records

Destroy the information within three years after completion of contract performance in accordance with agency procedures.

Performance Rating of the COTR (see Attachment Eleven, http://www.governmenttraininginc. com/The-COTR-Handbook.asp)

To hold COTRs accountable for their contracting work, agencies must first ensure that COTRs are clearly informed about their responsibility and authority, and then assess their

performance in completing these duties. This essential communication of the authority and responsibility a COTR has for a particular contract is expressed through the formal delegation of contracting authority to the COTR.

COTRs who are rated on the performance of their contracting work report more positive contract outcomes, especially in terms of timeliness, quality, and cost, than did COTRs who are not rated on their contracting work. While the practice of evaluating or rating COTRs on the performance of their contracting work is positively related to better contract outcomes, not all COTRs are formally delegated the authority to perform their contracting work. This means that some COTRs are being held responsible for performing their contracting work, but are not necessarily being given the authority to carry out these duties.

1.1. Exercise: Advancing the State of the Art

On April 12, 2008, Techtronics, Inc., was awarded a $2.2 million firm, fixed-price contract for satellite maintenance for the GOES and POES satellites managed by NOAA. A few days after award of the contract, but before Techtronics had begun the work, Dr. Lawrence Abbott, project manager in NOAA, wrote to the company asking it to hold up its services until he could complete an investigation of his own. Dr. Abbott said he felt that his review would add greater merit to whether a contractor was to do the maintenance or it was to be done in-house.

Hearing nothing further from Dr. Abbott, Techtronics wrote to the CO in August to inquire about the status of the doctor's study and the disposition of its own contract. In answer, the CO informed Techtronics that Dr. Abbott was no longer with NOAA, that he knew nothing of a review the doctor was conducting, and that he was surprised to learn that the company had not been working on the contract.

In December, the contractor received a second letter from NOAA. This letter, from Dr. Abbott's successor, said that Dr. Abbott's review had no bearing on the work and directed Techtronics to proceed with the maintenance services as specified in the original contract.

Assignment:

How did this situation arise?

What will Techtronics do now?

What would have been the proper procedure?

Is there a role for a COTR here? If so, what is it?

STEP THREE – KEY SKILL AREAS

There are three central facets of a COTR's role: (1) a technical information conduit, (2) a contracting and regulatory liaison, and (3) a business partnership manager. The changing nature of acquisition work places significant importance on COTR activities. It is essential that all COTRs understand their responsibilities and are provided with appropriate support, training experiences, and developmental tools to effectively perform these responsibilities.

A. Strategic Expertise

The four areas that comprise a complete collection of effective capabilities to fully participate and manage the technical acquisition processes are:

Business/Program/Industry Knowledge and Performance – i.e., sufficient knowledge of laws, regulations and terminology, etc., for a particular field sufficient to work with, understand, and evaluate technical information, and advise on technical issues related to a particular field.

General Management Knowledge and Performance – i.e., skillful application of knowledge or cognitive ability to lead teams by building coalitions, and applying communication, change management, problem solving, influence, business acumen, and conflict resolution skills while remaining focused on results.

Project Management Knowledge and Performance – i.e., the knowledge and skillful application of the principles, techniques, methods, or tools for developing, scheduling, coordinating, and managing projects and resources, including monitoring and inspecting costs, work, and contractor performance.

Acquisition Knowledge and Performance – i.e., the skillful application of knowledge of various types of contracts, techniques for contracting or procurement, contract negotiation and contract administration.

The management competencies that a COTR need bring to bear to achieve this strategic expertise are:

A.1. COTR Professional Management Competencies

Competency	Definition
Oral communication	Expresses information to individuals or groups effectively, taking into account the audience and nature of the information; makes clear and convincing presentations, listens to others; attends to nonverbal cues.
Decision-making	Makes sound, well-informed, and objective decisions; perceives the impact and implications of decisions; commits to action even in uncertain situations to accomplish organizational goals; causes change.
Teamwork	Encourages and facilitates cooperation, pride, trust; fosters commitment; works with others to achieve goals.
Problem solving	Identifies problems; determines accuracy and relevance of information; uses sound judgment to generate and evaluate alternatives, makes recommendations.
Attention to detail	Is thorough when performing work and conscientious about attending to detail.
Reasoning	Identifies rules, principles, or relationships that explain facts, data or other information; analyzes information and makes correct inferences and accurate conclusions.
Flexibility	Is open to change and new information; adapts behavior or work methods in response to new information, changing conditions, or unexpected obstacles; effectively deals with ambiguity.
Interpersonal skills	Shows understanding, courtesy, tact, empathy; develops and maintains relationships; deals with difficult people; relates well to people from varied backgrounds; is sensitive to individual differences.
Self-management and initiative	Sets well-defined and realistic personal goals; displays a high level of initiative, effort, and commitment towards completing assignments in a timely manner; works with minimal supervision; is motivated to achieve; demonstrates responsible behavior.
Integrity and honesty	Contributes to maintaining the integrity of the organization; displays high standards of ethical conduct and understands the impact of violating these standards on an organization, self, and others; is trustworthy.
Planning and evaluating	Organizes work, sets priorities, determines resource requirements, determines goals and strategies; coordinates with other organizations, monitors progress; evaluates outcomes.
Influencing and negotiating	Persuades others to accept recommendations, cooperate, or change their behavior; works with others towards an agreement; negotiates to find mutually acceptable solutions.

Competency	Definition
Writing	Recognizes or uses correct English grammar, punctuation, and spelling; communicates information in a succinct and organized manner, produces written information appropriate for the intended audience.
Project management	Identifies a need for and knows where or how to gather information; organizes and maintains information or information management systems.

B. Acquisition Lifecycle Expertise

B.1. Overview

The COTR's capability and competency areas described above enable the COTR to better perform the technical and communication aspects of the acquisition lifecycle. When COTRs know of potential procurement activities, they will seek to be involved in the technical aspects of the contract beginning with contract development. Their involvement in pre-award technical activities is critical because a well-developed contract lays a foundation for more positive contracting outcomes.

COTRs provide the technical expertise to ensure that the Performance Work Statement requirements are complete and accurate, to establish sound technical review criteria, and to appropriately establish the scope within which all parties to the contract must work. It makes sense that a COTR can more effectively, and perhaps more efficiently, oversee a contract if he or she is involved in establishing the technical aspects of the contract. COTR involvement in the pre-award technical aspects of the contract correlates to more positive contract outcomes. Similarly, technical competencies that a COTR need bring to bear to achieve acquisition lifecycle expertise are:

B.2. COTR Technical Competencies

Competency	Definition
Strategic planning	Advises customers on their acquisition-related roles and the development and implementation of strategies needed to ensure that supplies and services are available when needed to meet mission requirements.
Discover acquisition strategy	Determines which source selection means is appropriate to the purchase. Assesses whether competition, set aside, sole source or other means will be used. Provides "business case analysis" to the CO.

Competency	Definition
Understanding the marketplace	Collects and analyzes relevant market information from government and non-government source; analyzes and provides business advice on the procurement request; reviews and provides business advice in the preparation of requirements documents and related elements of the procurement request.
Articulating requirements	Based on market research plus previous requirements, structures and expresses performance-based requirements for this activity.
Effective publicizing communication	Assists with: publicizing proposed procurements, appropriate subcontracting and make-or-buy requirements, preparing written solicitation that includes appropriate provisions and clauses tailored to the requirement; responds to inquiries about the solicitation received prior to contract award or a request for information under the Freedom of Information Act. Helps conduct pre-proposal conference when appropriate. Recommends amendment or cancellation of a solicitation.
Defining solicitation evaluation elements	If source selection is being done through negotiated procurement, suggests appropriate technical evaluation factors and proposal preparation instructions for incorporation into the solicitation that tie back to technical requirements. Also, assesses whether oral presentations will occur.
Effective negotiation skills and effective analytical skills	Receives proposals for evaluation; assesses compliance with minimum solicitation requirements. Identifies proposals that will not receive further consideration. Applies non-price factors in evaluating proposals and past performance. Assists with determining what pricing information (if any) to require from offerors, adequacy of a firm's accounting and estimating systems, obtaining any necessary audit support. Helps establish pre-negotiation positions including: the need to cancel and re-solicit for price-related reasons, the need for communications, the need for cost information, and the need to negotiate; provides pre-negotiation positions related to cost reasonableness and cost realism by analyzing cost and technical data from the offeror and other sources. Helps develop pre-negotiation positions on terms and conditions other than price, and whether to award without discussions. Conducts communications to enhance government understanding of proposals; allows reasonable interpretation of a proposal; or facilitates the government's evaluation process. Assists with selecting offerors for discussions, negotiation strategy, negotiation session, and documents in the contract file the principal elements of the negotiated agreement.

Competency	Definition
Effective communication of contract requirements	Plans for contract administration. Helps conduct a post-award orientation. Recommends contract modifications when needed. Determines whether or not to exercise an available option. Uses task order contracts, delivery order contracts, and basic ordering agreements.
Effective performance management	Monitors contract performance and takes necessary action related to delays in contract performance or the need to stop work under the contract. Applies remedies to protect the rights of the government under contracts. Documents past-performance information.

The various specific aspects to be accomplished by exercising the Management and Technical Competencies are:

B.3. Management and Technical Competencies for Source Selection

☐ Advise on or determine a need for a product or service

☐ Analyze technical requirements of the product or service

☐ Conduct market research to establish technical requirements or identify potential contractors

☐ Provide technical information to assist in determining type of contract and level of competition

☐ Plan the technical aspects of the source selection process

☐ Establish the solicitation's technical terms and conditions

☐ Help prepare the statement of work (SOW) and other terms and conditions of the solicitation

COTR involvement in contract planning is important to ensure that the contract, from the start, accurately and completely delineates the Government's technical needs and how the deliverables will be assessed to determine if they meet those needs. In the contract planning stage, COTRs work with program managers to determine whether there is a need for the Government to contract for a particular product or service. Then, COTRs work with COs to conduct a more detailed analysis of the Government's needs, including defining the technical requirements or performance standards the contract must meet. COTRs also help establish the initial timeframes for the contract because they know when the deliverable must be provided and/or how long a deliverable could take to be produced. COTR input regarding the contract timeframes is especially important if the deliverable is a subcomponent of a larger agency initiative of which the COTR is thoroughly familiar.

COTRs may use their expertise and familiarity with those contractors to conduct market research to gather information about technical criteria, or to obtain a list of potential sources (contractors).

Sources are companies, organizations, institutions, or individuals capable of providing a product or service that meets Government requirements. The COTR can obtain source information from a wide variety of information sources including:

☐ Recommendations from technical experts.

☐ Past contracts for similar products and services.

☐ Responses to public announcements published on-line.

☐ Small Business Development Office.

The CO uses this information to promote competition and ensure the agency gets a sufficient number of high quality proposals from which to select a final contractor.

B.4. Type of Contract

The Type of Contract means the financial arrangement and who assumes the risk of contract performance. There are basically to ends to the contract type spectrum. On the one side, is the Fixed Price family of contracts in which the contractor's payment is tied to performance that meets the requirements and is therefore accepted by the Government. By contract, the Cost-Reimbursement family of contracts occurs where the Government assumes the performance risk, the contractor is guaranteed reimbursement of all allowable costs and so the contractor's mandate is to show up and attempt to provide full performance. See Attachment Two for a fuller discussion.

COTRs also provide technical expertise to help the CO determine the appropriate type of contract to allow the Government to obtain what it needs at a reasonable cost and at an acceptable level of risk. The type of contract chosen determines the appropriate level of competition and negotiation and the pricing structure of the contract. The two major families of contract types are: fixed price and cost reimbursement. The basic differences between the "families" are that with fixed price contracts, the performance risk is on the contractor's shoulders and payment occurs for performance accepted by the Government. By contrast, cost-reimbursement contracts have the Government assuming the performance risk and paying the contractor all allowed costs, so that the contractor's obligation is to "try his or her best."

Now the type of contract will vary depending on what is purchased. The gamut of purchases can range from the simple purchase of commercial products (e.g., office supplies)

to long-term research and development services (e.g., advanced technical system design and testing) to capital construction (e.g., building courthouses, prisons or roads). There are certain types of contracts, such as those for major research and development services that are particularly difficult to develop and manage. For these kinds of contracts, the Government may not know what the final product or service will look like or how it will perform because of rapidly changing needs or technology. Instead, the product or service is developed in partnership with the contractor, which makes the involvement of highly skilled Government employees even more important to ensuring positive outcomes.

Commercial, fixed-price contracts, such as those used to purchase office supplies or facilities maintenance services, typically have price ranges associated with specific levels of quality and quantity that have been established over time to the point of becoming recognized standards. Commercial, fixed-price contracts do not typically require complex negotiation to obtain a fair price for the Government and several contractors are usually able to provide competitive prices. The risk to the Government is more limited as it is easier to show when a commercial item does or does not meet established standards. The involvement of COTRs is useful in these types of contracts to ensure that the appropriate quality of the commercial product is obtained at the appropriate time, at an appropriate cost.

By contrast, purchasing professional services, major integrated hardware systems, research and development services, or construction services can be more complex. The types of contracts used here vary more than with commercial buys. However, in today's "performance-based environment" more effort and expertise is used by the technical community to do a better job of defining what is needed. In complex, cutting-edge research and development contracts, the Government may not always know what the optimal deliverable of the contract will look like. In either case, the overall costs cannot be well estimated, and the risk of contract failure is borne by the Government in those instances when more money must be paid to compensate contractors required to put in more effort than was initially estimated. Given the level of uncertainty in estimating final costs and the risks to the Government, the role of the COTR is essential. Under these circumstances, the COTR (and technical colleagues) plans the technical aspects of the contract, anticipates the risk and potential challenges the contractor and the Government may face and how those risks may be managed over time, and helps establish appropriate intervals and milestones for the contract.

B.5. Purpose of the Factors and Subfactors

Evaluation factors permit an objective assessment of the merits of individual proposals against standards, rather than against other proposals. Each RFP must identify the specific evaluation factor and the relative importance of the factor used so prospective offerors may

judge the basis by which their proposals are to be evaluated, and how they may best devote their efforts in preparing their proposals. Factors will be definable in specific qualitative terms that are readily understandable by both the offerors and the evaluators.

Development of evaluation factors and the assignment of the relative importance or weight to each factor require the exercise of judgment on a case by case basis because they must be tailored to the requirements of the individual acquisition. Because the factors will serve as a standard against which all proposals will be evaluated, it is imperative that they be chosen carefully to emphasize those factors considered to be critical in the selection of a contractor.

The final evaluation factors and indications of their relative importance or weights, as included in the RFP, cannot be changed except by a formal amendment to the RFP issued by the Contracting Officer. No factors other than those set forth in the RFP can be used in the evaluation of proposals.

B.5.a. Develop Technical Evaluation Criteria

Technical evaluation criteria are used to determine which offeror's approach to satisfying Government's requirements is most advantageous. The Contracting Officer may request the COTR to prepare a technical evaluation criteria and plan that describes:

☐ The criteria to be used for evaluating offerors' technical proposals.

☐ Guidelines for a technical evaluation panel on how to evaluate technical proposals.

☐ Be specifically applicable to the acquisition—they will not merely be restatement of factors from previous acquisitions

☐ Represent only the significant areas of importance that must be emphasized, rather than a multitude of factors (All factors tend to lose importance if too many are included. Using too many factors and subfactors will prove as detrimental as using too few.)

Examples of topics that form a basis for the development of evaluation factors are listed below. These examples are intended to help Project Officers develop actual evaluation criteria for a specific acquisition and will only be used if they are applicable to that acquisition.

☐ Understanding of the problem and statement of work

☐ Method of accomplishing the objectives and intent of the SOW

☐ Soundness of the scientific or technical approach for executing the requirements of the statement of work (to include, when applicable, preliminary layouts, sketches,

diagrams, other graphic representations, calculations, curves, and other data necessary for presentation, substantiation, justification, or understanding of the approach)

☐ Special technical factors, such as experience or pertinent novel ideas in the specific branch of science or technology involved

☐ Feasibility and/or practicality of successfully accomplishing the requirements (to include a statement and discussion of anticipated major difficulties and problem areas and recommended approaches for their resolution)

☐ Availability of required special research, tests, and other equipment or facilities

☐ The managerial ability to achieve delivery or performance requirements as demonstrated by the proposed use of management and other personnel resources, and to successfully manage the project, including subcontractor and/or consultant efforts, if applicable, as evidenced by the management plan and demonstrated by previous experience

☐ Availability, qualifications, experience, education, and competence of professional, technical, and other personnel, to include proposed subcontractors and consultants (as evidenced by resumes, endorsements, and explanations of previous efforts)

☐ Soundness of the proposed staff time or labor hours, propriety of personnel classifications (professional, technical, others), necessity for type and quantity of material and facilities proposed, validity of proposed subcontracting, and necessity of proposed travel

The FAR requires the following factors be included:

☐ Price or cost;

☐ Past Performance (all solicitations with an estimated value in excess of $100,000).

B.5.b. Weighting Factors and Significant Subfactors

A statement or indication of the relative importance or weight must be assigned to each evaluation factor. This informs prospective offerors (and evaluators) of the specific significance of each factor in comparison to the other factors. Similarly, if a factor is subdivided into significant subfactors, each of the subfactors must be assigned a statement or indication of the relative importance of weight.

Evaluations may be conducted using any rating method or combination of methods, including color ratings, adjectival ratings, numerical weights, or ordinal ratings. The numerical score method is preferable because it is more precise and informative. However, in some instances the use of the adjective description method may be more appropriate.

The relative strengths, deficiencies, significant weaknesses, and risks supporting proposal evaluation must be documented in the contract files.

B.5.c. Cost or Price as a Factor

Cost or price to the Government shall be included as an evaluation factor in every source selection. A statement must be included in the RFP to reflect the relationship of cost or price in comparison to other factors. The Contracting Officer must ensure that this statement accurately reflects the appropriate balance between cost or price and the technical factors. The Contracting Officer and Project Officer will work together in arriving at the final determination regarding the relationship.

The solicitation must state whether all evaluation factors other than cost or price, when combined are:

☐ Significantly more important than cost or price;

☐ Approximately equal to cost or price; or

☐ Significantly less important than cost or price.

B.5.d. Sample Evaluation Factors

The two formats that follow are for general guidance and will be varied to suit the requirements for each individual project. The items identified may be expanded or modified to reflect technical factors considered to be critical to the specific acquisition. The specific points assigned to each factor must be identified in the RFP, and the factors are listed in their relative order of importance.

Format I
Understanding of the Problem (40 Points)

Provide a comprehensive statement of the problem, scope and purpose of the project to demonstrate your complete understanding of the intent and requirements. This understanding indicates a clear awareness of the contract objectives.

Soundness of Approach (30 Points)

Proposal describes the proposed approach to comply with each of the requirements specified in the Statement of Work. The proposal is consistent with the stated goals and objectives. The proposed approach of ensuring the achievement of timely and acceptable performance is well documented and sound. Milestone and/or phasing charts illustrate a logical sequence of proposed events.

Personnel (20 Points)

(1) The staff is competent and experienced in the skills required in the Statement of Work. Resumes of staff and consultants reflect not only academic qualifications, but also length and variety of experience in similar tasks and clearly demonstrate relevant training and experience. If subcontractors are proposed, information is provided to support the qualifications of the subcontractors.

2. Information is provided as to which key personnel will be used on this project. Documentation is provided on the decision making authority of the project director as related to other elements of the organization. The percentage of time each staff member will contribute to the program is adequately identified. The extent to which outside consultants or specialists will be used is documented and evidence of their availability is provided.

Facilities (10 Points)

A description and location of your organization's research, test, and other facilities to be used on this project is to be provided.

Award will be made to that responsible offeror who can best perform the required work in a manner most advantageous to the Government, considering cost and all of the above factors.

Format 2
Technical Approach   Total: 40 Points

1. Understanding and awareness of tasks required including the quality of approaches offered for dealing with these tasks.   8 points

2. Data collection techniques that are practical, sound and timely and that reflect both an awareness of potential methodological and inferential problems and proposed solutions for resolving them. 8 points

3. An administrative framework satisfactory for maintaining quality control over the implementation and operations of the study.   8 points

4. Data handling and analysis techniques are relevant and sound.   8 points

5. An overall approach that reflects clarity, conciseness, general responsiveness, and the ability to comply with the requirements of the Statement of Work. 8 points

B.6. Oral Presentations (OFPP "Guidance for the Use of Oral Presentations")

The use of oral presentations as a substitute for a portion of the traditional written proposal in competitive negotiated procurements is gaining increased interest. This concept is viewed as a method of streamlining the proposal evaluation and source selection process. Procurement and program staff who have tried this approach have found it to be an exciting and effective way of doing business.

The purpose of using oral presentations is to reduce or eliminate the need for written material where information can be conveyed in a more meaningful and efficient way through verbal means. Its major use has been to permit evaluators to receive information regarding the offeror's ability to perform the work directly from the key members of the offeror's team who will actually perform the work. In many cases, the evaluators conduct the oral presentation in interview form, posing sample tasks, probing for additional information, or using other techniques to determine the ability of the offeror.

The advantages of using oral presentations include the reduction of time and cost in the source selection process. The process can also reduce the offeror's costs and increase competition. In addition, the "face to face" interaction improves communication and enhances the exchange of information between the Government and the offerors. Oral presentation provides a more level playing field for those offerors with expertise to satisfy the Government's requirement, but less experience in preparing written Government proposals. This method can also help the Government determine which offerors truly possess the capability to perform versus those offerors who have the resources of great proposal writers, but less ability to produce the actual work. All the advantages of the oral presentation method mentioned work together to improve the ability of the Government to select the most advantageous offer.

Oral presentations are most useful in situations where the Government's Statement of Work is clear and not overly complex in nature. Oral presentations are also useful in requirements where the offeror's qualifications and demonstrated understanding of the work serves as the prime evaluation criterion.

In terms of application, agencies are free to design an approach that best fits the nature of the procurement and available resources. Variations in approach have included:

☐ Media used to record the presentation

☐ Restrictions on the extent and nature of material used in the presentation

☐ Type, number, and background of Government participants

☐ Type, number, and background of offeror's presentation team

☐ Amount of time permitted for the presentation

In all instances, the RFP must notify that oral presentations will be used to evaluate and select the contractor, and explicit instructions must be included regarding the extent and nature of the approach. Setting a firm time limit ensures that each offeror has an equal amount of time and controls the amount of material used during the presentation. All of the Government evaluators who are responsible for evaluating the offers for a specific requirement will be present at each oral presentation. Further, requiring the presenters to be the same individuals who will perform or direct the work will avoid use of "professional" presenters. Rejecting submission of video tapes or other types of media during the presentation will also ensure that presentations are made in person and are representative of the offeror's true capabilities.

Evaluations can be performed after all the presentations are held or after each individual presentation. There is no firm rule, however there are benefits to promptly evaluating each presentation while the information is still fresh and the evaluation team is still assembled.

In conclusion, the use of oral presentations appears to be an effective method of streamlining source selection and enhancing the ability of the Government to discern the most advantageous offer. Based upon an examination of the procurement statutes and regulations, and GAO and court cases, there are no legal impediments to the use of oral presentations. Used appropriately, it is a proven alternative to the costly and time-consuming method of written proposals. If you are interested in pursuing this method for one of your requirements, contact your Contracting Officer early in the acquisition process to obtain more information and specific guidance geared to your acquisition.

B.7. Technical Source Selection Assistance

Finally, COTRs can work with the CO to prepare the technical portions of the solicitation which is: the formal request for contractors to submit proposals to accomplish specified work for the Government. Fundamentally, the COTR helps develop the Government's technical requirements as the "core" of the solicitation information and subsequent contractor performance.

B.7.a. Contract Formation and Selection

☐ Develop and issue the solicitation

☐ Serve on panels to evaluate bids and proposals—using a source selection plan

☐ Provide award recommendations to the CO with written justification

The contract formation phase begins with the formal solicitation for proposals and ends with the awarding of the contract. The solicitation is published in a "request for proposal" or "request for bid" to inform potential contractors (those who wish to provide the product or service to the Government) of the Government's needs for goods and/or services. The solicitation is the basis on which contractors "propose" to the Government how and what they will provide, when they will provide it, and at what cost. If significant aspects of the Government's requirements were overlooked or not sufficiently specified in the contract planning phase, then the contract formation phase will probably not result in a contract that can accomplish the work intended.

COTRs work with the CO to develop the source selection process including the technical criteria for evaluating contractors' proposals.

B.7.b. Chair the Technical Evaluation Panel

A technical evaluation panel is used to assess offeror's proposals. The COTR assembles individuals who are technically competent in identifying the strengths and weaknesses of offeror's proposals. The panel may be chaired by the COTR.

B.7.c. Solicitation Assistance to the CO

The solicitation phase is the time between issuing a solicitation and receiving offers. During this time, the Contracting Officer relies on the COTR for technical assistance, and may request the COTR to:

☐ Draft answers to questions about the technical requirement, delivery or performance schedule.

☐ Participate in pre-proposal conferences.

☐ Advise on amending or canceling the solicitation before the due date for proposals.

☐ Refer all calls and correspondence from potential offerors to the Contracting Officer.

B.7.d. Evaluation and Award Assistance

The evaluation phase is the time in the procurement cycle used for evaluating, selecting and notifying the contractor about contract award. Contracting Officer may seek COTR assistance on any of the following tasks:

☐ Chair or serve as a member on the technical evaluation team.

☐ Prepare findings and recommendations on offeror's proposals:

☐ Technical strengths, weaknesses, or deficiencies.

☐ Reasonableness or realism of proposed labor hours, skill mix, material, etc.

☐ Proposal rankings.

☐ Reference checks and contractor past-performance evaluations.

☐ Fact-finding sessions.

☐ Preparation for negotiations.

☐ Discussions with offerors.

☐ Evaluating contractor's subcontracting plan, make-or-buy program, equipment, and facilities.

☐ Reviewing unsolicited proposals and advising whether offered products or services are innovative, unique, and independently originated and developed.

☐ Participating in debriefings of unsuccessful offerors.

☐ Gathering facts or preparing justifications on technical issues to respond to protests.

The technical assessment of the contract proposals is the primary activity of COTRs during this phase. Once proposals or bids are received, they are evaluated against a preestablished set of criteria to determine which contractor offers the best value for the Government. COTRs are helpful in interpreting or assessing the proposals to determine which ones provide complete information from which to judge the capability of the contractor. COTRs will also be involved in assessing contractor proposals to ensure that the technical criteria for bid evaluation established during contract planning are accurately and completely applied and that any technical issues are resolved so that each contractor can compete fully and fairly for the Government's business. COTRs may also serve on panels established to provide formal review and rating of proposals.

Often, COTRs are involved with the CO in negotiations between the Government and the contractor(s) to ensure that the final agreement will meet the Government's technical requirements and be satisfactory to all parties. COTRs may be involved in other contract activities during contract formation including investigating contractor past performance and providing input for estimating contract costs. The contract formation stage results in a signed contract between the Government and a specified contractor or contractors. This contract will clearly and completely lay out the Government's requirements, the roles of both the contractor and the Government, and the means to effectively assess that the Government's requirements (quality, timeliness, completeness, and cost) are met.

B.8. Contract Management Overview

The next stage of the contract is the contract management phase (see also Section E under Step Two). This phase begins with the initiation of work by the contractor and ends

with the closeout or termination of the contract. The goal of this phase is to ensure the contractor meets the government's technical requirements for quality and completeness, at the cost, and within the timeframes established by the contract. Assuming a well-developed contract, the success of the contract depends on the contractor's performance in delivering services and products and the government's performance in monitoring the contract and assessing that these technical requirements are met. COTRs generally perform this technical oversight function because they are usually the only people with the expertise and position within the agency to assess the contractor's performance. Typical activities in the contract management phase include initiation of work and administration of the contract, monitoring the technical work of the contractor (including quality assurance and inspection of deliverables), contractor personnel oversight and payment and accounting of contract funds, modification of the contract, satisfying any special terms of the contract, and closeout or termination of the contract.

Contract management is the most critical phase from the program office's perspective because it is during this phase that the contract will either succeed or fail to satisfy the government's requirements. If the contract succeeds, it means that the contractor has produced the products and services required, and that the government's representative — usually the COTR — accurately and effectively judged that the products and services satisfy the government's requirements in terms of quality, timelines, completeness, and cost. In the end, the government has gotten what it needs, and the contractor is paid a fair price for those deliverables. In this case, the contractor did what was expected and the government's representatives did their job in overseeing and certifying the contractor's work. Contract management is often extremely challenging and problems in managing contracts can result in the failure of the contract.

COTRs are intimately involved in all parts of contract management, but their key responsibility is to ensure that all the technical issues of the contract are managed effectively. COTRs must work hand in hand with the CO to resolve any problems that arise. Technical issues in contract management, such as monitoring contractor performance, judging the quality of deliverables, and knowing when contracts will be modified, are complex. Inspection standards for some products and deliverables are well established, but standards for more complex deliverables may have to be created for each contract. More complex and costly contracts, or contracts that require more judgment on the part of the COTR, make the COTRs job more difficult. It is under these circumstances that it is especially critical to effectively select, train, and manage COTRs, so they can do their part to ensure positive contract outcomes.

Administration

- Serve as agency's technical representative for contract administration
- Represent agency in technical meetings, record important facts
- Confer with program office and user groups on contract performance
- Maintain COTR file
- Assist contractor in understanding technical requirements
- Monitoring the technical work of the contractor, quality assurance, and inspection of deliverables
- Determine and list the deliverables required from the contractor, with due dates
- Monitor the contractor's compliance with submitting deliverables
- Review and approve or reject technical deliverables
- Give technical direction to contractor
- Ensure all work is in accordance with the contract requirements
- Review and monitor progress reports and work plans
- Ensure the contractor is complying with its quality control systems
- Advise the CO of work that is accepted or rejected
- Ensure the contractor properly corrects all defects and omissions
- Changes and modifications
- Advise the CO of the need to issue change orders, develop estimates for equitable adjustments, assist in evaluating contractor claims
- Perform a technical review of contractor proposed changes
- Contractor human resources and financial oversight issues
- Ensure contractor exhibits required materials for EEO, contract laws, and job safety
- Report violations of labor standards to the CO
- Monitor time worked and contractor record-keeping procedures
- Ensure contractor enforces all health and safety requirements
- Ensure contractor assigns employees with the necessary capabilities, qualifications, and experience
- Review and quickly process contractor invoices
- Determine if progress or advance payment requests will be processed
- Contract closeout or termination
- Provide technical information for contract termination decisions
- Forward COTR file to CO when COTR duties end

It is always hoped that contract difficulties will be minor and easily resolved. However, when the contract deliverables significantly fail to meet the technical requirements, are not timely, are not complete, or are more costly than originally agreed upon, then the government or the contractor must take action to correct the situation. Regardless of the cause of the problem, or who takes the action, the problem is likely to increase costs to the government and to reduce the chances for a successful outcome. COTR involvement in these situations is critical to ensure successful resolution of contract problems. When the structure of the contract is such that the risk of non-performance is borne more by the government, the potential costs to the taxpayer for contract problems and/or contract failure are even greater. In these situations, it is imperative that the COTRs involved in the technical aspects of the contract have the expertise, authority, and managerial support to effectively perform their contracting duties on behalf of the government.

The final activities in contract management involve closing out or terminating the contract, each of which requires different but important work for the COTRs. If the contractor was successful in meeting the government's requirements, the contract is closed out. Close-out activities include certifying completion of all deliverables, reviewing and storing records used during the contract, and completing the final payments to the contractor. A contract can also be terminated before its completion. If there were significant problems during the execution of the contract resulting in the contractor's failure to perform, the contract can be terminated for cause. Alternately, if the government's requirements have changed significantly, the contract can be terminated based on those changing needs. Termination of contracts may require more work for the COTR, such as providing evidence of technical insufficiency and furnishing other administrative documentation that will withstand contract review, as well as audit and appeals procedures. The purpose is to end the contract and minimize the cost to the government. Often, a failed contract will require additional effort and money to hire a new contractor to complete or redo the work.

C. Building cooperative relationships among the stakeholders

COTRs work with many other federal employees in performing their contracting duties including program supervisors, program managers, executives, COs, and other employees in a variety of other occupations. The perceptions COTRs have of these employees have an important relationship to how well COTRs are able to perform their role in the contracting process. When COTRs rate these other employees as being competent, ethical, and supportive of the COTRs' work, it is easier for the COTRs to perform their contracting duties, thus having a positive effect on contract outcomes. Conversely, having to work with employees whom COTRs perceive as less competent, less supportive, and having questionable ethics

could make the COTRs job more challenging, thus having a potential negative effect on contract outcomes. In these more adverse kinds of circumstances, the COTR may have to spend effort accomplishing work that others will be doing, or may otherwise have to spend effort avoiding or overcoming ethical dilemmas. These efforts may take away from the COTRs ability to deal with the more technical issues of the contract, and thus can negatively affect contract outcomes.

A cooperative relationship between the CO and the COTR, at least from the COTR's perspective, is related to improved contract outcomes. Agencies will heed these perceptions in terms of the contracting structure and processing requirements COs and COTRs must use. When COs and COTRs work well together, the data suggest that better contract outcomes will result.

COTRs also work with other agency employees in doing contract work. For example, they work with administrative, finance, logistic, and legal staff, as well as technical experts in other functional areas related to the contract. In some agencies, COTRs routinely work with only one or two of these employees. In other agencies, and especially for large, complex, and costly contracts, COTRs are members of a team of such professionals who work together to oversee and manage the contract. Agencies need to ensure that the right people, with the right skills are tapped to perform the various roles in the contracting process.

D. Communications expertise

There are two threads that are interwoven in ensuring successful COTR carrying out of responsibilities. They are: technical and communication. We have discussed both of them. Here, focus is provided on how you can "slow the action down" and pick up insights and tips for strengthening the way you interact with others.

D.1. Seven Guidelines for Communications

1. Prepare your message in advance.

2. Transmit your message in terms the receiver will accept.

3. Be aware of the feelings on both sides.

4. Time your message carefully.

5. Listen for the receiver's message.

6. Draw the receiver out.

7. Test to make sure your message has been accepted.

Preparing Your Message

Identify the problem or issue to be communicated by:

A. Clarifying the problem through eliminating nonessential information

B. Gathering all available data

C. Assessing possible alternatives or solutions

D. Selecting the best course of action

BE PREPARED! YOUR BEST SOLUTION MAY NOT BE THE SAME AS YOUR RECEIVER'S

Transmitting Your Message

As the transmitter, you are responsible for getting the message across without misunderstanding or misinterpretation. How can you keep the message clear?

☐ Keep it simple.

☐ Avoid fear or antagonism.

☐ Be constructive.

☐ Watch your semantics.

☐ Repeat/summarize.

☐ Check nonverbals.

☐ Get feedback.

Implications:

☐ Practice the message before sending it.

☐ Obtain feedback on your communication content and form from colleagues before encountering the actual receiver.

☐ Pay particular attention to the gender and ethnic context of your transmission.

☐ Be Aware of Feelings

What can affect how the receiver interprets your message?

☐ The message

☐ Tone of voice

☐ Emotions

☐ Attitudes

☐ Relative rank

☐ Project priority

☐ Syntax

☐ Context

☐ History of interactions

☐ Nonverbals

☐ Policies

☐ Distractions

Implications:

☐ Interpreting any message means handling several factors.

Distinguishing which factors have more influence in any communication becomes one way of improving your ability.

Check out the receiver's attitude, or emotional state, or nonverbal behavior, or level of distraction, or context of message, or etc., before communicating the actual message.

Timing Your Message Carefully

☐ When is the best time?

☐ When it is convenient.

☐ When the recipient is free.

☐ When you are expected.

☐ When you have established a rapport.

When is the worst time?

☐ When the recipient is busy.

☐ When the recipient is pre-occupied.

☐ When the recipient is disinterested.

☐ When the recipient is upset.

Implications:

☐ Plan to speak as much as speak to plan.

☐ Check out the recipient's situation before communicating.

☐ The more important the message, the more critical timing becomes.

☐ Listening to the Receiver's Message

Effective listening means:

☐ Giving the receiver a chance to respond.

☐ Accepting the receiver's input without criticism.

☐ Being aware of body language, voice tone and choice of words.

☐ Listening for what is not said.

Implications:

☐ Give responses indicative of listening.

☐ Question and paraphrase as a means of sustaining what you have heard.

☐ Demonstrate nonverbal, attentive behavior to the speaker.

☐ Draw the Receiver Out

☐ Encourage full disclosure from the recipient:

☐ Evoke - Ask general questions about your message.

■ Examples – What do you think of the idea? Has your office ever dealt with anything like this?

☐ Reiterate - Summarize and repeat the recipient's responses.

■ Examples – Are you saying that while this might work on a mainframe, it is not likely to be feasible on a LAN?

☐ Follow Up - Pursue partial responses.

■ Examples – You said that this system meets only the requirement for data storage. What other requirements need also to be met?

Implications:

Through these three means, try to obtain the entire communication.

If appropriate, listen for feedback about other facets of the message not communicated at first.

☐ The major thrust is mutual understanding.

☐ Ensure Your Message is Accepted

☐ Getting the message and buying into it is not the same thing:

☐ Review interpretations of the message with the receiver.

☐ Review the receiver's opinion of the message.

☐ Evaluate differences between .the receiver's opinion and yours.

Understand how to resolve the differences between what is sent and what is received, as well as the respective understandings of the message.

Implications:

☐ Need to have a clear message that is also sent and received clearly.

☐ Sustain mutual involvement to resolve any communication errors.

☐ If message acceptance is still elusive, discover why and how to mitigate this situation.

☐ Needing to Modify Communication

☐ Circumstances will arise in which the facets of communication may be changed:

Sender -

Choose a different person to communicate the message when personalities, content or influence necessitate it.

Receiver -

Choose a different person for similar reasons to sender.

Message -

In communicating, there is always the chance of misunderstanding. Thus, be prepared to rephrase, use analogies, try another time for communication, reorder message logic, repeat, speak with the receiver alone, or speak with the receiver together with others, and so forth.

Transmission-

Substitute or add mediums to sustain the message. Examples are: face-to-face, telephone, fax or written, or teleconference; informal or formal; major point of contact or any point of contact; impersonal or personal.

D.2. Connections between Communication Tools & Contract Management

A valuable means of assessing how well the message is understood is feedback. Pointers include:

☐ Reiterate the message as you have received it as clearly as possible.

☐ Review interpretations of the message with the sender.

☐ Provide feedback on the message only when the communicators are ready.

☐ Limit feedback to issues the listener can do something about.

☐ Ensure that all communicators are given the opportunity to provide feedback.

☐ Request clarification of any part of the message which is not clear.

☐ Be descriptive rather than evaluative with your comments.

☐ Review how feedback will strengthen actions taken as result of communication.

Relationship between Communication Techniques and Procurement Process for Administration

Post-award orientation:

☐ Presentations

☐ Avoid misunderstanding

☐ Clarification

Technical direction:

☐ Meetings

☐ Presentations

☐ Establish understanding

☐ Ethics

☐ Avoid misunderstanding

☐ Clarification

☐ Reach technical agreement

Monitor key personnel assignments:

☐ Interviewing

☐ Monitor performance

Monitor project progress and performance, meetings, presentations

☐ Establish understanding

☐ Ethics

☐ Avoid misunderstanding

☐ Clarification

Approve deliverables

☐ -- Monitor performance

Resolve performance problems

☐ Meetings

☐ Reach technical agreement

☐ Communicate problems

☐ Resolve problems

☐ Negotiations

☐ Listening

Approve payment

☐ Monitoring contractor performance

Closeout contract

☐ Establish understanding

Define changes in Task Order requirements

☐ Establish understanding

☐ Negotiating

☐ Reach agreement

D.3. Resolving Problems

Embedded in almost every communication instance developed here is the intention to identify and resolve problems. But with the focus on a particular communication mode, attention is not always clear or recognized about this area. Thus, the rationale for this topic being treated separately: to be better able to integrate problem solving with the other surveillance activities.

Definition: Process by which a performance concern is identified, understood, resolved and prevented –

I. Warning signs of a project in trouble:

A. Delays

B. Cost overruns

C. Quality shortcomings

D. Chronic technical problems

E. Excuses

F. No action plan

II. Identifying effective courses of action:

A. Recognition that a problem exists

B. Definition of the problem

C. Causes of the problem

D. Alternative ways of resolving the problem

E. Choice of alternatives

F. Implementation and control

III. *Process for curing performance discrepancies:*

    A. Informal discussion via telephone, face-to-face, discrepancy letter or the like

    B. Repeat communication using different means

    C. Partially implement solutions, if possible

    D. Follow-up communication results

    E. Ask contracts office to send official notice of performance deficiencies

    F. Follow-up, informal communication about notice

    G. Discuss stronger measures to protect government interest with contracting officials

    H. Continue follow through of actions taken

IV. *Role of the COTR in effective communication:*

    A. First line of response in sensing performance problems

    B. Need well-document interactions and responses

    C. Can use differing communication styles in dealing with the contractor:

        1. Acceptance

        2. Observation

        3. Motivation

        4. Confrontation

        5. Persuasion

V. *Implications:*

    A. Process not used to punish contractor

    B. Explain that firm's performance failure may affect earnings, completion and future work

    C. Dialogue about preventive measures

Example: Getting Contractor Performance Back on Track

Performance gets off track – what is your legitimate role and responsibility in correcting this situation?

Demonstrate effective communication tools

Focus as much on problem resolution as prevention through follow up

Causes of contractor problems: i) unforeseen events, ii) government-caused delays, iii) technical difficulties, iv) competing demands, and v) inability to access data

D.4. Communication which Exceeds Authority

I. Concept: Constructive change –

A. Approval for change done without proper authority; that is, violation of technical guidance procedures

B. Such approval has only negative consequences on effective performance

II. Reasons why Constructive Change occurs:

A. Not knowing proper administrative procedures to follow

B. Not understanding the requirement, keeping accurate administrative records, or knowing the limits to your authority

C. Willing to violate contract clauses to obtain needed outputs

D. Having informal agreement from authorized officials allowing changes to be made by COTR

E. Coercion from a contractor

III. Process: Ratification –

A. CO must step in and clean up the contractual mess

B. COTR or other technical person must explain in writing and in person all circumstances surrounding the change

C. Impacts of ratification are to create delays, increase costs, reduce quality and endanger government technical personnel influence over task order or contract affairs

IV. Avoidance Procedures:

A. Contract clauses provide remedies for most situations

B. Use effectively technical direction to mitigate "unnecessary changes" (Based on the results, if a change is required, then proceed to C.)

C. COTR can carry out all change steps discussed herein, but cannot in any way leave the contractor with the impression that the change is official

D. COTR works with contractor on a potential change, and the procurement office is informed at every step

E. If the procurement office gives cautionary feedback to COTR, it is to be used in further handling the change

F. COTR can give "green light" for change only if given delegated authority up to certain dollar limit by the CO

G. Except within delegated authority, COTR can only direct the contractor to modify work activities if there is a clear and present danger to life, limb or property

D.4.a. Communication Cautions

☐ Do not have a well-documented file to provide complete picture of the problem

☐ Unable to study file, postulate problem, substantiate with causes and present findings to contractor for concurrence

☐ Fail to discuss and reach agreement on what the problem is, why it exists, what will be done to resolve it and what will be done to prevent it

☐ Not willing to discover any subsequent contractor communication responses which tip you to performance problems

☐ Exceed authority through unauthorized changes

☐ Discussion leads into other areas beyond the scope of the issues and/or the contract/order

☐ Not prepared to have thorough discussion of technical issues

☐ Have insufficient information from prior communications which thwart ability to reach technical agreement

D.5. Ethics in Communications

Communication is the medium through which ethical behavior is spread or not. The key is not to change morals; rather, it is to become more aware of what communication instances can straddle or cross the ethics line.

Definition: Ethics are the guidelines to convey what types of behaviors are morally wrong or could appear morally wrong.

D.5.a. Situations Leading to Potential Abuse

A. Failure to consider any interest but your own

B. Passing the ethical "buck" elsewhere

C. Getting the job done at the expense of ethical considerations

D. "Protecting" some interest through withholding information

E. Inappropriately releasing confidential or secure information

F. Responding to unethical behavior in kind

G. If it does not hurt anyone, then ethical infractions are permitted

H. It is OK if I do not gain personally

I. Receiving gifts, favors or benefits because of public position

J. Exercising inappropriate co-employment or allowing contractor employment marketing

K. Using public resources for private gain

L. Not deciding public issues on their merit due to real or apparent conflict of interest

Using influence: sustaining stewardship relations with the contractor.

The government has primary duty to ensure its contractual efforts bring expected, agreed-to-results.

Obtaining the above objective means having frequent discussions or reviews of the contractor's performance. If the contractor is fully meeting the contractual requirements, then the dialogue is in the "check-up" mode. If the contractor is not meeting the requirements, then the communication options become more diverse and tricky.

The impact of the government-initiated discussion is to resolve performance concerns, not create new problems based on the communication.

The challenge then becomes to focus the interaction to the issues at hand, being clear where both the government's and the contractor's responsibilities start and stop.

Protecting the government's interest forms the basis for any feedback to the contractor. Yet, giving no feedback does not absolve the performance from reflecting what is legally mandated.

Having undue influence by the contractor (in tangible or intangible forms) threaten the "arms length" relationship and create potential judgment bias.

The influence challenge for government representatives is to exert it as a direct function of:

☐ The complexity of the work;

☐ The past purchasing history;

☐ The past experience with the contractor;

☐ The level of rapport; and

☐ The need to reiterate the government's interest in this effort.

D.5.b. Practical Examples of Potential Ethical Infractions

Conflict of Interest – having a pre-determined interest, relationship or influence which can reduce one's objectivity in evaluating the contractor's effort. Instances include:

☐ Financial

☐ Friendship

☐ Corporate knowledge

☐ Inside information

☐ Prior experience

☐ Contract with former employee

Managing the Contractor's Performance – giving feedback on "how" to perform rather than monitor what has been done. This is a fundamental undoing of the legal arrangement between the government and the contractor.

Keeping Independent Records – failure to do this leaves no choice but to rely on the contractor's written and oral interpretation of performance. The inability to corroborate the event sequence by having a second version of monitoring and performance actions implies the lack of protecting the government interest.

Abdicating Performance Standards – the technical elements of a contract or task order contain the standards of performance to judge if the actual effort is meeting the requirements. Abandoning the "enforcement" of such standards demonstrates:

☐ Not living up to the government's responsibility to communicate in a timely manner about performance

  ■ Not protecting the government's interest

■ Not communicating performance evaluation findings to the contractor

Unauthorized Discussion or Commitment – the actions of giving the green light to the contractor to act or perform in ways which are:

☐ Beyond the scope of the government individual's authority

☐ Outside the purview of the contract or order

Such behavior (whether perceived or actual) must be avoided since the breach of authority undermines the government s ability to sustain its interest. Instances include, in part:

☐ Changes to the original scope of effort, voluntary work, increase or decrease to original time or cost, movement of contractor employees among contracts or requests for additional deliverables.

Not keeping an "arms-length" social relationship, although the contractor contact outside working hours in and of itself may have no effect on the working relationship, it is the potential or the appearance of negative impact that cautions this interaction. That is, attendance at each other's functions is prohibited.

Failure to Report Ethical Infractions -- as an extension of agency policy, such communication must occur for contractor behavior and because it also violates the contract.

Procurement Integrity Summary – 1) During the conduct of procurement, a procurement official shall not knowingly solicit or accept future employment or business opportunities from a contractor; solicit or accept money or anything of value from a contractor or disclose proprietary of source selection information to unauthorized individuals. 2) After leaving government service, a procurement official may not represent the contractor in contract award, modification or extension negotiations and/or participate substantially in the contract performance for two years after the last date of procurement participation.

D.6. DOs and DON'Ts in Government/Contractor Communication

Means of Enhancement

DOs

☐ Have a copy of the contract and the current order readily available and be familiar with all facets of the contract and the order.

☐ Understand the limits of your authority.

☐ Acknowledge other government representatives and how your role connects and interfaces with theirs.

☐ Establish and maintain a separate file for documents and correspondence pertaining to each order.

☐ Whenever communicating, if possible: i) prepare your message in advance, ii) transmit your message in terms the receiver will accept, iii) be aware of the feelings on both sides, iv) time your message carefully, v) listen for the receiver's message, vi) draw the receiver out, and vii) test to make sure your message has been accepted.

☐ Give instructions to the contractor primarily in writing or orally followed up with a written confirmation.

☐ Allow for easy access to dialogue to prevent problems or problems becoming crises.

☐ Whenever the objective is the need for information, use interviewing well to rapidly discover it.

☐ Ensure that meetings further rapport and, as outcomes occur, they: explain what must be done, who will do it, their authority, expected results and schedule, contingencies and follow through.

☐ Have regular and frequent contact (as necessary) with the contractor to become aware of any potential concerns.

☐ Assist the contractor wherever possible, within your authority, to resolve any communication misunderstandings.

☐ Use active listening so your rapport and your message can be furthered.

☐ Negotiate to seek better ways of resolving issues.

☐ Ensure that information is collected well, reviewed properly and presented with impact.

☐ Know that a strong relationship means: when in doubt, talk it out.

☐ Keep thorough records such to provide substantive evaluation of the contractor's effort.

☐ Periodically monitor the contractor's work to ensure high performance within the time and cost parameters stated in the contract.

☐ Stress clarification (in writing) since both sides have the flexibility to talk first, act second – thereby not wasting resources.

☐ Ensure technical discussions do not lead to changes.

☐ Ascertain that government property is being used properly and appropriate measures are being taken to protect and safeguard it.

☐ Ensure that the contractor is providing timely response to all correspondence.

☐ Verify that the contractor has the correct personnel performing the contract work.

☐ Ensure satisfactory subcontractor performance by observing the contractor's surveillance.

☐ Sustain that the delivery schedule is adhered to or immediate action taken to resolve delays.

☐ Approve but do not accept item until ready to become government owned.

☐ Ascertain that all emergencies are attended to and resolved immediately.

☐ Keep the CO fully informed and current on any major problem areas concerning the contractor's performance, costs or adherence to clauses.

☐ Validate that unsatisfactory contractor performance is corrected in a timely fashion.

☐ Ensure discrepancies don't end up as deviations or waivers without cause.

☐ Continue the "same wavelength" theme as government and contractor representatives change.

☐ Ensure that your replacement is thoroughly briefed, both verbally and in writing on all important issues.

☐ Be proactive in ensuring that the contractor identifies, resolves and prevents performance problems on an ongoing basis.

☐ Means of Alleviation

DON'Ts

☐ Fail to plan your meetings since this reduces viability of results.

☐ Be too easily distracted, not give feedback or be unable to really hear the substance and tone of the speaker.

☐ Tell the contractor how to carry out his/her responsibilities with any facet (technical, management, cost or provisional) of the contract.

☐ Not reach agreement due to:

- defining the wrong problem
- having a "hidden agenda"
- having an unclear understanding about each other's roles or authority
- believing compromise means settling for less rather than finding mutually acceptable solutions

Neglect to document significant actions, conversations, etc., as they occur.

☐ Delay or cause to be delayed any correspondence or reports that require immediate response from the contractor or government officials.

☐ Presume and assume in dialoguing, presenting and furthering rapport.

☐ Not provide timely feedback about performance checks.

☐ Exhibit lack of technical agreement since it leads to poor quality work, claims and additional time spent on administrative not technical matters.

☐ When corrective actions are needed, fail to follow-up to ensure they are completed.

☐ Accept an appointment as a COTR if there is an apparent conflict of interest.

☐ Allow undue influence by the contractor (in tangible or intangible forms), since this threatens the "arms length" relationship and creates potential judgment bias.

☐ Accept special favors or gratuities from the contractor.

☐ Approve requests just because the contractor asked. Ascertain that it is required.

☐ Give feedback in "how" to perform, rather than monitoring "what" has been done.

☐ Permit the contractor to act or perform in ways which are :

☐ Beyond the scope of the government individual's authority

    ■ Outside the purview of the contract or order

☐ Obligate, in any way, the payment of money by the government.

☐ Provide information on other contractors or contracts unless approved by the CO.

☐ Monitor the contract so closely that you interfere with the contractor's work.

☐ Discuss new proposed effort or encourage the contractor to perform additional effort on an existing contract.

☐ Commit the equipment, supplies, or personnel of the contractor for use by others.

☐ Create an employer-employee relationship with contractor personnel through supervisory or administrative practices.

☐ Offer advice to the contractor which may adversely affect contract performance, compromise the rights of the government, provide the basis for a constructive change, or impact any pending or future effort.

☐ Ever exceed your authority as expressed (or implied).

E. What has gone well and means to improve

COTRs sit in the center of a multi-pronged acquisition process, with stakeholders distributed across departmental lines, as well as within and outside the federal government.

The aspects of this section are focused to balance the ongoing technical challenges with stronger communication and relationship development. These capabilities present COTRs with a vibrant, challenging acquisition environment in which to contribute.

Successful acquisitions now require a fresh, results-oriented view of the process with acquisition professionals serving as business advisors to their respective agency stakeholders. A key guiding principle for any acquisition contributor is to develop a sound business solution that links short-and long-term goals. The capabilities described herein give the COTR much greater potential to achieve these business solutions.

STEP FOUR – COTR APPLICATIONS

A. Detailed Overview of Acquisition Lifecycle

Specific tasks for a COTR vary with the type of contract and complexity of the acquisition. Each contract must be treated on an individual basis, because it may place responsibilities on the COTR unique to that contract or task order. The information presented here is to provide a full "picture" of the everyday duties and activities that a COTR can do. The thrust is to start "walking the walk" to more effective contracting using the previous Three Steps.

A.1. Pre-award Tasks

The primary duties of the COTR are specified by the CO appointment; however it is advantageous for the COTR to take part in various pre-award activities. Early involvement by the COTR can make for a better contract. It will also give the COTR better insight into the contract requirements to make the post-award tasks easier to accomplish.

A.1.a. Acquisition Planning

Acquisition planning is the process of identifying and describing requirements and determining the best method for meeting those requirements. Acquisition planning focuses on the business and technical management approaches designed to achieve the customer's objectives within specified resource constraints and the procurement and contracting strategies necessary for implementation. Acquisition planning involves determination of need, market research, source selection procedures and socioeconomic considerations as follows:

A.1.b. Determination of Need

☐ Forecast future acquisition requirements and look for long-range strategies to maximize competition, minimize costs, and reduce lead times.

☐ Prepare initial cost estimates and schedules, and determine priorities.

☐ Describe needs in terms of desired outcomes and objectives.

☐ Perform a cost/benefit analysis to prioritize the objectives.

☐ Determine the need for test equipment/tooling, software, and government-furnished property.

☐ Identify documentation/data requirements.

A. 1. c. Market Research/Market Surveillance

☐ Obtain data from acquisition histories and other agency sources. Collect and compile additional market information.

☐ Conduct trade studies to evaluate alternatives and associated risks. As part of the trade study, consider supportability, reliability, cost and schedule, as well as performance.

☐ Estimate the proper price level or value of needed supplies or services.

☐ Determine if commercial-off-the-shelf or non-developmental items (COTS/NDI) are applicable.

A. 1. d. Purchase Requests

Use market research results to determine, as appropriate:

☐ Available sources

☐ Contractor vs. government performance

☐ Budgeting and funding needs

☐ Product descriptions

☐ Priorities, allocations, and allotments

☐ Management information requirements

☐ Security considerations

☐ Government-furnished property/information needs

☐ Environmental considerations

☐ Performance milestones

Identify deliverable requirements, including options and foreign military sales, and work with the assigned contracting office to prepare the contract line item structure and any data requirements.

Plan the requirements for the contract, including as appropriate the Performance Requirements Summary (PRS), Quality Assurance Surveillance Plan (QASP), specification, project design reviews, acceptance requirements, and schedule.

☐ Ensure adequate funding to support technical requirements.

☐ Submit PR using e-DARTS.

A.1.e. Source Selection

☐ The objective of source selection is to select a source that will provide the best value to the government, in meeting the customer's needs.

☐ Establish technical criteria for price-related factors and their relative importance. Determine the product's expected quality and lifecycle cost.

☐ Establish technical requirements for evaluating performance, quality, maintenance concept, technical/logistics documentation, and skills.

☐ Perform technical/non-price factor trade-off analyses and determine the best value or minimum technical requirements for award.

Socioeconomic Programs

The government's policy is to offer maximum opportunities in its acquisitions for small businesses and other disadvantaged businesses. Acquisitions for goods or services under $100,000 are restricted to small businesses unless the CO determines otherwise. The COTR will work with the CO and the local Small Business Specialists to seek, identify, and tailor requisitions to permit participation by qualified small and disadvantaged businesses. The COTR shares in the responsibility for meeting small business program goals and can participate actively towards their achievement.

A.2. Post-award Tasks

A.2.a. Contract Administration Planning

After award, the CO will send the following documents to the COTR:

☐ The COTR appointment letter

☐ A complete copy of the contract

☐ The Quality Control Plan (QCP) of the contractor

☐ The Quality Assurance Surveillance Plan (QASP)

The COTR will read the contract in its entirety to ensure complete understanding of the tasks, milestones, clauses, and other terms and conditions of the contract, in order to:

☐ Establish a list of documents due from the contractor each month

☐ Establish what information must be sent to the CO during performance of the contract

☐ Determine the priorities of tasks that must be monitored

☐ Understand the surveillance and monitoring techniques for which the COTR is responsible

☐ Determine the contractor's obligations under the contract

☐ Identify potential problem areas in the contract

☐ Prepare for the initial visit to the work site or contractor's office to meet key players

A.2.b. Post-award Conferences

While it is not required for all contracts, the post-award or pre-performance conference can be a valuable tool for post-award planning. Although not the time to change a contract, sometimes the need for a modification may surface at this meeting. It is the opportunity for both parties to:

☐ Meet one another face-to-face and work out administrative details

☐ Identify government and contractor personnel and their roles

☐ Achieve clear and mutual understanding of the contract requirements

☐ Identify and resolve potential problems

This meeting will focus on establishing a good working relationship between government and contractor personnel and in clarifying any remaining questions or issues.

A.2.c. Contract Oversight and Surveillance

Normally, the COTR has the responsibility/authority to monitor all aspects of the day-to-day administration of a contract. The COTR must immediately identify to the CO specific areas of concern for corrective action (i.e., Inspection of Work, Technical Progress Reports, Technical Direction, Constructive Changes, etc.). The COTR is expected to maintain effective surveillance of the contract and document the surveillance performed. Surveillance activities include the following:

Ensure there is a common understanding with the contractor on its responsibilities in implementing the surveillance plan.

Provide technical interpretations of the requirements to the contractor.

Document in the contract file any technical assistance given to the contractor.

☐ Respond to the contractor in writing for significant matters, with a copy to the CO.

☐ Notify the CO immediately whenever the contractor disagrees with or refuses to comply with any technical aspects of the contract as interpreted by the COTR.

☐ Refer any disagreements with the contractor to the CO.

☐ Strive to void misunderstandings and conditions that could lead to a claim or dispute.

Take corrective action, contacting the CO as necessary when contractor performance is unsatisfactory.

Report any instance of suspected conflict of interest or fraud, waste, and abuse to the CO or the local Office of General Counsel.

Maintain access to and/or furnishing all technical publications and regulations included in the contract.

Ensure that the contractor has current security clearances for facilities and personnel.

Provide recommendations to the CO relative to approval/disapproval requests for public release of information regarding work under the contract.

Ensure that contractor personnel working on a government facility wear identification at all times and identify themselves as contractor employees when attending meetings, using the telephone, and in all correspondence (whether written or electronic).

Perform property surveillance and/or oversight over accountability on government furnished-property, except when a property administrator serves this function.

- ☐ Initiate action for government-furnished property for contractor use and ensure that the contractor receives property in accordance with the contract.
- ☐ Furnish disposition instructions to the contractor for government-furnished property or contractor-acquired property when requested by the CO.

Monitor the contractor's performance, including submittal of required reports and other documentation.

- ☐ Ensure prompt review of all reports.
- ☐ Provide approval/disapproval and comments to the contractor through the CO.

Monitor financial management controls and coordinate with government resource managers on actions relating to funding and changes in the contract.

- ☐ Evaluate monthly cost data on a quantitative and qualitative basis to include trends and projections, if appropriate.

Monitor contractor expenditures under cost-reimbursable contracts to ensure that the contractor provides proper notice to the CO and to provide appropriate recommendations to the CO.

Request that the CO de-obligate excess funds, when appropriate.

Review reimbursable contractor purchases to ensure that the contractor has provided evidence.

☐ Ensure proper billing of any contractor-acquired property and documentation in property accountability records.

Notify the CO when the contractor is behind schedule or not performing within cost.

☐ Explain the reasons for the contractor's problems.

☐ Identify the work related to the overrun or schedule delay.

☐ Recommend corrective actions to the CO.

☐ If a contract change is called for, submit a funded requisition to the CO, describing the required changes related to the overrun.

Document your recommendations to the CO for the need to modify the contract or for other contract actions.

Ensure that the CO has issued the contract modification before the contractor may proceed with any changes in the work/services or delivery schedule.

Provide oversight of contractor in processing QA procedures.

Provide appropriate coordination between the CO and any technical inspectors or QA evaluators/inspectors assigned to the contract.

Perform inspection of delivered supplies or services.

Reject nonconforming supplies or services.

Verify that the contractor has performed the technical and management requirements of the contract in accordance with the contract terms, conditions, and specifications.

Certify receipt of supplies/services for payment purposes.

☐ Ensure that the process is performed with IAW contract quality provisions and within the contract performance period.

Verify that the contractor has successfully corrected any deficiencies in delivered supplies and services.

Notify the CO in sufficient time to put the contractor on notice to avoid losing the government's right to exercise an option.

Make evaluations and recommendations concerning Task Order awards.

Prepare the contractor's past-performance assessments.

The following chart brings together all facets of the acquisition lifecycle (discussed previously) in the context of the COTR's responsibilities and influence. These are then described in terms of COTR involvement and success.

A.3. Summary of Acquisition Lifecycle

In more detail, this chart fully describes the COTR's involvement and influence in source selection (see G. for the equivalent Phases and Steps for Contract Administration).

Acquisition Phase	Source Selection Process	Source Selection Activities
Pre-Solicitation	Market Research	Gather information about Requirement.
		Effectively Interact with Industry.
	Prepare Purchase Request	Develop Purchase Request and, as needed, Acquisition Plan.
	Devise Source Selection Plan	Formulate the Source Selection Plan and Designate Key Players.
	Obtain Reviews, Approvals, and Authorization	Request/Receive Agency-level Reviews/ Approval.
Solicitation	Prepare and Issue Solicitation	Write the Solicitation.
		Create Monitoring Plan.
		Develop an Independent Government Cost Estimate.
		Obtain Industry Comments on the Draft Solicitation. (optional)
		Develop detailed Source Selection Materials.
		Publicize the Solicitation in FEDBIZOPPS.
		Issue the Solicitation.
		Hold Pre-proposal Conference. (optional)
		Answer Questions and Amend the Solicitation.

Acquisition Phase	Source Selection Process	Source Selection Activities
Evaluation	Evaluate Proposals	Train Source Selection Team.
		Receive Proposals.
		Determine Whether Proposals Comply with Proposal.
		Evaluation Instructions.
		Evaluate Proposals Against the Evaluation Factors and the
		Requirements' Description.
		Request Clarification or Correction. (as needed)
		Rate Technical Proposals.
		Conduct Initial Cost Evaluation.
		Select Contractor or Establish Competitive Range. (optional)
Award	Select Contractor	Conduct Discussions and Oral Presentations. (as needed)
		Request Best and Final Offers (BAFOs).
		Rate updates to Proposals Based on Evaluation Criteria.
		Select the Apparent Winner.
		Conduct Responsibility Reviews.
		Approve the Selection.
		Award the Contract and Publicize.
		Notify Unsuccessful Offerors.
		Debrief Offerors.
		Handle Any Protests.
Post Award	Contract Administration	Effectively ensure Performance meets Established Baseline.

B. Developing the need

The acquisition process has three discrete phases:

☐ Preparing for the solicitation (requirements development, pre-solicitation, or planning phase);

☐ Soliciting, evaluating, and awarding the contract; and

☐ Administering the awarded contract.

B.1. Pre-solicitation activities

These are tasks that the government must complete before approaching the business community for proposals. The steps in the first phase of the acquisition process are accomplished in a logical sequence and are designed to produce one major document: the request for contract (RFC). This involves development of the acquisition planning data as required by FAR Part 7, and the information must specify which special approvals and clearances are required. Other elements of the RFC document are its purpose, and contents. The RFC is a detailed document. Many of its components are critical to ensuring that the government receives quality supplies and services at a fair price once a contract is signed.

B.1.a. Planning

Planning for an acquisition is the best way of ensuring that the product or service will be acquired in the most efficient, trouble-free manner. This process will begin as soon as a program need is identified and it is obvious that the need must be met outside the government. Acquisition planning involves a general consideration of all the elements that will be required in connection with a particular acquisition. This process may be quite simple or very elaborate, depending on the cost, political sensitivity, complexity, or importance of the item or service being acquired. Acquisition planning helps both the CO and the COTR to efficiently procure outside services by enabling them to allocate and schedule the work involved in an acquisition, and to resolve potential problems early in the process.

Failure to schedule the overall acquisition workload of an agency results in an inordinate percentage of contract awards being made in the closing months, weeks, and, even, days of the fiscal year. This excessive year-end spending invites increased intervention and scrutiny from Congress, the Office of Management and Budget, and the media. The key to avoiding this is to begin advance acquisition planning early in the fiscal year.

Concept development is the first step in an acquisition. In this phase the agency realizes that an acquisition is necessary and defines, in broad terms, what this effort will entail. Concept development may include assessment of prior contract results, in-depth literature searches, and discussions with technical and scientific personnel, both within and outside the government. These discussions may serve to determine interest, scientific approaches, technical capabilities, and the state-of-the-art relevant to the subject area. In holding such discussions with people outside the government, care must be taken not to disclose advance information on any specific acquisition, proposed or contemplated. To do so might create

the impression that the government has given the recipient an unfair advantage over other organizations solicited subsequently.

Once the concept has been formulated, it must be reviewed for program relevance, need, merit, priority, and timeliness by the appropriate management staff. In many agencies, the concept development phase is intimately connected with the agency's budget process because these agencies use the budget process as the primary means of identifying, defining, and approving agency acquisitions.

Although most COTRs do not become involved with an acquisition until after the initial budgeting has been accomplished, they always have to deal with budget considerations. This happens, for example, when the initial cost of an acquisition is underestimated and additional funds are required. Although it is important to have funds for an acquisition, especially a major one, included in the agency's budget, occasionally one that has not been included is turned over to a COTR. If funds have not been budgeted, it still may be possible to fund a particular acquisition. COTRs who are faced with this situation will contact their budget component for advice and guidance.

B.1.b. Determining Whether to Bundle Requirements

Another important step in initial acquisition planning is the decision whether or not to bundle requirements. FAR 2.101 defines bundling as consolidating two or more requirements for supplies or services, previously provided or performed under separate smaller contracts, into a consolidation for a single contract that is likely to be unsuitable for award to a small business concern due to:

☐ The diversity, size or specialized nature of the elements of the performance specified;

☐ The aggregate dollar value of the anticipated award;

☐ The geographical dispersion of the contract performance sites; or

☐ Any combination of the above.

While bundling was at one time encouraged for efficiency and pricing reasons, it has become much less fashionable in recent years. FAR 7.107 cautions agencies to consider bundling only when market research demonstrates that bundling is likely to save the government:

Ten percent of the estimated value (including options) if the value is $75 million or less; or

Five percent of the estimated contract value (including options) or $7.5 million, whichever is greater, if the value exceeds $75 million.

Reduction of administrative or personnel costs alone is not sufficient justification for bundling unless the cost savings are expected to be at least 10 percent of the estimated contract value (including options) of the bundled requirements. However, without power of delegation, the service acquisition executable for the military departments, the Under Secretary of Defense for Acquisition, Technology and Logistics for the Defense agencies, or the Deputy Secretary or equivalent for the civilian agencies, may determine that bundling is necessary and justified when:

The expected benefits do not meet the above thresholds but are critical to the agency's mission success; and

The acquisition strategy provides for maximum practicable participation by small business concerns.

For short, bundling will not be entered into lightly, and, when it is considered, the benefits will clearly be identified in a supporting justification. When bundling is being considered, do the following:

When performing market research, consult with the local Small Business Administration Procurement Center Representative (PCR) or, if a PCR is not assigned to the procuring activity, the SBA Office of Government Contracting Area Office serving the area in which the primary activity is located.

Prepare and incorporate justification for anticipated bundling in the acquisition planning data portion of the Request for Contract (RFC).

An OFPP Report on Contract Bundling was issued in October 2002, which detailed the increased use of bundling by federal agencies and the reduced involvement of small business in the acquisition process. The OFPP made numerous recommendations in the report for reducing bundling and increasing small business involvement including increased vigilance in review of bundling requirements by senior management. It appears that, if small business opportunities do not increase, tighter restrictions on bundling will be implemented.

B.1.c. Market Research

FAR Part 10 (see FAR Excerpts Appendix) requires agencies to conduct market research. It prescribes policies and procedures for conducting market research to arrive at the most suitable approach to acquiring, distributing, and supporting supplies and services. Market research is conducted to determine if commercial items or non-developmental items are available to meet the government's needs, or could be modified to meet the government's needs.

FAR Subpart 2.101 defines market research as "collecting and analyzing information about capabilities within the market to satisfy agency needs." The results of market research are used "to arrive at the most suitable approach to acquiring, distributing, and supporting supplies and services requirements." Market research accomplishes the goal of fulfilling government needs by acquiring commercial products when such products would adequately satisfy those needs. In addition, market research is further required to:

☐ Promote full and open competition

☐ Ensure that the need is met in a cost-effective manner

☐ Typical types of data that are collected during market research are:

☐ Availability

☐ Warranty information

☐ Cost to modify commercial products

Market Research Table

This table illustrates techniques to use in compiling data necessary for making the best decisions when planning the procurement.

Technique	Application	Impact
1. Investigate the market. Determine current status of technology, extent of commercial applications, and source availability,	Buys where rapid technological changes influence the way the requirement is stated.	Market indicators influence the specifications and the contracting approach (e.g., multi-year, options, type of contract). Significant savings by adapting commercial items.
2. Brief Industry. Conduct widely publicized briefings on future requirements to gain interest and to solicit comments on planned approach.	When seeking out new companies.	Acquire information that will affect the specification development and contracting approach.
3. Contact potential contractors to discuss requirements and get recommendations about planned acquisitions.	All buys.	Enhanced requirements definition, solicitation development, and competition.
4. Visit potential sources. Target qualified potential sources who typically do not respond to solicitations.	Where history suggests that responses may be insufficient.	Identify and encourage new and possibly better sources to submit offers.

Technique	Application	Impact
5. Attend industry and scientific conferences.	Key personnel who need to keep abreast of new developments, industry trends, and make contacts.	Knowledge of current technology and commercial successes and failures as applied to agency requirements.
6. Acquire literature about commercial products, industry trends, product availability, reliability, and prices.	All requirements.	More sources to solicit. Affects how requirements are stated, facilitates price analysis, identifies new products.
7. Analyze procurement history by examining quality and extent of competition, prices, and performance results.	All buys.	Revise requirements, specifications, and contracting approach based on "lessons learned."
8. Evaluate and test commercial items fully, as appropriate.	Whenever seemingly artificial barriers to the use of commercial items exist.	Develop data about performance of commercial items. Determine necessary adaptations and develop cost estimates.
9. Advertise in trade journal and other publications to solicit inquiries.	Any buy where competition is limited and fbo.gov announcements are not reaching potential sources.	More responses from new, perhaps better, sources.
10. Use the fbo.gov; provide complete data and synopsis far in advance of a solicitation.	All nonexempt procurements over $25,000.	More inquiries and responses. Sufficient time to receive expressions of interest about a requirement and alert potential contractors to release of a solicitation.
11. Determine why selected contractors do not respond to a solicitation.	All procurements where responses are insufficient or apparently well-qualified sources do not respond.	Identify the impediments to effective competition. Document and publicize "lessons learned."
12. Examine business and trade association directories.	All buys.	Identify additional sources to solicit and acquire basic information about these sources.

Technique	Application	Impact
13. Use Federal Procurement Data System information.	All buys where an insufficient number of sources are responding (e.g., you can search FPDS for the SIC codes for your product and obtain a printout of contractors who have previously supplied it).	Identify current government contractors, what was purchased, and if the purchase was competitive. Also, information about past procurements of the same/similar supplies, products, or services.
14. Examine Federal Supply Schedule.	All requirements that might be satisfied by commercially available products or services.	Identify products or services on schedules at a favorable price and terms.
15. Contact the agency small business advisor to assist in locating qualified small and minority suppliers.	All requirements.	Identify qualified small and minority businesses for inclusion in a sources list.

Note: In considering the priority of sources to obtain Market Information, note that federal procurement policy mandates considering use of GSA Schedules (www.gsaadvantage.gov) before going with an "open market" buy.

B.1.d. Exchanges with Industry Before the Solicitation is Issued

Exchanges of information among all interested parties, from the earliest identification of a requirement through receipt of proposals, are encouraged. Any exchange of information must be consistent with procurement integrity requirements found at FAR 3.104. "Interested parties" is defined as potential offerors, end users, government acquisition and supporting personnel, and others involved in the conduct or outcome of the acquisition.

The purpose of exchanging information is to improve the understanding of government requirements and industry capabilities, thereby allowing potential offerors to judge whether or how they can satisfy the government's requirements. It also enhances the government's ability to obtain quality supplies and services, including construction, at reasonable prices, and increases efficiency in proposal preparation, proposal evaluation, negotiation, and contract award.

Agencies are encouraged to promote early exchanges of information about future acquisitions. An early exchange of information among industry and the program manager, CO, and other participants in the acquisition process can identify and resolve concerns regarding:

The acquisition strategy, including proposed contract type, terms and conditions, and acquisition planning schedules;

The feasibility of the requirement, including performance requirements, SOW, and data requirements;

The suitability of the proposal instructions and evaluation factors and significant subfactors, including the approach for assessing past-performance information;

The availability of reference documents; and,

☐ Any other industry concerns or questions.

☐ Some techniques to promote early exchanges of information are:

☐ Industry or small business conferences

☐ Public hearings

☐ Market research

☐ One-on-one meetings with potential offerors

Any that are substantially involved with potential contract terms and conditions will include the CO.

General information about agency mission needs and future requirements may be disclosed at any time.

☐ Pre-solicitation notices

☐ Draft RFPs

☐ Request for Information

☐ Pre-solicitation or pre-proposal conferences

☐ Site visits

FAR 5.205(e) suggests using its special notices of proposed contract actions, or electronic notices, to publicize the government's requirement or solicit information from industry.

Requests for Information (RFIs) may be used when the government does not presently intend to award a contract, but wants to obtain price, delivery, other market information, or capabilities for planning purposes. Responses to these notices are not offers and cannot be accepted by the government to form a binding contract.

After release of the solicitation, the CO must be the focal point of any exchange with potential offerors. When specific information about a proposed acquisition that would be necessary for the preparation of proposals is disclosed to one or more potential offerors, that information must be made available to the public as soon as practicable, but not later than the next general release of information, in order to avoid creating an unfair competitive advantage.

Information provided to a particular offeror in response to that offeror's request must not be disclosed if doing so would reveal the potential offeror's confidential business strategy, and would be protected by the Procurement Integrity Act or Freedom of Information Act.

When a pre-solicitation or pre-proposal conference is conducted, materials distributed at the conference will be made available to all potential offerors, upon request. The FAR recognizes special situations that apply to exchanges with industry before proposals are transmitted. These situations are discussed next.

B.1.e. Research and development (R&D) advance notices

COs may transmit to the fbo Web site advance notices of their interest in potential R&D programs whenever market research does not produce a sufficient number of concerns to obtain adequate competition.

Advance notices must not be used where security considerations prohibit such publication.

Federally Funded Research and Development Centers (FFRDC)

Before establishing a FFRDC or before changing its basic purpose and mission, the sponsor must transmit at least three notices over a 90-day period to the GPE and the Federal Register, indicating the agency's intention to sponsor an FFRDC or change the basic purpose or mission of the FFRDC.

B.1.f. Special notices

COs may transmit to the fbo Web site special notices of procurement matters such as business fairs, long-range procurement estimates, pre-bid or pre-proposal conferences, meetings, and the availability of draft solicitations or draft specifications for review.

Architect-engineering (A&E) services

COs —

Must publish notices of intent to contract for A&E services (unless exempted by FAR 5.202) when the total fee is expected to exceed $25,000;

When the total fee is expected to exceed $10,000 but not exceed $25,000, must display a notice of the solicitation or a copy of the solicitation in a public place at the contracting office.

Section 8 (a) competitive acquisition

When a national buy requirement is being considered for competitive acquisition limited to eligible 8(a) concerns, the CO must transmit a synopsis of the proposed contract action to the SBA.

B.2. The Purchase Request Responsibilities

The FAR requires agencies to perform acquisition planning. It outlines a schedule of the steps to be taken to accomplish the acquisition, and serves to resolve problems early in the acquisition cycle, thereby avoiding delay of the award.

Responsibilities for the Purchase Request (PR) or Request for Contract (RFC)

The Request for Contract (RFC) usually is prepared jointly by the COTR and the CO, although the Head of Contracting Activity (HCA) may request that a different procedure be followed.

COTRs who expect to initiate acquisitions will discuss their requirements with the responsible CO. These discussions will result in understandings on:

- ☐ The details of the acquisition plan
- ☐ Preliminary discussion on the work statement or specifications and appropriate evaluation criteria
- ☐ Preliminary discussions on the content and timing of the PR or RFC
- ☐ COs are required to coordinate with program personnel to ensure:
- ☐ Timely and comprehensive planning for acquisitions
- ☐ Timely initiation of requests for contracts
- ☐ That program personnel have been instructed in proper acquisition practices and methods
- ☐ Format and Content of the Acquisition Plan (AP)

B.3. The Acquisition Plan Contents

For larger procurement efforts (over $500,000), along with the PR, an Acquisition Plan (AP) is needed. According to FAR 7-105, the AP must address all the technical, business, management, and other significant considerations that will control the acquisition. The specific content of plans will vary, depending on the nature, circumstances, and stage of the acquisition. In preparing the AP, the planner must address the acquisition background and objectives and a plan of action. APs for service contracts must describe the strategies for

implementing performance-based contracting methods or must provide rationale for not using those methods, which are in FAR Part 37.6.

B.3.a Acquisition Background and Objectives:

Statement of need – Introduce the plan by a brief statement of need. Summarize the technical and contractual history of the acquisition. Discuss feasible acquisition alternatives, the impact to prior acquisitions on those alternatives, and any related in-house effort.

Applicable conditions – State all significant conditions affecting the acquisition, such as:

Requirements for compatibility with existing or future systems or programs

Any known cost, schedule, and capability or performance constraints

Cost – Set forth the established cost goals for the acquisition and the rationale supporting them, and discuss related cost concepts to be employed, including, as appropriated, the following items:

☐ Lifecycle cost

☐ Design-to-cost

☐ Application of should-cost

Capability or performance – Specify the required capabilities or performance characteristics of the supplies or the performance standards of the services being acquired and state how they are related to the need.

Delivery or performance-period requirements – Describe the basis for establishing delivery or performance requirements. Explain and provide reasons for any urgency if it results in concurrency of development and production or constitutes justification for not providing for full and open competition.

Trade-offs – Discuss the expected consequences of trade-offs among the various costs, capability or performance, and schedule goals.

Risks – Discuss technical, cost, and schedule risks and describe what efforts are planned or underway to reduce risk and the consequences of failure to achieve goals. If concurrency of development and production is planned, discuss its effects on cost and schedule risks.

Acquisition streamlining – If specifically designated by the requiring agency as a program subject to acquisition streamlining, discuss plans and procedures to:

Select and tailor only the necessary cost-effective requirements;

State the timeframe for identifying which of those specifications and standards originally provided for guidance only shall become mandatory.

B.3.b. Plan of Action

This part of the plan will include the following:

Sources – Indicate the prospective sources of supplies or services that can meet the need. Consider required sources of supplies or services. Include consideration of small business, veteran-owned small business, service-disabled veteran-owned small business, HUBZone small business, small disadvantaged business, and women-owned small business concerns. The impact of any bundling that might affect the participation of small business in the acquisition will also be considered. Address the extent and results of the market research and indicate their impact on the various elements of the plan.

Competition -- Describe how competition will be sought, promoted, and sustained through the course of the acquisition. If full and open competition is not contemplated, cite the authority in FAR 6.302. Discuss the basis for the application of that authority, identify the source(s), and discuss why full and open competition cannot be obtained. Describe how competition will be sought and when feasible and desirable how subcontract competition will be sought, promoted, and sustained throughout the course of the acquisition.

Source Selection procedures – Discuss the procedures including timing for submission and evaluation of proposals and the relationship of evaluation factors to the attainment of the acquisition objectives.

Contracting considerations – Discuss the contract type selection, use of multiyear contracting, options, or special contracting methods. Any special clauses, provisions or FAR deviations required will be discussed. Discuss any other contracting consideration, such as equipment lease or buy, and sealed bidding or negotiation procedures that you intend to use.

Budgeting and funding -- Include budget estimates, explain how they were derived, and discuss the schedule for obtaining adequate funds at the time they are required.

Product of service descriptions -- Explain the choice of product or service description types to be used in the acquisition.

Priorities, allocations, and allotments – When there is urgency for a requirement, specify the method for obtaining and using priorities, allocations, and allotments, and the reasons for them.

Contractor versus government performance

Inherently governmental functions

Management information requirements – Discuss, as appropriate, what management system will be used by the government to monitor the contractor's effort.

Make or buy – Discuss any consideration given to make-or-buy programs.

Test and evaluation – To the extent applicable, discuss the test program of the contractor and the government. Describe the test program for each major phase of a major system acquisition. If concurrency is planned, discuss the extent of testing to be accomplished before the production release.

Logistics considerations – Describe the assumptions determining contractor or agency support; reliability, maintainability and quality requirements; the requirements for contractor data and data rights; and standardization concepts.

Government-furnished property – Indicate if any property is to be furnished to the contractor including material and facilities.

Government-furnished information – Discuss government-furnished information.

Environmental consideration – Discuss all applicable environmental and energy conservation objectives.

Security considerations – For items dealing with classified matters discuss the establishment, maintenance and monitoring of such.

Contract administration – Describe how the contract will be administered. In contracts for services, include how inspection and acceptance corresponding to the work statement's performance criteria will be enforced.

Other considerations – Discuss other matters that may be germane to the plan not covered elsewhere.

Milestones for the acquisition cycle – In addition to the above topics the following and other appropriate steps will be addressed:

☐ Acquisition plan approval

☐ SOWs

☐ Specifications

☐ Data requirements

☐ Completion of acquisition-package preparation

☐ Purchase request

Justification and approval for other than full and open competition where applicable and/or any required determination and funding approval

☐ Issuance of synopsis

☐ Issuance of solicitation

☐ Evaluations of proposals, audits, and field reports

☐ Beginning and completion of negotiations

☐ Contract preparation, review, and clearance

☐ Contract award

Identification of participants in acquisition plan preparation – List the individuals who participated in preparing the acquisition plan, giving contact information for each individual.

Approvals: All acquisition planning documents must be signed by the COTR and the contract negotiator. Acquisition planning documents for acquisitions estimated to be between $100,000 and $1,000,000 must be approved by the CO. Acquisition planning documents for acquisitions established to be in excess of $1 million must be approved by the HCA (Head of Contracting Activity) or his/her designee. The designated official must be in a position no lower than the level above the CO. One copy of all acquisition planning documents must be filed with the PORA (Principal Official Responsible for Acquisition) or the designated official for planning purposes. The original acquisition planning document must be retained in the contract file.

B.4. Purchase Request Contents

B.4.a. Purpose of contract

Provide a brief description of the requirements, including the citation of the legislation that authorizes the program or project, and a statement as to the intended purpose/use of the proposed contract.

B.4.b. Period of Performance

The number of months (or other time period) required for total performance and, if applicable, for each phase of work indicated in the SOW, as well as the proposed starting date.

B.4.c. Estimated cost and funds citation

An estimate of the total cost of the proposed contract and, if applicable, the estimate for each phase indicated in the Requirements' Description. The COTR must provide a cost breakdown of all contribution cost factors, an estimate of the technical staff hours, direct material, subcontracting, travel, etc. The COTR may consult with contracting and cost advisory personnel in developing this information. This section must include the certification of funds availability for the proposed acquisition. Along with the appropriation and accounting information, citations will be included. When funds for the proposed acquisition are not currently available for obligation but are anticipated, a statement of intent to commit funds from the financial management officer shall be included in lieu of the certification that funds are available.

B.4.d. Requirements' Description

A work description of the work to be performed that may be in the form of a specification, purchase description, or SOW must be included in the RFC. Use of the specification is primarily limited to supply or service contracts where the material end item or service to be delivered is well defined by the government. To the maximum extent possible, requirements will be defined as performance-based work statements that focus on outcomes or results. If the RFC for a service contract is not utilizing a performance-based SOW, with associated measures and a quality surveillance plan, the rationale for this determination must be documented. If a performance-base service contract is utilized, the RFC must detail the performance standards that must be met, the quality surveillance plan that will be implemented and the performance incentives to be used, if applicable.

B.4.e. Schedule of deliverables/reporting requirements

B 4.f. COTR and alternate

If applicable to the acquisition the PR must include:

Background and need – The background, history, and necessity for the proposed contract are discussed in this section. It will include prior, present and future planned efforts by the program office in the same or related areas, and a description of efforts by other departmental activities and federal agencies in the same or related efforts if known. In addition, specific project information, such as the relevance or contribution to the overall program objectives, reasons for the need, priority, and project overlap are to be provided.

Reference materials – A list will be provided by title and description, of study reports, plans, drawings, and other data to be made available to prospective offerors for use in preparation of proposals and/or the contractor for use in performance of the contract. The

COTR must indicate whether this material is currently available or when it will be available, and how it may be accessed by potential offerors.

Technical evaluation criteria and instructions – Information concerning the technical evaluation and instructions that pertain to the specific requirements of the project must be included in the RFC. Evaluation factors may include understanding of the problem, technical approach, experience, personnel, facilities, etc. Criteria areas discussed in the SOW and the relative order of importance or weights assigned to each of these areas for technical evaluation purposes must be identified by the PO.

Special program clearances or approvals – Any required clearance or approval must be included with the PR. The servicing contracting office will work with the COTR and provide comprehensive checklists that include special approvals, clearances, and other requirements that are needed. It is the responsibility of the COTR to obtain the necessary clearances and approvals.

B.5. Special Purchase Request Approvals and Clearances

There are numerous types of acquisitions, or elements within an acquisition, that require particular approvals or clearances. The following special program approvals or clearances will be reviewed to see if they are applicable to the acquisition in question. Those that are applicable must be addressed in the acquisition planning document.

B.5.a. Information Technology

The policies and procedures for use in acquiring information technology are found at FAR Part 39, OMB Circular No. A-130, Management of Federal Information Resources and in each agency's IRM manual.

B.5.b. Evaluation Contracts

Evaluation studies are defined as those seeking to formally assess existing federal policies, programs, or their components. Such studies are performed to inform policy decision-making officials about program performance, with respect either to program objectives or other significant intended or unintended effects. The Assistant Secretary for Planning and Evaluation (ASPE) must approve all evaluation projects for proposed solicitations, except those that have been included in an evaluation plan previously approved by the ASPE.

B.5.c. Paid Advertising

Paid advertisements and notices to be published in newspapers and periodicals may be authorized by the CO in accordance with the requirements and conditions set forth in FAR

Subpart 5.5. Requests for advertising must be accompanied by written authority to advertise or publish, giving the names of the newspapers or journals, frequency and dates of proposed advertisements, estimated cost, and other pertinent information. Paid advertisements will be limited to the publication of essential details of grant announcements, invitations for bids, and requests for proposals, including those for the sale of personal property, and for the recruitment of employees.

B.5.d. Printing

FAR Subpart 8.8 defines "Government printing" as printing, binding, and blank-book work for use of an executive department, independent agency, or establishment of the government. Government printing must be done by or through the Government Printing Office (GPO). The COTR must coordinate with the CO to determine if there are any applicable exceptions.

B.5.e. Fraud, Abuse, and Waste

All proposed acquisitions that concern the subjects of fraud, abuse, and waste must be reviewed and approved by the Inspector General or Deputy Inspector General. Written approval from either must be included in the request for contract.

B.5.f. Paperwork Reduction Act

Under the Paperwork Reduction Act of 1995 (PL 104-13), a federal agency obtaining information from persons, other than from federal employees within the scope of their employment, (that is, asking persons to provide information beyond what they would ordinarily provide in the course of doing their jobs) must obtain advance written approval from the department or Office of Management and Budget.

B.5.g. Contracts with Federal Employees

Contracts between the government and government employees, or between the government and organizations that are substantially owned or controlled by government employees, may not knowingly be entered into, except for the most compelling reasons (See FAR Subpart 3.6). Authority to enter into such a contract must be obtained before contract award from either the Assistant Secretary for Management and Budget, the head of the OPDIV, or the regional director, or their designees. (See 45 CFR Part 73.)

B.5.h. Publications

All projects that will result in contracts in excess of $2,500, and that include publications, must be reviewed and approved by Public Affairs.

B.5.i. Public Affairs Services

Projects for the acquisition of public affairs services in excess of $5,000 must be submitted to the Office of the Assistant Secretary for Public Affairs (OASPA) for review and approval.

B.5.j. Audiovisual Services

All audiovisuals must be acquired under the government-wide Contracting System for Motion Picture and Videotape Productions, unless they are included in the exceptions to the mandatory use of the uniform system. Any proposed acquisition of an audiovisual project requires submission of Standard Form 282, Mandatory Title Check, to the National Audiovisual Center. When the results of this title check have been reviewed and approved, and the COTR has determined that existing materials are not adequate to fulfill the requirement, the COTR must prepare a statement to that effect. For acquisitions in excess of $5,000, a copy of that statement, together with Standard Form 202, Federal Audiovisual Production Report and any other agency forms must be submitted through the Public Affairs Office for review and approval. As an Addendum, the Purchase Request will also have the Acquisition Plan for all Procurements over $500,000.

Privacy Act

All agencies have a policy to protect the privacy of individuals to the maximum possible extent, while permitting the exchange of records required to fulfill their administrative and program responsibilities and their responsibilities for disclosing records to which the general public is entitled under the Freedom of Information Act. The Privacy Act is applicable whenever an agency contracts for the design, development, operation, or maintenance of a system of records on individuals in order to accomplish a departmental function. The key factor is whether a departmental function is involved. Therefore, the Privacy Act requirements apply to a departmental contract when, under the contract, the contractor must maintain or operate a system of records to accomplish a departmental function.

The COTR will consult with the activity's Privacy Act Coordinator, and, as necessary, with the Office of the General Counsel, to determine whether or not the Act applies to the proposed contract. The RFC must contain a statement regarding applicability. When the Act is applicable, the COTR must prepare a "system notice" for publication in the Federal Register. This notice must describe the agency's intent, i.e., to establish a new system of records on individuals, to make modifications to an existing system, or to disclose information in regard to an existing system. A copy of the "system notice" will be attached to the request for contract. The contract cannot be awarded until the "system notice" has been published in the Federal Register.

B.5.k. A-76 Review (FAR Subpart 7.3)

OMB Circular No. A-76, Performance of Commercial Activities, provides that it is the policy of the government to rely generally on private commercial sources for supplies and

services, if certain criteria are met. At the same time, it recognizes that some functions are inherently governmental and must be performed by government personnel. It also provides that it is government policy to give appropriate consideration to relative cost in deciding between government performance and performance under contract. In comparing the costs of government and contractor performance, the circular provides that agencies shall base the contractor's cost of performance on firm offers. The circular and the Cost Comparison Handbook, Supplement No. 1 to the circular, prescribe the overall policies and detailed procedures required of all agencies in making cost comparisons between contractor and government performance. Note: Little activity of this sort is occurring now.

Given the previous planning documentation, setting a schedule for timely source selection is now done. The key challenge about the Procurement Milestone Schedule graphic below is to "cut out" the "Revised Dates" column so that the Projected Dates column can become the Actual Dates column with little time delay.

B.6. Procurement Milestone Schedule

Contract Specialist	Buyer Code	
Req. No.	Received Req:	
Requiring Act:	Priority	
Supplies/Services	Negotiation Procedures	
Solicitation No:	Contract Type	
Est. Dollar Amt:	Type of Funds	Funds Expiration Date:
Avg. Palt Days:	Current Contract:	Expiration Date:

Event	Responsibility	Projected Dates	Revised Dates	Actual Dates
1. Funding				
2. Small Business/S(a) review				
3. Final Specs (SOW)				
4. Quantity				
5. Quality				
6. Packaging/Marketing				
7. Inspection/Acceptance				
8. Deliveries or Performance				
9. Special Provisions/Clauses				

Event	Responsibility	Projected Dates	Revised Dates	Actual Dates
10. Sources				
11. Source Selection Plan/Factors				
12. Special Approvals (technical, etc.)				
13. Justifications/Approvals (legal, etc.)				
14. Preparation of PR				
15. Presolicitation Conference				
16. Determination & Findings				
17. Synopsize in CBD				
18. FRP Released				
19. Preproposal Conf.				
20. Issue Clarifications/Changes				
21. Closing Date				
22. Request Technical Evaluation				
23. Receive Technical Evaluation				
24. Initiate Audit Request				
25. Receive Audit Results				
26. Price Cost Analysis				
27. Competitive Range				
28. Subcontract Plan				
29. Negotiations				
30. Request Best & Final Offer (BAFO)				
31. Receive BAFOs				
32. Complete Evaluation of BAFO				
33. Conduct Preaward Survey				
34. EEO Clearance				
35. Analyze Contractor Responsibility				
36. Final Contract Document				
37. Legal Review				
38. Contract Clearance				
39. Notification of Award				
40. Debriefing				
41. Notice to Proceed				

Event	Responsibility	Projected Dates	Revised Dates	Actual Dates
42. Administration Assigned				
43. Other				

B.7. Statement of Work (SOW)

The SOW, or in performance-based contracting the Performance Work Statement (PWS), is probably the single most critical document in the acquisition process. It must define requirements in clear, concise language identifying specific work to be accomplished. It also defines the respective responsibilities of the government and the contractor, and provides an objective measure so that both the government and the contractor will know when the work is complete and payment is justified. In this section we will use the SOW synonymously with PWS unless noted otherwise.

The COTR must also define requirements in terms that enable and encourage the offerors to supply commercial or non-developmental items. In describing its requirements, the government is rapidly moving to using performance-based SOWs. FAR Subpart 37-602 provides guidance on using them. Performance-based SOWs are to:

Describe the work in terms of what is to be the required output rather than either how the work is to be accomplished or the number of hours to be provided;

Enable assessment of work performance against measurable performance standards;

Rely on the use of measurable performance standards and financial incentives in a competitive environment to encourage competition to develop and institute innovative and cost-effective methods of performing the work; and

Avoid combining requirements into a single acquisition that is too broad for the agency or a prospective contractor to manage effectively.

Quality Assurance Surveillance Plans (QASP) must be developed when acquiring services using a performance-based SOW. These plans must recognize the responsibility of the contractor to carry out its quality control obligations and must contain measurable inspection and acceptance criteria corresponding to the performance standards contained in the SOW. The QASPs must focus on the level of performance required by the SOW, rather than the methodology used by the contractor to achieve that level of performance.

The SOW must be precisely worded because it will be read and interpreted by a variety of people, such as attorneys, acquisition personnel, cost estimators, accountants, technical

specialists, etc. If the SOW does not state exactly what is wanted, or does not state it precisely, it will generate contract administration problems for both the COTR and the CO. Ambiguous SOWs often result in unsatisfactory contractor performance, delays, disputes, and higher contract costs. The Comptroller General and the courts generally interpret ambiguous requirements against the drafter.

SOWs are sometimes referred to administrative boards or the courts for interpretation. These interpretations represent what an objective third party thinks is the intention of the document. Generally speaking, the court or board will not concern itself with what the drafter intended to express, but will look at what was expressed. This determination is usually made solely on the basis of the words used and the context in which they appear.

How the SOW is written affects the entire acquisition cycle. It determines the type of contract that is awarded, it influences the number and quality of proposals received, and it serves as a baseline against which to evaluate proposals, and later, contractor performance. Thus, the SOW is the key element in shaping and directing all three stages of the acquisition cycle: pre-solicitation, solicitation and contract award, and post-award administration.

In the pre-solicitation phase, the SOW establishes the parameters of the government's requirements so that the COs can determine the best way to accomplish them. Therefore, the SOW must articulate program objectives. It must also establish actual minimum requirements for performance of the proposed work. In the solicitation, evaluation, and award phase, the SOW is the vehicle that communicates the government's requirements to prospective offerors. At this stage, the SOW guides the offerors on the content of their technical proposals. When a contract is awarded, the SOW becomes part of the contract between the two parties, stating what has been offered by the proposer and accepted by the government. Therefore, the SOW defines the scope of work, including tasks the contractor must undertake, types or stages of work, number and type of personnel, sequence of effort, and reporting requirements. The SOW must also establish a guide for technical evaluation of the proposals. Both the offeror and the evaluators need a list of factors that clearly state how the agency will compare the offers. The technical evaluation criteria are not part of the SOW itself but, because they relate directly to the requirements specified in the SOW, they must be carefully considered when preparing it. At the post-award stage, the SOW provides the mechanism for defining the work or supplies that are to be produced and the deadlines for producing them. To be effective at this stage, the SOW will provide a guide for monitoring the progress of work by specifying what supplies will be delivered or tasks accomplished at specific times during the course of the contract. The SOW also will describe the supplies or results from the work effort and set the standards of contractor performance.

B.7.a. Common Elements of Statements of Work

Because each acquisition is unique, each SOW must be tailored to the specifics of the project. The elements of an SOW will vary with the objective, complexity, size, and nature of the acquisition. In general, it will cover the following matters, as appropriate.

Background – Describes the requirements in general, non-technical terms, and explains why the acquisition is being pursued and how it relates to past, current, or future projects. Include a summary of statutory program authority and any regulations that are applicable. If any techniques have been tried and been found effective, they will be included here.

Project objectives – Provides a succinct statement of the purpose of the acquisition. It will outline the results that the government expects, and may also identify the benefit to the program that is contemplated.

Scope of work – Provides an overall, non-technical description of the work to be performed. It expands on the project objectives, but does not attempt to detail all of the work required. Identify and summarize the various phases of the project, and define its limits in terms of specific objectives, time, special provisions, or limitations. This information must be consistent with the detailed requirements. Contractor responsibilities are often summarized here, as are the results or supplies expected.

Detailed technical requirements – States most precisely what is expected of the contractor in the performance of the work. It describes the specific tasks and phases of the work and specifies the total effort each task or phase is to receive. Considerations that may guide the contractor in its analysis, design, or experimentation on the designated problems will also be included. Specify the requirements (i.e., training, computer modeling, tests, verification, etc.), and indicate the scope of each. Include the parameters of tests, for example, and the criteria governing the number of designs, numbers of tests, performance, etc. Also identify any budgetary, environmental, or other constraints. If more than one approach is possible, and the government prefers a particular approach, it will be identified. When applicable, state the criteria on which a choice of alternative approaches will be based. If end supplies or deliverables are required under the contract, they will be clearly and firmly defined and the criteria for acceptance will be given. Delivery or completion schedules are expressed either by calendar date or as a certain number of days from the date of contract award. When using the latter method, specify whether work days or calendar days are meant.

Reporting schedule – Specify how the contractor shows that it has fulfilled its obligations. Define the mechanism by which the contractor can demonstrate progress and compliance with the requirements, and present any problems it may have encountered. This is usually

accomplished through monthly or bimonthly progress reports. Discuss what areas the reports are to cover, the report format, number of copies the contractor will submit, and to whom they will be submitted. Clearly identify the criteria to be used by the government for acceptance. It is important to require the preparation and submission of technical and financial progress reports to reflect contractor certification of satisfactory progress. If possible, the reports will be coordinated to provide a correlation between costs incurred and the state of contract completion.

Special considerations – Include if there is any information that does not fit neatly or logically into one of the other sections. For example, to explain any special relationships between the contractor and other contractors working for the government.

References – Provide a detailed list and description of any studies, reports, and other data referred to elsewhere in the SOW. Each document will be properly described, cited, and cross-referenced to the applicable part of the work statement. If documents are limited or hard to get, and will not be attached to the RFP, tell where they can be obtained, or when and where they will be available for review. Examples of references include: field memoranda, technical reports, scholarly studies, articles, specifications, and standards.

B.7.b. Term versus Completion Statements of Work

Careful distinctions must be drawn in the SOW between a term (or level-of-effort) acquisition and a completion acquisition. Term SOWs require that the contractor furnish a report on technical effort during a specified period of time, while completion SOWs often require the contractor to develop a tangible end item that is designed to meet specific performance characteristics.

A term or level-of-effort SOW is used where the fundamental "buy" is having the contractor manage, operate and/or maintain. Here the work itself is the primary "output" with deliverables supporting the work done.

A completion-type SOW is appropriate to development work where the feasibility of producing an end item is already known. Completion-type statements of work may describe what is to be achieved through the contracted effort, such as the development of new methods, new end items, or other tangible results. For example, a completion requirement might entail delivering a final study report, submitting test results, or developing and delivering documentation on a computer program.

In many situations there can be a hybrid SOW consisting of both Term and Completion elements. Whichever method is selected, the SOW will be definitive and precise. In

describing an end item, for example, be specific about the characteristics it must possess and the standards it must meet. In a level-of-effort SOW, where results of the effort are not measurable, be specific about the goals and directions toward which the contractor is to deploy resources.

B.7.c. Phasing

Individual research, development, or demonstration projects frequently lie well beyond the present state of the art, and entail procedures and techniques of great complexity and difficulty. Under these circumstances, a contractor, no matter how carefully selected, may be unable to deliver the desired result. Moreover, the job of evaluating the contractor's progress is often difficult. Such a contract is frequently divided into stages (or phases) of accomplishment, each of which must be completed and approved before the contractor may proceed to the next. When phases of work can be identified, the SOW will provide for phasing and the request for proposals will require the submission of proposed costs by phases. The resultant contract will reflect costs by phases, require the contractor to identify incurred costs by phases, establish delivery schedules by phases, and require the written acceptance of each phase.

Phasing makes it necessary to develop methods and controls, including reporting requirements for each phase of the contract and the factors for evaluating the reports submitted that will provide, at the earliest possible time, appropriate data for making decisions relative to all phases. A phased contract may include stages of accomplishment, such as research, development, and demonstration. Within each phase, there may be a number of tasks that will be included in the SOW. Phasing will not be used for projects where several tasks must proceed simultaneously because if each task is made a separate phase, progress will be blocked by lack of data.

B.7.d. Steps in Writing a Statement of Work

Because the SOW is the most influential document in an acquisition, it must be carefully planned and written. It expresses what the contractor is to accomplish and determines whether the government receives the supplies or services it needs.

B.7.d.i. Planning the Statement of Work

Carefully planning the SOW will save time in the writing phase and will make it possible to develop a concise, trouble-free RFP. The first step is to determine the project's objectives. This involves developing clear statements about why the agency is undertaking the acquisition, and what it hopes to achieve. Such a statement is critical because it is impossible to communicate a requirement to potential offerors unless the need can be clearly stated.

Once the project's objectives have been stated clearly in writing, the next step is to meet with the CO, who will help lay out the requirements for the acquisition and the schedule that must be met if a contract is to be awarded by a specific date. The CO can also identify sources of information on regulations and contracting, as well as in-house experts who may be able to help. The next step is to determine all of the individual requirements that must be accomplished if the agency is to meet its objectives. Requirements that need to be considered at this stage include:

☐ Deliverables

☐ What supplies/services are required?

☐ Who will use the supplies and how?

☐ Standards of Performance

☐ What performance/accuracy standards can be specified for the supplies or services?

☐ Personnel

☐ What categories of staff will conduct the project for the contractor?

B.7.d.ii. Hints for Writing Statements of Work

The basic purpose of all writing is to convey a meaning to a reader. The quality and clarity of the writing will determine whether or not that purpose is accomplished. If the writing is unclear, the reader will not understand the message; if it is wordy, the reader will waste time trying to determine the meaning and may misinterpret it. If the language is unfamiliar or too technical, the reader may misunderstand or lose interest. The list that follows contains some writing pitfalls, along with some suggestions for how to avoid them.

Use simple, direct, and clear language. Considerable clarity can be achieved by using short, clear, well-understood words. Avoid technical language unless its meaning is well understood or unless it is defined in the SOW itself. Words with multiple meanings and vague words also should be avoided unless they are defined.

Use active verbs. Passive verbs can be vague. For example, say "the contractor shall perform ..." not "it shall be performed ..." because the latter leaves the question of who shall do the performing open. This is particularly important in research and development acquisitions where many of the contractor's activities depend on the government supplying certain information first.

Use adjectives carefully. Many times adjectives soften nouns and make their meaning vague instead of adding clarity. For example, using adjectives such as "workmanlike,"

"successful," "substantial," and "reasonable" to modify the description of work the contractor is to perform tends to decrease the contractor's obligation rather than increase it.

Use language consistently. Do not change a word or phrase unless a change in meaning is intended. The repetition of long, awkward phrases can often be avoided by inventing an arbitrary name and using that consistently; thus, "the XYZ Company, Inc. (herein called the Contractor)."

Take care in employing modifiers and exceptions. These can cause confusion when the reader is unsure of the reference. If a modifier comes at the end of a long series of phrases, it is sometimes impossible to determine if the modifier refers to the entire series or merely to the last item.

Use and/or sparingly. The use of and/or can be confusing. This is one place where the rule of using as few words as possible can be ignored. For example, if the SOW says, "The contractor shall supply A, B, and/or C," is the firm in compliance if it supplies A and C? Or can it merely supply C, under the assumption that "and/or" meant that supplying C was sufficient? If the writer really means that the contractor has the choice of supplying any or all of the three items, it is better to say, "The contractor shall supply either, A, B, or C, all of them, or any combination of them."

In addition to the specific uses of language mentioned above, there are certain elements in the SOW that often cause confusion:

Time – One of the big problems in writing an SOW is to specify when something must be done. It is best if the obligation is made certain. "On February 1, the contractor shall submit a report ..." But sometimes the report will depend on certain other contingencies. One of the most annoying contingencies is the uncertainty as to the time when the contractor is to start work or is permitted by the government to start work. For this purpose, drafters like to say, "Deliver within 90 calendar days ..." Be sure to specify 90 days from when. Avoid "90 days from the award of the contract" because this is ambiguous. "Awarded" might mean the time the government decided who the contractor was to be, the date of approval by the CO, or the date the contract was signed. To avoid this kind of ambiguity, say "90 days from the effective date of the contract." The "effective date" is a definitive date, i.e., November 2, 20XX, and it gives a firm base from which to start.

Notices – Frequently, SOWs require that a report be delivered to a certain person. Generally, it is better to specify this person by title rather than by name, because personnel can change.

Incorporation by reference – Often there is a need to incorporate some other document into the SOW. When this is done, it will be clear. The incorporated document will be completely identified by date, by title, and by revision number, if applicable. It will be attached, unless it is too cumbersome; then its location will be identified. If "standard tables" are incorporated, the drafter will be clear about which tables these are and know exactly what they say. They may include material that might be objectionable to the government.

Agreements to agree – Exercise caution in "agreeing to agree" on some significant points. If "the model is to be painted a color to be mutually agreed upon" and the drafter really does not care what color it is, then no harm is done. But if the color is significant, the matter should not be left open.

Theoretical discussion – Sometimes theoretical discussion is included in a SOW, with confusing results. If it is necessary to include scientific background or theoretical reasons for doing the work, the drafter will try to do this in a separate part of the SOW so that there will be a clear line of demarcation between the "why" and the "what." The SOW ideally will consist of a description of work, not theoretical discussion. The inclusion of the latter may have the effect of modifying the instructions so that the contractor is given a reason for not performing in accordance with the drafter's wishes or for doing something that was not desired.

Government obligations – Care will be taken in describing what the government is supposed to do. Frequently the contractor's obligation to perform will depend on what the government does first. If the government does not perform its part, the contractor will be excused from performing. If it appears that the government has not performed, then the contractor will have the foundation for an excuse, even if the government has done its part. This situation may arise when it is not sufficiently clear what the government is to do and when.

As an example, the phrase, "Based on information supplied by the government the contractor shall ..." leaves open what information the government will supply. It could be a great deal; it could be very little. There is no way of knowing whether it is significant or not, costly or inexpensive.

There is no way of determining when the government has supplied this information. But the contractor is in a position at any time to claim that whatever it was, the firm did not have it. Furthermore, the contractor is in a position to claim that even if it did get it, it did not get it soon enough. Tell precisely the kind of information the government will supply, and when. Limit the obligation to supplying information or services that are readily available to the

government. Do not agree to give information or services that the government does not have or that may cost a great deal to get.

B.7.d. iii. Revising the Statement of Work

When the first draft is complete, it will need to be rewritten and revised. The writer will read the SOW several times with a view to revising it. The first time, check only the content.

☐ Does it contain sufficient information?

☐ Are more examples needed?

☐ Are the sources the best obtainable?

☐ Has too much material been included?

☐ Is the writing based on sound reasoning?

The second time, check the effectiveness of the organization.

☐ Is the subject stated clearly?

☐ Is the subject advanced in clear stages?

☐ Is the connection between the stages clear?

During the third reading, check the sentence structure and grammar. Revise the SOW, read it again, and continue this process until it is logical and readable, conveys exactly what is required of the contractor, and emphasizes the critical elements. One of the best ways of determining if the SOW meets these design objectives is to have it reviewed by someone else in the program office. Writers often have trouble critiquing their own writing because they tend to read into their own work what they intended it to say instead of what it actually says.

B.7.e. *Performance Statement of Work Checklist*

A.   Is the stage "properly set" for this procurement? That is, are the purpose, background, results and implications providing a clear understanding of the requirement?

B.   Are the applicable documents listed with a complete citation?

C.   Is it clear which performance standards are contained in each applicable document?

D.   Has extraneous material been expunged or put in an applicable document?

E.   Has the work been organized into a logical sequence of tasks which can be effectively performed?

F.   Are specific tasks stated such that it is clear what is required and that there are related performance standards to tell whether the contractor has complied with the effort?

G. Is there a schedule for doing the tasks? Is it necessary? Why?

H. Are the deliverables cross-referenced to their respective tasks?

I. Does each deliverable have its format and content described?

J. Is there a complete delivery schedule and distribution list?

K. Are an overall period of performance and a place of performance stated?

L. Are the elements of quality assurance (inspection, handling nonconformance and acceptance) completely described?

M. If government property is to be provided, are the nature, condition, availability and estimated value stated, including nomenclature, number and timeframe to be furnished?

N. Have headings been checked for consistent format and grammatical usage? Are subheadings comparable? Is the text compatible with the title? Is a multidecimal numbering system used?

O. Are definitive sentences used which precisely identify work to be done, in clear and understandable terms? Are work words, such as analyze, install, develop, detail, update, review and test, used? Are words, such as assist, as required, as necessary, or as directed, avoided?

P. Are there performance standards (as appropriate) related to each task and deliverable to tell whether the contractor has complied with the effort? Do the standards take into account the limits and contingencies for any task or deliverable?

Q. Are the performance standards measurable and can they be monitored straightforwardly?

R. Are acronyms and abbreviations defined?

S. Are there labor categories descriptions for "key" personnel?

T. Is the SOW impartial concerning who can perform it?

U. Will any task have the government directing or supervising the contractor personnel?

V. Are any inherent government functions specified in the various task descriptions?

W. Does the PWS define the government's minimum needs?

X. Is the SOW sufficiently specific to permit the government and the would-be contractors to identify the resources required for each task, and then do a cost estimate?

Y. Does the PWS match the proposal preparation instructions and the proposal evaluation criteria?

Z.   Does the SOW for the basic contract define all anticipated work tasks which may be required under individual task orders?

AA. If government property is to be provided, are the nature, condition, availability, number and timeframe known?

B.8. Work Package

The procurement work package is developed when a need will be satisfied through a contract. The COTR may be required to:

☐ Finalize requirements

☐ Inherently Governmental Function Determination

☐ Prepare an independent government cost estimate

☐ Prepare evaluation factors

☐ Prepare a surveillance plan

☐ Prepare other documentation and obtain necessary approvals

☐ Distribution and support capabilities

B.8.a. Finalize Requirements

Providing an adequate description of government requirements is one of the COTR's most important duties, when assigned. Final requirements are described in a specification, SOW, or other description that defines what the contractor must accomplish to meet government needs.

The following illustrates the importance of a good description of requirements:

The degree to which requirements can be defined shape the procurement strategy and contract type.

The description of requirements may affect the number of vendors willing and able to respond to the solicitation. If a description is not definitive, some vendors may not respond because of uncertainty about the risks or because they do not understand the relationship of the requirement to their own capabilities. If a description is too restrictive, competent vendors may decline to respond because they believe that the government will inhibit their creativity or opportunity to propose alternatives.

The clarity of requirements influences the quality of proposals. A definitive description is likely to produce definitive proposals, reducing the time to evaluate them.

Clear and precise requirements allow the government to establish conclusive baselines on which to structure sound technical evaluation criteria. This reduces delays and administrative effort when evaluating proposals.

The description becomes the standard for measuring contractor performance. When a question arises over work to be performed, the specification or SOW is the baseline document for resolving the question. Language in the specification or SOW that defines the limits of contractor efforts is crucial. If limits are hazy, it will be difficult to determine if the contractor met requirements or if there has been an increase in the scope of work. Negotiation of cost and schedule modifications will be impaired, if not impossible.

B.8.b. Inherently Governmental Function Determination

An agency cannot contract for inherently governmental functions. Inherently governmental functions are those activities so closely related to the public interest that only federal employees can perform them. These functions include activities that require discretion in applying government authority or value-judgments in making decisions for the government. Governmental functions normally fall into two categories: (1) the act of governing, which requires discretionary use of government authority; or (2) decisions affecting monetary transactions and entitlements. The following functions are inherently governmental (this list is not all inclusive):

☐ Determining agency program priorities and budget requests;

☐ Conducting monetary transactions or entitlements;

☐ Interpreting and executing laws that bind the agency to take or not take some action by contract, policy, regulation, authorization, or order;

☐ Determining agency policy;

☐ Exercising ultimate control over a procurement, including collecting, controlling, or disbursing funds, and on what terms;

☐ Use or disposal of government property;

☐ Determining budget policy, guidance and strategy;

☐ Directing and controlling federal employees;

☐ Approving position descriptions and performance standards for federal employees;

☐ Determining and defining supplies or services to be acquired by the agency (a contractor may not identify its own work requirements or write its own SOW or task assignments);

☐ Approving contractual documents such as those defining requirements, incentive plans, and evaluation criteria;

☐ Awarding, administering, and terminating contracts (including functions delegated to a COTR);

☐ Determining whether contract costs are reasonable, allocable, and allowable; and

☐ Drafting congressional testimony, responses to congressional correspondence, or agency responses to audit reports from the Inspector General, General Accounting Office, or other federal audit entity.

The COTR will review requirements to ensure no inherently governmental functions are included.

B.8.c. Prepare an Independent Government Cost Estimate

The independent government cost estimate is a detailed assessment of what the agency expects to pay for work described in the SOW or specifications. It is developed by the COTR or other government subject-matter experts, and cannot be shared with any potential vendor. Cost estimates for complex or non-commercial requirements include a detailed breakdown by cost element, e.g., labor, material, and overhead. The COTR will ensure the government cost estimate:

☐ Covers all program needs or technical objectives

☐ Identifies and sequences tasks to accomplish each objective

☐ Identifies needed resources (materials, labor, etc.)

☐ Estimates length of time per task

☐ Accurately reflects available data on the project

☐ Lists probable line-items and probable quantity, cost, and milestones for each

☐ Describes factual information used to develop the estimate

An example of effective "Output Pricing" is shown below:

"OUTPUT" PRICING
I. INPUTS FROM LABOR USAGE
LABOR CATEGORIES/HOURS

Output	Researcher	Software Developer	Writer/Editor	Total Hours
Gathered Data	200	100	10	310
Decision Software	100	800	10	910

Output	Researcher	Software Developer	Writer/Editor	Total Hours
Simulation Results	25	600	10	635
Upgraded Software	25	250	40	315
Tested Software	50	250	80	380

"OUTPUT" PRICING
II. PRICES FOR EACH OUTPUT

Output	Researcher Price*	Software Developer Price*	Writer/Editor Price*	Total Price: The Sum Of Other Prices
Gathered Data	200 hrs. x $41.19/hr. = $8,238	100 hrs. x $51.50/hr. = $5,150	10 hrs. x $30.90/hr. = $309	$13,697
Decision Software	100 hrs. x $41.19/hr. = $4,119	800 hrs. x $51.50/hr. = $41,200	10 hrs. x $30.90/hr. = $309	$45,628
Simulation Results	25 hrs. x $41.19/hr. = $1,030	600 hrs. x $51.50/hr. = $30,900	10 hrs. x $30.90/hr. = $309	$32,239
Upgraded Software	25 hrs. x $41.19/hr. = $1,030	250 hrs. x $51.50/hr. = $12,875	40 hrs. x $30.90/hr. = $1,236	$15,141
Tested Software	50 hrs. x $41.19/hr. = $2,060	250 hrs. x $51.50/hr. = $12,875	80 hrs. x $30.90/hr. = $2,472	$17,407

CONTRACT PRICE IS: SUM OF ALL OUTPUT PRICES OR $124,112.

* Prices are taken from determined Loaded Rates.

NOTE 1: The Outputs become the CLINs in the contract.

NOTE 2: Input resources, such as Labor, are used to compute Output Prices.

NOTE 3: Such computations can be done in a similar way for Invoicing of actual Outputs provided.

Note 4: Other direct costs are now computed either with each specific Output or common across all Outputs.

B.8.d. Prepare Evaluation Factors

Some contracts, such as for complex products or services, may be awarded on the basis of price and other non-price factors. Other contracts may be awarded on the basis of lowest price, technically acceptable offer. The CO may require the COTR to develop a list of price and non-price factors for evaluating contractor proposals, such as:

Costs of government-furnished property

When contractors have government-furnished property, any competitive advantage that might arise from using such property must be eliminated.

Options

When options are required:

State whether options will be included in the evaluation. Options will be evaluated if the government reasonably intends to exercise them.

Inform offerors of the government's plan to exercise the option at the time of award.

Allow option quantities to be offered with no price limitation.

Allow offerors to submit varying prices for options.

In limited situations, require that option prices be no higher than prices for the initial requirement.

Lease versus purchase

When the economic advantages of lease versus purchase are unknown or minimal and when market research discloses that industry offers both alternatives, prices for both lease and purchase will be solicited. The solicitation will advise offerors that the government's award decision will be based on the best value offer, considering all associated costs of both alternatives.

Transportation costs

When shipping of supplies will be required, delivery may be:

Free on board (FOB) at origin; cost of shipping and risk of loss are borne by the government.

FOB destination; cost of shipping and risk of loss are borne by the contractor.

Both bases.

When lower freight rates are available to the government for shipment to final destinations, FOB origin offers generally may be more advantageous. When offers on both bases are permitted, the solicitation will advise offerors that the two FOB offers will be evaluated on the basis of lowest overall cost to the government.

Other costs

Other price-related factors include:

☐ Energy conservation and efficiency criteria

☐ Estimated quantities (for indefinite delivery contracts)

☐ Lifecycle costs

☐ Installation

☐ Maintenance

☐ Warranty protection or repair

☐ Training

☐ Technical manuals

☐ Spare parts

☐ Supplemental supplies

☐ Non-Price Evaluation Factors

The COTR will identify any non-price factors and a methodology for applying them. These evaluation factors could include potential contractors:

☐ Past performance

☐ Understanding of the government requirement

☐ Technical approach to performing the work

☐ Experience in performing similar work

☐ Qualifications of technical personnel

☐ Quality of the facilities to be used for performing the work

☐ Quality assurance programs and plans

☐ Management capabilities and organization for the proposed work

☐ Scheduling and delivery-related controls

☐ Subcontracting and make-or-buy plans

Environmental and energy objectives, including consideration for environmentally preferred or energy-savings products

B.8.e. Prepare a Surveillance Plan

Prepare a Surveillance Plan (see Attachment Eight for a composite example of a Performance Assessment Plan, http://www.governmenttraininginc.com/The-COTR-Handbook.asp.)

The surveillance plan outlines steps that the COTR will take to monitor contractor performance in delivering products and or services. Monitoring must conform to quality assurance policies and apply only to contract deliverables or outputs specified in the SOW or specification.

B.8.f. Prepare Other Documentation and Obtain Approvals

The COTR ensures the work package is accurate and complete, and has all necessary authorizations. The COTR consults with the program and contracting offices about any other documentation and approvals that may be required before submitting the work package, such as:

☐ Procurement request

☐ Contractor personnel security position risk designation

☐ Section 508 of the Rehabilitation Act non-availability determination

☐ Single source justification

B.9. Government Property

The COTR researches and recommends the need to use government property, identifies sources and availability of the property, and assists in any solicitation issues concerning government property. In fulfilling this duty, the COTR will:

Identify government property for the planned procurement

Notify the CO of the need to use government property

Identify Government Property for the Planned Procurement

To determine if government property will be used on a proposed procurement, the COTR:

Considers recommendations from program officials

Reviews acquisition histories of similar procurements

Reviews reports on existing property inventory

Once a determination is made that government property is required, the COTR determines whether the government property will be:

Furnished by the government to the contractor

Purchased by the government for the contractor to use

Acquired by the contractor for use under the contract

The COTR determines the date when government-furnished property is available and reserves it in the agency inventory system. The COTR specifies any special restrictions or conditions applicable to government-furnished property including:

Property to be provided "as is"

Security issues and other special handling

Minimum skills needed to operate the property

Notify the CO of the Need to use Government Property

The COTR submits written documentation to the CO that:

Includes all relevant factors justifying the use of government property

Addresses issues specific to the type of government property, such as:

☐ Government-furnished property issues

☐ Government liability for performance

☐ Administrative and logistics support costs

☐ Modification costs

☐ Opportunity costs (i.e., other ways the government could use the property)

☐ Potential impact on the contract price

☐ Reductions in direct costs, indirect costs, and fees

☐ Economic benefits of standardization

☐ Estimated residual value

☐ Amount offered by the contractor for the right to retain the property

☐ Effect on future competition and contract pricing

☐ Contractor-acquired property issues

☐ Potential performance problems if property is not delivered

☐ Ownership

☐ Use on other contracts

☐ Administrative and maintenance costs

☐ Government liability for storage

The COTR provides information about use, availability, and condition of government property before a solicitation is issued. After the solicitation is issued, the COTR may be asked by the CO to provide assistance when:

A comparison with offers based on contractor-acquired property is needed.

An offeror has proposed different terms and conditions for government-furnished property from those described in the solicitation.

C. Solicitation, evaluation and award

Expanding on the information provided in Steps Two and Three, the federal government uses different methods and approaches to acquire supplies and services. Contracting by Negotiation is the most commonly used approach in the department. It is also the most complex and places the most demands on the COTR. In this contracting approach, the government communicates its requirements to the business community by means of an RFP. In addition to the SOW discussed in detail in the previous section, this document contains various representations and/or certifications to be completed by prospective contractors, as well as the proposed terms and conditions of the resulting contract. Also included are instructions to offerors to guide them in preparing their proposals and information telling offerors how the government will evaluate proposals to determine which offer will be selected for contract award. The primary responsibility shifts to the CO during most aspects of the solicitation, evaluation, and award phase of an acquisition. The COTR primarily plays a supporting role at this stage.

C.1. The Request for Proposal (FAR Part 15)

The purpose of the RFP is to convey information that prospective offerors need to prepare a proposal. It describes all the information that prospective offerors must furnish to permit a meaningful and equitable evaluation of their offers. The RFP includes the SOW, and the terms, conditions, and provisions that will form the basis for the final definitive contract. The RFP must be clear, complete, accurate, and consistent with the requirements of the acquisition so that it provides all who receive it with the same understanding of the requirements.

The CO is responsible for preparing the RFP with the assistance of the COTR. However, much of the information in the RFP is derived directly from the Purchase Request (PR) or is otherwise furnished by the COTR. As a rule, the CO does not have the technical knowledge to uncover or correct any substantive deficiencies that may exist in the technical data. Therefore, the COTR must take care to develop a PR and supporting documentation during the

pre-solicitation phase that will fully satisfy program needs and objectives when included in the RFP. The COTR will review the final RFP before it is printed and released. Clear distinctions must be made as to the contents and purpose of the SOW, the instructions to offerors, and the evaluation factors and subfactors. The RFP will meet the following objectives.

The SOW must clearly specify the work to be done by the contractor (or, if it is an R&D acquisition, presents a clear statement of the requirements; see FAR Part 35).

The general, technical, and business instructions must delineate all the essential information prospective offerors need to prepare their proposals.

Evaluation factors must clearly indicate the technical, management, personnel, and cost or pricing factors that will be the major considerations in selecting the successful offeror.

The RFP must require that proposals be submitted in two parts — a "technical proposal" and a "business proposal." Each part is to be separate and complete so that one may be evaluated independently of the other. The technical and business proposal instructions must provide all the information deemed essential for proper evaluation of the proposals so that all prospective offerors are aware of all requirements, and so that differences in proposals will reflect each offeror's individual approach to the requirements, not different interpretations of the requirements.

The RFP must inform prospective offerors of all evaluation factors and of the relative importance or weight attached to each factor. Evaluation factors must be described sufficiently enough in the RFP to inform prospective offerors of the significant matters that will be addressed in the proposals. Only the evaluation factors set forth in the RFP can be used in evaluating proposals; these factors can only be modified by a formal amendment to the RFP. Generally, the RFP will require offerors to omit any reference to cost in their technical proposals. However, resource information, such as data concerning labor hours and categories, materials, subcontracts, travel, computer time, etc., must be included in the technical proposal so that the offeror's understanding of the scope of work may be evaluated.

C.2. Uniform Contract Format

The Federal Acquisition Regulation (FAR) requires COs to use the uniform contract format in preparing both RFPs and the resulting contracts. This format not only makes it easier for the government to prepare RFPs and contracts; it also makes it easier for offerors and contractors to use these documents.

Part I - The Schedule

A   Solicitation/contract form

B	Supplies or services and prices/costs
C	Description/specifications/work statement
D	Packaging and marking
E	Inspection acceptance
F	Deliveries or performance
G	Contract administration data
H	Special contract requirements

Part II - Contract Clauses

| I | Contract clauses |

Part III - List of Documents, Exhibits, and Other Attachments

| J | List of attachments |

Part IV - Representations and Instructions

K	Representations, certifications, and other statements of offerors or quoters
L	Instructions, conditions, and notices to offerors or quoters
M	Evaluation factors for award

C.3. Publicizing the Requirement

It is the government's policy that COs must publicize contracting actions in order to:

☐ Increase competition;

☐ Broaden industry participation in meeting government requirements; and

☐ Assist small business, small disadvantaged business, and women-owned small business concerns in obtaining contracts and subcontracts.

The two major Web sites for advertising the solicitation are: www.fbo.gov and www.gsaadvantage.gov.

The CO must establish a solicitation response time that will afford potential offerors a reasonable opportunity to respond to each proposed contract action in an amount estimated to be greater than $25,000, but not greater than the simplified acquisition threshold (SAT); or each contract action for the acquisition of commercial items in an amount estimated to be greater than $25,000.

Except for the acquisition of commercial items, agencies shall allow at least a 30-day response time for receipt of bids or proposals from the date of issuance of a solicitation, if the proposed contract action is expected to exceed the SAT. Agencies must allow at least a 45-

day response time for receipt of bids or proposals from the date of publication of the notice for proposed procurement actions categorized as research and development when the contract action is expected to exceed the SAT.

C.4. Pre-Proposal Conference

The government encourages exchanges of information among all interested parties. The purpose of exchanging information is to improve the understanding of government requirements and industry capabilities. One technique to promote early exchanges of information is the pre-solicitation or pre-proposal conference.

The CO and the COTR may decide that a pre-proposal conference is in the government's interest. Whenever possible, notice of such a conference will be included in the RFP. If the decision is made after the RFP is issued, all recipients must be provided adequate notice of the time, date, location, purpose, and scope of the conference, and invited to submit questions in advance for inclusion on the agenda. The pre-proposal conference may be used to:

Clarify complicated work statements;

Disseminate background data that offer further insight into the size and complexity of the acquisition, as well as the risks of undertaking the project;

Discuss anticipated difficulties during contract administration, including any exceptional demands on a prospective contractor's capacity and capability;

Disclose any ambiguities, errors, or omissions in the RFP that may later be corrected in a written amendment; and

Provide any additional information that is better presented at a conference or that may not have been known at the time the RFP was issued.

The pre-proposal conference is conducted by the CO or a designated representative, with the COTR in attendance to provide support. The CO is responsible for determining the agenda and ensuring that a record of conference proceedings is prepared for distribution to all recipients of the RFP, whether or not they attend the conference.

C.5. Communications with Offerors during Solicitation Period

In order to ensure that the competition is fair and equitable, every firm must be provided with the same information. Under no circumstances may any government employee take any action that might give one firm an advantage over another. In the interval between the time that the RFPs are mailed and the contract is awarded, only authorized acquisition personnel

will have any contact with the offerors. The RFP gives the name of the CO and states that only he/she represents the government. All correspondence to prospective contractors (relating to this acquisition) must be signed by the CO or the authorized representative, and all correspondence from prospective contractors (relating to this acquisition) must be received by the CO.

FAR 15.201 states that exchanges of information between the government and industry are encouraged at all stages of the process, but caution must be used to ensure no preference is given. Techniques that may be used include industry conferences, public hearings, pre-solicitation notices, draft RFPs, Requests for Information (RFIs), pre-solicitation or proposal conferences, site visits, and one-on-one meetings with potential offerors. If, for any reason, one offeror is given information that goes beyond what is contained in the RFP, the same information must be given to all other organizations responding to the solicitation. This must be done by means of a formal amendment that corrects, clarifies, or changes RFP requirements.

C.6. Amendment to the Solicitation

For a variety of reasons, it may be necessary to amend the RFP, either before or after receipt of the proposals. For example:

The CO determines that material changes need to be made in the SOW, terms, or conditions contained in the original solicitation; or quantities need to be increased or decreased;

The CO becomes aware that a number of potential offerors can be expected to be late, which would raise doubt as to whether adequate competition will be obtained. In this case, they may agree to extend the due date by amendment of the solicitation.

The CO makes these determinations in full cooperation and communication with the COTR.

Amendments to solicitations increase administrative effort and costs, and they may delay contract award and performance. For this reason, they will be held to a minimum through careful acquisition planning. When an amendment is unavoidable, the CO must prepare and distribute it to all recipients of the RFP. Any amendment requires that the CO must provide a reasonable time for potential offerors to respond to the change.

C.7. Receipt and Management of the Proposal

Proposals received under a competitive procurement may be accepted only by the CO. Their receipt will be recorded by time and date and they will be properly safeguarded by the CO until the deadline for submission has passed. No proposal received after the time and date specified in the RFP may be accepted unless it was:

Received before award is made; and

The CO determines that accepting the late proposal would not unduly delay the acquisition and:

If it was transmitted through an electronic commerce method authorized by the solicitation, it was received at the initial point of entry to the government infrastructure not later than 5:00 p.m. one working day prior to the date specified for receipt of proposals; or

There is acceptable evidence to establish that it was received at the government installation designated for receipt of proposals and was under the government's control prior to the time set for receipt of proposals; or

It was the only proposal received.

"However, a late modification of an otherwise successful proposal, that makes its terms more favorable to the government, will be considered at any time it is received and may be accepted." (FAR 15.208(b)(ii)). One of the most important administrative responsibilities of project and contract personnel during the pre-award period is to maintain the confidentiality of the proposals received. Unless offerors are assured that their data will not leak out to their competitors, they may be unwilling to provide the government with technical data and other essential information about their operations. However, care must be taken when considering the use or disclosure of technical data to ensure that the agency has sufficient rights to use the data in the desired manner.

To preclude the improper use or disclosure of the offerors' data, program personnel will familiarize themselves with agency policy as described in FAR 15.207. The receipt, storage, and handling of proposals must be treated with all the safeguards necessary to prevent offerors from receiving information that might give them a competitive advantage. In addition, project personnel must not reveal any information related to the identity of potential contractors, information concerning any proposal, or the status of any proposal in relation to others. Release of such information could jeopardize any resultant award and subject the persons involved to disciplinary action.

After the closing date, the CO uses a transmittal memorandum to forward the technical proposals to the COTR or review panel chairperson for evaluation and to establish a date for receipt of the technical evaluation report. The CO retains the business proposals until the technical evaluation report is completed.

Principal Source Selection Documentation

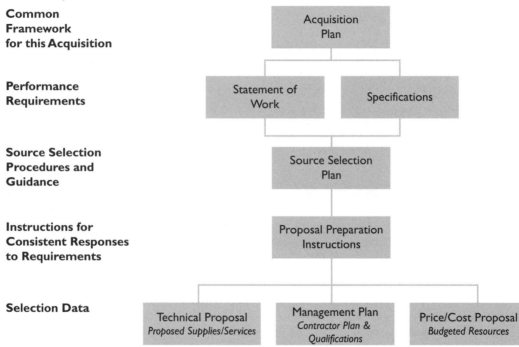

Common Framework for this Acquisition	Acquisition Plan
Performance Requirements	Statement of Work / Specifications
Source Selection Procedures and Guidance	Source Selection Plan
Instructions for Consistent Responses to Requirements	Proposal Preparation Instructions
Selection Data	Technical Proposal *Proposed Supplies/Services* / Management Plan *Contractor Plan & Qualifications* / Price/Cost Proposal *Budgeted Resources*

C.8. Source Selection Plan

When Negotiated Procurement is being used, the Program and Procurement offices need to be synchronized about how source selection will be executed. The preceding graphic and the outline that follows show that proper preparation and understanding of what will be done to select the contractor are key factors to enabling a fair and effective process.

C.8.a. Source Selection Plan Outline

Source selection of ………………………..

1. Description of property or service to be acquired

2. Description of organizational structure, including:

(a) Duties of the SSA

(b) Duties of the SSEB

3. Proposed presolicitation activities

4. A summary of the acquisition strategy

5. A statement of the proposed evaluation factors, including technical/business and price or cost, and their relative importance

6. A description of the evaluation process, methodology, and techniques to be used, including evaluation standards

7. A schedule of significant milestones, such as:

☐ Release of the RFP

☐ Date proposals due

☐ Date evaluation starts

☐ Date evaluation completed

☐ Competitive range determination

☐ Discussions

☐ BAFOs

☐ SSEB Briefs SSA on Findings and Evaluation

☐ SSA Decision Due

☐ Contract review

☐ Execution/award

8. A conflict of interest form

9. Procurement Integrity Certificates

10. Non-disclosure forms

11. Provision for a secure meeting place

Evaluation of Technical Proposals

This review is performed by a technical evaluation panel convened by the program office funding the procurement.

C.8.b. Technical Evaluation Panels

The technical evaluation panel reviews all proposals submitted in response to an RFP to determine which are technically acceptable. A technical evaluation panel is required for all acquisitions that are expected to exceed $500,000. The CO may require a technical evaluation panel for acquisitions that do not exceed $500,000, depending on their complexity. The technical evaluation panel is responsible for evaluating the original proposals; making recommendations to the chairperson regarding weaknesses and deficiencies; reviewing supplemental, revised, and/or final proposal revisions; and, if required, assisting the CO during discussions and negotiations and reviewing supplemental, revised and/or final proposed revisions.

To the extent possible, the same evaluators will be available throughout the entire evaluation and selection process to ensure continuity and consistency in the treatment of proposals. It is usually necessary to conduct a second technical evaluation of proposals submitted as final proposal revisions. The following are examples of circumstances when it would not be necessary for the technical evaluation panel to evaluate revised proposals submitted during the acquisition:

☐ The answers to the questions do not have a substantial impact on the proposal;

☐ Final proposal revisions are not materially different from the original proposals, or

☐ The rankings of the offerors are not affected because the revisions to the proposals are relatively minor.

The chairperson, with the concurrence of the CO, may decide not to have the panel evaluate the revised proposals. Whenever this decision is made, it must be fully documented by the chairperson and approved by the CO. Attendance by the evaluators is mandatory when the CO considers the technical evaluation panel meeting to be necessary. When the chairperson determines that an evaluator's failure to attend the meetings is prejudicial to the evaluation, the chairperson may replace the individual after discussing the situation with the CO and obtaining both his/her concurrence and the approval of the program official responsible for appointing the panel members. Whenever continuity of the evaluation process is not possible, and new evaluators are selected or a reduced panel is used, each proposal being reviewed at that stage of the acquisition will be reviewed by all members of the revised panel unless this is impractical because of the receipt of an unusually large number of proposals.

The technical evaluation panel will be composed of government employees. Outside evaluators may be used when expertise is required that is not available within the government, or as required by law. The research entities of agencies are required to have a peer review

of research and development projects in accordance with Public Law 93-352 as amended by PL 94-63; 42 USC 298 I-4. This legislation states that not more than one-fourth of the members of a peer review group may be officers or employees of the federal government.

Business proposals are evaluated after the CO has accepted the technical evaluation. Evaluations of business proposals are conducted only for those proposals that are in the competitive range. Although the panel's primary responsibility is to evaluate technical proposals, it also may be asked to comment on some aspects of the business proposal. Generally, these will be limited to quantitative elements of cost, such as the number of hours of a given skill required to accomplish a task, the amount and destinations for travel, etc. These cost elements will also help the technical evaluation panel judge an offeror's understanding of the requirement.

C.8.c. Role of the COTR

As the CO's technical representative for the acquisition, the COTR's responsibility is to recommend panel members who are knowledgeable about the technical aspects of the acquisition, and who are competent to identify the strengths and weaknesses of the various proposals. At least 50 percent of the program personnel appointed to a technical evaluation panel for any competitive solicitation must have successfully completed the basic COTR training course or its equivalent. This requirement applies to the initial technical proposal evaluation, as well as to any subsequent technical evaluations that may be required. The determination of course equivalency must be made by the HCA (not delegable) of the cognizant contracting activity. The CO is responsible for ensuring that the COTR and technical proposal evaluators have successfully completed the required training.

If a panel member has an apparent or real conflict of interest related to a proposal being evaluated, that member must be replaced with another evaluator. If a suitable replacement is not available, the panel must perform the review with one less evaluator. The COTR will submit the recommended list of panel members to an official within the program office in a position at least one level above the COTR or in accordance with contracting activity procedures. This official reviews the recommendations, appoints the panel members, and selects the chairperson.

C.9. Reading and Scoring Proposals

Normally the technical evaluation panel convenes to evaluate the proposals, unless the CO decides this is not feasible or practicable. When a panel convenes, the chairperson is responsible for keeping track of all copies of the technical proposals provided by the CO. The chairperson generally distributes the technical proposals at the initial panel meeting and

establishes procedures for securing the proposals whenever they are not being evaluated. After the evaluation is complete, all proposals must be accounted for by returning them to the CO, destroying them, or filing them in a way that will maintain their confidential nature. The CO will address the initial meeting of the panel and state the basic evaluation ground rules. The CO will provide written guidance to the panel if he/she is unable to attend the initial meeting. The guidance will include:

☐ An explanation of conflicts of interest;

☐ The necessity of reading and understanding the solicitation, especially the SOW and evaluation criteria, before reading the proposals;

☐ The need for evaluators to restrict the review only to the solicitation and the contents of the technical proposals;

☐ The need for each evaluator to review all the proposals;

☐ The need to watch for ambiguities, inconsistencies, errors, and deficiencies that will be noted;

☐ An explanation of the evaluation process and what will be expected of the evaluators;

The need for the evaluators to be aware of the requirement to have complete written documentation of the individual strengths and weaknesses that affect the scoring of the proposals; and

An instruction directing the evaluators that, until the award is made, information concerning the acquisition must not be disclosed to any person not directly involved in the evaluation process.

Every evaluator will read each proposal, describe strengths and weaknesses, and develop preliminary scores in relation to each evaluation criterion set forth in the solicitation. The evaluators use either the rating sheets in the technical evaluation plan (discussed later) or rating sheets approved by the CO when a technical evaluation plan is not required. Each evaluator individually scores each proposal, judging the merits of each against the evaluation criteria published in the RFP. No factors other than those set forth in the RFP may be used.

After individual review, the evaluators will discuss in detail the strengths and weaknesses described by each evaluator. Evaluators may change their numerical scores at this time if they believe they have gained a new understanding of the requirements and the proposed approach. However, they will not feel pressured to make changes to conform to the group if they do not wish to do so. The panel collectively ranks the proposals. Generally, this is done by totaling the numerical scores assigned to the criteria by each evaluator, and developing an average rating

for each offeror. Other methods are permissible, depending on the rating plan employed. In any case, numerical scores must be accompanied by a supporting narrative that discusses what was considered in the scoring. When the proposals have been ranked, the evaluators will then identify each as either acceptable or unacceptable. A proposal may be rated as technically unacceptable if it does not meet a design or performance requirement, or if it deviates from the criteria set forth in the RFP. Predetermined cutoff scores cannot be used.

C.10. Exchanges with Offerors After Receipt of Proposals

As stated in FAR 15.306, during the evaluation process, communications between the agency and the offerors are extremely limited. This is particularly true in situations where award without discussion is contemplated. In this situation, offerors may only be given the opportunity to clarify certain aspects of proposals (e.g., the relevance of an offeror's past-performance information and adverse past-performance information to which the offeror has not previously had an opportunity to respond) or to resolve minor or clerical errors. If a competitive range is to be established, communications are somewhat less restricted and:

Shall be limited to –

Offerors whose past-performance information is the determining factor preventing them from being placed within the competitive range. Such communications shall address adverse past-performance information to which an offeror has not had a prior opportunity to respond; and

Those offerors whose exclusion from, or inclusion in, the competitive range is uncertain.

Enhance government understanding of proposals; allow reasonable interpretation of the proposal; or facilitate the government's evaluation process. Such communications shall not be used to cure proposal deficiencies or material omissions, materially alter the technical or cost elements of the proposal, and/or otherwise revise the proposal. Such communications may be considered in rating proposals for the purpose of establishing the competitive range.

Addressing issues that must be explored to determine whether a proposal will be placed in the competitive range. Such communications shall not provide an opportunity for the offeror to revise its proposal, but may address –

Ambiguities in the proposal or other concerns (e.g., perceived deficiencies, weaknesses, errors, omissions, or mistakes); and

Information relating to relevant past performance.

Addressing adverse past-performance information to which the offeror has not previously had an opportunity to comment.

C.11. The Technical Evaluation Report

A technical evaluation report must be prepared and signed by all voting panel members for submission to the CO. The report is maintained as a permanent record in the contract file. The report will reflect the ranking of proposals and identify each proposal as acceptable or unacceptable. The report must also include a narrative evaluation specifying the strengths and weaknesses of each proposal, a copy of the rating sheet and any reservations, qualifications, or areas to be addressed that might affect the selection of sources for negotiation and award. The report also will include specific points and questions that are to be raised in discussions or negotiations. A determination of technical unacceptability must be supported with concrete technical data. The use of phrases, such as "it could not be determined" and "sketchy presentation," is not adequate support for unacceptable ratings. The narrative forms the basis for later debriefings; therefore, specific references and terms must be used.

C.12. Determining the Competitive Range

Agencies shall evaluate all proposals solely on the factors and subfactors specified in the solicitation. Then, if discussions are to be conducted, the agencies must establish the competitive range. Based on the ratings of each proposal against all evaluation criteria, the CO must establish a competitive range that includes all proposals most highly rated, unless the range is further reduced for purposes of efficiency pursuant to the paragraph below.

After evaluating all proposals in accordance with the standards above, the CO may determine that number of most highly rated proposals is too high for conducting an efficient competition. Provided the solicitation notifies offerors that the competitive range can be limited for purposes of efficiency, the CO may limit the number of proposals in the competitive range to the greatest number that will permit an efficient competition among the most highly rated proposals. If the CO, after complying with the other FAR provisions, decides that an offeror's proposal will no longer be included in the competitive range, the proposal will be eliminated from consideration for award. Written notice of this decision shall be provided to unsuccessful offerors. Offerors excluded or otherwise eliminated from the competitive range may request a debriefing.

Discussions with Offerors after Establishment of the Competitive Range
Negotiations are exchanges, in either a competitive or sole source environment, between the government and offerors that are undertaken with the intent of allowing the offeror to revise its proposal. These negotiations may include bargaining. Bargaining includes persuasion,

alteration of assumptions and positions, and give-and-take. They may apply to price, schedule, or technical requirements, type of contract, or other terms of a proposed contract. When negotiations are conducted in a competitive acquisition, they take place after establishment of the competitive range and are called discussions.

Discussions are tailored to each offeror's proposal and shall be conducted by the CO with each offeror within the competitive range. The primary objective of discussions is to maximize the government's ability to obtain best value, based on the requirements and the evaluation factors set forth in the solicitation. The CO shall indicate to or discuss with each offeror, still being considered for award, significant weaknesses, deficiencies, and other aspects of its proposal (such as cost, price, technical and past performance, and terms and conditions) that could, in the opinion of the CO, be altered or explained to enhance materially the proposal's potential for award. The scope and extent of discussion are a matter of CO judgment. In discussing other aspects of the proposal, the government may, if the solicitation stated that evaluation credit would be given for technical solutions exceeding any mandatory minimums, negotiate with offerors for increased performance beyond any mandatory minimum.

If, after discussions have begun, an offeror originally in the competitive range is no longer considered to be among the most highly rated offerors still being considered for award, that offeror may be eliminated from the competitive range, whether or not all material aspects of the proposal have been discussed or the offeror has been afforded an opportunity to submit a proposal revision.

Government personnel involved in the acquisition shall not engage in conduct that –

Favors one offeror over another;

Reveals an offeror's technical solution, including unique technology, innovative and unique uses of commercial items, or any information that would compromise an offeror's intellectual property to another offeror;

Reveals an offeror's price without the offeror's permission. However, the CO may inform an offeror that its price is considered by the government to be too high, or too low, and reveal the results of the analysis supporting that conclusion. It is also permissible, at the government's discretion, to indicate to all offerors the cost or price that the government's price analysis, market research, and other reviews have identified as reasonable;

Reveals the names of individuals providing reference information about an offeror's past performance; or

Knowingly furnishes source selection information.

C.13. Proposal Revisions

The CO may request or allow proposal revisions that clarify and document understandings reached during negotiations. At the conclusion of discussions, each offeror still in the competitive range shall be given an opportunity to submit a final proposal revision. The CO is required to establish a common cut-off date for receipt of final proposal revisions. Requests for final proposal revisions shall advise offerors that the final proposal revisions must be in writing and that the government intends to make award without obtaining further revisions.

C.14. Negotiation

Developing Negotiation Objectives

Developing the government's negotiation goals is a process that will require close coordination between the CO and the COTR. They will discuss uncertainties or deficiencies included in the technical evaluation report for each proposal in the competitive range. Additional clarifying technical questions can be developed by the COTR. The management and cost or price questions will be prepared by the CO with assistance from the COTR and cost analyst, as required.

The CO (based on input from the technical evaluation group, the competitive range determination, the COTR's Technical Questionnaire and additional coordination, and business audit review) is responsible for developing the government's objectives and the strategy for meeting those objectives in contract negotiations. It is expected that the CO will hold a pre-negotiation meeting with the COTR and other government attendees to discuss negotiation goals and strategy and to develop a unified negotiating position. In establishing this strategy, the following will be considered:

Subjects to be discussed;

☐ Content and presentation of revised positions;

☐ Requirements for support of positions; and

☐ All other technical procedures for reaching agreement.

Technical and Business Discussions

Because contract awards are based usually on factors other than costs, technical and business discussions with offerors within the competitive range are a significant aspect of negotiations. The discussions give offerors an opportunity to clarify, correct, or support the proposals; they must therefore be meaningful and address the findings and recommendations from advisory and staff reviews, and may include judgmental cost and business management responsibility issues, as well as technical factors.

Either written or oral discussions may be conducted with each offeror determined to be among the most highly rated. In some cases, the CO represents the government in negotiating with offerors; in other cases there will be a negotiation team composed of those individuals with skills and backgrounds appropriate for the specific acquisition. Either way, the CO shall be the focal point and control the discussions, with the other members present in an advisory capacity. The CO may elect to have various members of the team lead the negotiations in particular areas. However, the CO will always be in control of the overall negotiations.

Discussions are carried on separately with each offeror in the competitive range and may take the form of site visits. The goal is to maximize the government's ability to obtain best value, based on the requirement and the evaluation factors set forth in the solicitation. There will be no reference in discussion with any offeror to the proposal of any other offeror. In fact, no offeror will even be told whether there are any other offerors. The CO shall point out to each offeror the ambiguities, uncertainties, and deficiencies, if any, in its proposal. Each offeror shall be given a reasonable opportunity to support, clarify, correct, improve, or revise its proposal. No offeror may be given information that will give a competitive advantage over other offerors. The discussions shall aim primarily to identify proposal deficiencies and ambiguities, improve their clarity from both technical and business standpoints, and eliminate unnecessarily elaborate provisions exceeding agency requirements. Discussions must not attempt to improve the quality of proposals up to levels of higher-ranking proposals, nor introduce new evaluation elements.

The CO shall:

Control all discussions;

Advise offerors of deficiencies, ambiguities, errors and other uncertainties of the proposals; and

Provide opportunity for offerors to submit technical, cost/price, or other corrections to satisfy the agency requirements fully.

In those processes, all personnel must avoid:

Technical leveling, i.e., helping any offeror improve its proposal to the level of other proposals by discussing weaknesses resulting from the offeror's lack of diligence, competence, or inventiveness in preparing the proposal;

Technical transfusion, i.e., disclosure of technical information from other proposals, resulting in improvement of a competing proposal; and

Auction techniques, e.g. –

Indicating a price that an offeror must meet to obtain further consideration;

Advising an offeror of its price standing relative to other offerors; or

Providing information about other offerors' prices.

C.15. Site Visits and Negotiation Memorandum

Competitive Range Site Visits

Competitive range site visits may be necessary to assess information regarding certain offerors' capabilities, resources, organization, physical facilities, etc., and to clarify necessary proposal details unfamiliar to evaluators and staff. Site visits are considered as included within the technical and business discussions. COs will conduct site visits together with appropriate program staff since they generally involve, or at least can be construed to involve, oral discussions. COs are responsible for conducting and documenting competitive range site visit discussions, although program staff take the lead in technical aspects of the proceedings, including selection of appropriate scientific or technical consultant reviewers to participate in the site visit. These may be Technical Evaluation Group members.

The Negotiation Memorandum

The negotiation memorandum or summary of negotiations is a complete record of all actions leading to award of a contract. It is prepared by the CO in sufficient detail to explain and support the rationale, judgments, and authorities upon which all actions were predicated. The memorandum documents the negotiation process and reflects the negotiator's actions, skills, and judgments in concluding a satisfactory agreement for the government. The COTR will assist the CO in providing documentary evidence to support the justification for award.

C.16. Review of Business/Cost Proposal

The CO is responsible for evaluating business considerations, i.e., those factors relating to cost/price analysis and determination of the contractor's responsibility (e.g., adequate financial resources, ability to comply with delivery or performance schedule, satisfactory record of performance, etc.). Business evaluations normally center on cost analysis and analysis of the contractor's financial strength and management capability.

Each business proposal requires some form of price or cost analysis. The CO must exercise judgment in determining the extent of analysis in each case. The record must be carefully documented to disclose the extent to which the various elements of cost, fixed fee, or profit contained in the contractor's proposal were analyzed. Elements considered in cost

analysis generally include direct material and labor costs, subcontracting costs, overhead rates, general and administrative expenses, travel costs, and profit or fee. Elements considered in evaluating the contractor's financial strength and management capability include:

- ☐ Organization
- ☐ Past performance on similar contractual efforts
- ☐ Reputation for reliability
- ☐ Availability of required facilities and personnel
- ☐ Cost controls
- ☐ Accounting policies and procedures
- ☐ Purchasing procedures
- ☐ Personnel practices (Equal Employment Opportunity, etc.)
- ☐ Property accounting and control
- ☐ Financial resources

In addition, adequacy of the contractor's facilities and key personnel critical to contract performance will be evaluated. The COTR and/or the technical evaluation panel will analyze such items as:

The number of labor hours proposed for various labor categories;

The mix of labor hours and categories of labor in relation to the technical requirements of the project;

The types, numbers, and hours/days of proposed consultants;

The logic of proposed subcontracting;

The proposed travel, including number of trips, locations, purpose, and travelers.

The type and quantity of data processing.

The COTR and/or the evaluation panel will tell the CO whether these elements are necessary and reasonable for efficient contract performance. Exceptions to proposed elements will be supported in sufficient detail to allow the CO to negotiate effectively. In addition, the CO may request that the technical evaluation panel review cost or pricing data as a means of facilitating the decision about including a proposal in the competitive range. Situations that may make such a review necessary include:

A suspected "buy-in" (i.e., a deliberately low bid made with the expectation that the resulting loss will be made up in modifications to the contract or in future contracts);

Large difference in cost or price among the proposals;

Proposals receiving a high technical rating that have relatively high costs; and

Proposals receiving low technical rating that have relatively low costs.

The comparison of cost data with technical factors and information about whether prices are realistic will help the CO decide which proposals to include in the competitive range.

C.17. Selection

The FAR requires that the CO select the source or sources whose proposal is the best value to the government. As stated earlier, at the conclusion of discussions, each offeror still in the competitive range may submit a final proposal revision, which may be subject to a final evaluation by the technical evaluation panel and a cost/price analysis, as necessary. This final evaluation produces a ranking of proposals that aids in the selection of one (or more) offer that achieves the "best value" edict. The department does not specify a formal source selection procedure. Agency heads are responsible for source selection. In most cases the CO is the source selection authority, unless the agency head appoints another individual for a particular acquisition or group of acquisitions. When the CO makes the source selection it will be made on the basis of input from the COTR.

In some cases, where large and/or potentially sensitive acquisitions are involved, the source selection authority will establish an evaluation team, tailored for the particular acquisition. The team will include appropriate contracting, legal, logistical, technical, and other expertise to ensure a comprehensive evaluation of offers. In a formal source selection, the evaluation panel will consist of technical personnel who are knowledgeable about the subject area and the project. They will evaluate and score the proposals and determine the proposals that are in the competitive range. The COTR usually chairs the panel. The panel's recommendations are then made to the source selection authority that is responsible for making the final selection decision.

Sometimes in a more complex or highly visible project the Source Selection Authority (SSA) may appoint a source selection advisory counsel (SSAC). The SSAC represents disciplines that have an inherent interest in the project. They are usually personnel that represent various departments within the agency, such as comptrollers, technical, contracting, legal, etc. Their purpose is to advise the SSA on business and technical matters pertaining to the final source selection.

C.18. Completion of Contract Award

The CO is responsible for preparing the final contract document. The CO coordinates with all parties to the negotiation to ensure that the final document fully delineates the agreement reached at negotiations and is representative of the needs of the program office. The CO reviews the entire contract and file documents for completeness, accuracy, and compliance with requirements. The CO signs the contract on behalf of the government. The contract becomes effective on the date signed by the CO, unless otherwise specified in the contract. Finally, a copy of the fully executed contract is forwarded to the contractor, as well as to the COTR.

C.19. Publicizing the Award

C.19.a. Government-wide Point of Entry

The CO must transmit all required notices to the government-wide point of entry (GPE). The GPE means the single point where government business opportunities greater than $25,000, including synopses of proposed contract actions, solicitations, and associated information, can be accessed electronically by the public. The GPE is located at http://www.fedbizopps.gov.

Except for contract actions described in FAR subpart 5.301(b), COs must synopsize through the GPE awards exceeding $25,000 that are:

Subject to the Trade Agreements Act; or

Likely to result in the award of any subcontracts.

The dollar threshold is not a prohibition against publicizing an award of a smaller amount when publicizing would be advantageous to industry or to the government. There are exceptions to publicizing awards, such as:

Security;

Perishable subsistence supplies;

Award for utility services, other than telecommunications, and only one source is available; and

Award as a result of an unsolicited research proposal that demonstrate unique ideas.

Public Announcement

Federal regulations require the CO to make information available on awards over $3 million to the department in sufficient time for an official announcement by 5:00 p.m. (Washington, DC time) on the day of award. No information shall be released on such awards prior to this public release time.

C.20. Unsuccessful Offeror Notification

Pre-award Notices

Pre-award notices of exclusion from competitive range. The CO shall notify offerors promptly in writing when their proposals are excluded from the competitive range or otherwise eliminated from the competition. The notice shall state the basis for the determination and that a proposal revision will not be considered.

Pre-award notices for small business set-asides. In addition, for a small business set-aside, the CO shall, upon completion of negotiations and determinations of responsibility but prior to award, inform each unsuccessful offeror in writing of the name and location of the apparent successful offeror.

Post-award Notices

Within three days after the date of contract award, the CO shall provide written notification to each offeror whose proposal was in the competitive range but was not selected for award (10 USC 2305(b)(5) and 41 USC 253b(3)) or had not been previously notified under paragraph (a) of this section.

Debriefing Unsuccessful Offerors
Any agency employee who receives either a written or oral request for a debriefing from an unsuccessful offeror will immediately refer the request to the CO. If the request is made orally, the CO will require that the request be made in writing. The CO must be present at all debriefings and must review written debriefings prior to release.

Pre-award debriefing of offerors – Offerors excluded from the competitive range or otherwise excluded from the competition before award may request a debriefing before award (10 USC 2305 (b) (6) (A) and 41 USC 253b (f) - (h)).

The offeror may request a pre-award debriefing by submitting a written request for debriefing to the CO within three days after receipt of the notice of exclusion from the competition.

At the offeror's request, this debriefing may be delayed until after award. If the debriefing is delayed until after award, it shall include all information normally provided in a post-award debriefing.

Post-award debriefing of offerors –

An offeror, upon its written request received by the agency within three days after the date on which that offeror has received notification of contract award, shall be debriefed and furnished the basis for the selection decision and contract award.

To the maximum extent practicable, the debriefing will occur within five days after receipt of the written request. Offerors that requested a post-award debriefing in lieu of a pre-award debriefing, or whose debriefing was delayed for compelling reasons beyond contract award, also shall be debriefed within this time period.

An offeror that was notified of exclusion from the competition (FAR 15.505(a)), but failed to submit a timely request, is not entitled to a debriefing.

D. Protests

Offerors may object to an award by filing a protest with the CO or higher authority. The CO is primarily responsible for resolving it, with assistance from the PO. Protests frequently occur when:

A solicited source is provided with information on the acquisition requirements that is not provided to all other solicited sources;

A program attempts to direct an acquisition to a sole source who is only one of a number of sources who might perform the work;

One source improperly receives information on another's proposal during negotiation;

Solicitation requirements are unnecessarily restrictive.

Protest regulations impose very tight time requirements on the government to respond to inquiries and produce and prepare file documentation if the government wants to receive a favorable opinion in the matter of a protest. Protests received before award prohibits the award action from taking place. The COTR, CO, and other staff necessary to prepare protest documentation files shall be required to devote full and immediate attention to the protest issue until the matter is resolved.

E. Circumstances permitting other than full and open competition

Based on the discussion in Step One, there are seven circumstances that permit for other than full and open competition. Illustrations of the use for three of those circumstances are presented here:

There is only one responsible source and no other supplies or services will satisfy agency requirements. For example, follow-on contracts for the continuation of major research and development studies on long-term social and health programs, major research studies, or clinical trials may be deemed to be available only from the original source when it is likely that award to any other source would result in unacceptable delays in filling the requirements of the agency.

When the agency office head has determined that a specified item of technical equipment or parts must be obtained to meet an activity's program responsibility to test and evaluate certain kinds and types of supplies, and only one source is available. (This criterion is limited to testing and evaluation purposes only and may not be used for initial outfitting or repetitive acquisitions. COTRs will support the use of this criterion with citations from their agency's legislation and the technical rationale for the item of equipment required.)

When the agency office head has determined that there is existing equipment that, for reasons of compatibility and interchangeability, requires an item that is manufactured only by one source. This criterion is for use in acquisitions where a particular brand name item is required, and an "or equal" will not meet the government's requirements. This criterion may not be used when there are other manufacturers available that may be able to produce acceptable items, even though their supplies might require some adjustments and modifications. The other manufacturers must be given the opportunity to compete.

Each contracting activity within the agency has appointed a Competition Advocate who is responsible for promoting full and open competition and challenging barriers to competition.

Justifications and Approvals Required

The program office will discuss prospective "other than full and open competition" requests with their supporting contracting office as early as possible during the acquisition planning stage (see FAR Part 7.1), and before developing the Purchase Request. The discussions may resolve uncertainties, provide program offices with names of other sources, allow proper scheduling of the acquisition, and avoid delays that might otherwise occur, should it be determined that the request for other than full and open competition is not justified. When a program office desires to obtain certain supplies or services by contract without full and open competition, it must — usually at the time of forwarding the requisition

or request for contract — furnish the contracting office with a justification explaining why full and open competition is not feasible. All justifications must be initially reviewed by the CO.

Justifications in excess of $100,000 (simplified acquisition threshold) must be in the form of a separate, self-contained document, prepared in accordance with the agency's acquisition regulation and called a "JOFOC" (Justification for Other than Full and Open Competition). Justifications of $100,000 or less may be in the form of a paragraph or paragraphs contained in the requisition or request for contract. The JOFOC must be approved in writing:

For a proposed contract not exceeding $500,000, by the CO unless a higher approval level is established in agency procedures.

For a proposed contract over $500,000 but not exceeding $10,000,000, by the competition advocate for the procuring activity designated pursuant to FAR Part 6.501. This authority is not delegable.

For a proposed contract over $10,000,000 but not exceeding $50,000,000, by the head of the procuring activity, or a designee who is serving in a position in grade GS-16 or above (or in a comparable or higher position under another schedule).

For a proposed contract over $50,000,000, by the senior procurement executive of the agency designated pursuant to the OFPP Act (41 USC 414(3) in accordance with agency procedures. This authority is not delegable.

Justifications, whether over or under $100,000, must fully describe what is to be acquired, offer reasons that go beyond inconvenience, and explain why it is not feasible to obtain competition. Justifications must be supported by verifiable facts rather than mere opinions. Documentation in the justification will need to be sufficient to permit an individual with technical competence in the area to follow the rationale. Justifications must contain sufficient facts and rationale to justify the use of the specific authority cited. As a minimum, each justification shall include the following information:

Identification of the agency and the contracting activity and specific identification of the document as a "Justification for Other than Full and Open Competition."

Nature and/or description of the action to be approved.

Description of the supplies or services required to meet the agency's needs (including the estimated value).

Identification of the statutory authority permitting other than full and open competition.

Demonstration that the proposed contractor's unique qualifications or the nature of the acquisition requires use of the authority cited.

Description of efforts made to ensure that offers are solicited from as many potential sources as is practicable.

Determination by the CO that the anticipated cost to the government will be fair and reasonable.

Description of the market research conducted and the results found, or a statement of the reasons market research was not conducted.

Any other facts supporting the use of other than full and open competition, such as an explanation of why technical data packages, specifications, engineering descriptions, SOWs, or purchase descriptions suitable for full and open competition have not been developed or are not available.

A list of the sources, if any, which expressed an interest in the acquisition in writing.

A statement of the actions, if any, the department may take to remove or overcome any barriers to competition before any subsequent acquisition for the supplies or services required.

CO certification that the justification is accurate and complete to the best of the CO's knowledge and belief.

Signature lines are:

Recommended	Date

Contract Officer's Technical Representative

Concur	Date

COTR's Immediate Supervisor

Concur	Date

Contracting Officer

Approved	Date

Approving Official

The CO, who receives a JOFOC for processing after ascertaining that the document is complete, forwards the JOFOC exceeding $500,000, with his or her concurrence or nonconcurrence, to the appropriate competition advocate for his or her approval. When the CO does not concur with the JOFOC, a written explanation setting forth the reasons must

be provided to the competition advocate. If the JOFOC is disapproved by the competition advocate, the CO must promptly notify the concerned program office.

F. Unsolicited proposals – A special case of no competition

Unsolicited Proposals

It is the policy of the government to encourage the submission of new and innovative ideas in response to Broad Agency Announcements, Small Business Innovation Research topics, Small Business Technology Transfer Research topics, Program Research and Development Announcements, or any other government initiated solicitation or program. When the new and innovative ideas do not fall under topic areas publicized under those programs or techniques, the ideas may be submitted as unsolicited proposals. A valid unsolicited proposal must meet each of the following criteria:

It must be innovative and unique.

It must be independently originated and developed by the offeror.

It must be prepared without government supervision, endorsement, direction, or direct government involvement.

It must include sufficient detail to permit a determination that government support could be worthwhile, and the proposed work could benefit the department, research and development, or other mission responsibilities.

It must not be an advance proposal for a known department requirement that can be acquired by competitive methods.

Any unsolicited proposals received by any organizational element will be forwarded immediately to the contracting office. The contracting office will acknowledge the receipt of all unsolicited proposals and assign an appropriate control number to the proposal. In the acknowledgment letter, the CO will request any additional information that is required in order to make the proposal complete. The contracting office will then forward the unsolicited proposal to the appropriate program office for preliminary review.

All unsolicited proposals must contain a certification that provides the following statement:

Unsolicited Proposal Certification by Offeror

This is to certify, to the best of my knowledge and belief, that:

a.   This proposal has not been prepared under government supervision.

b.   The methods and approaches stated in the proposal were developed by this offeror.

c.   Any contact with employees of the (named government agency) has been within the limits set forth in FAR 15.604, Agency points of contact.

d.   No prior commitments were received from (named government agency) employees regarding acceptance of this proposal.

Date:

Organization:

Name:

Title:

(This certificate shall be signed by a responsible official of the proposing organization or a person authorized to obligate the organization contractually.)

The following information must be provided as part of the unsolicited proposal:

☐ Name and address of the organization or individual submitting the proposal

☐ Date of preparation or submission

☐ Clear and concise title and abstract of the proposal

☐ An outline and discussion of the purpose of the proposed effort or activity, the methodology to be used, and the nature and extent of the anticipated results

☐ Names of the key personnel to be involved, brief biographical information, including principal publications and relevant experience

☐ Proposed starting and completion dates

☐ Equipment, facility, and personnel requirements

☐ Proposed budget, including separate cost estimates for salaries and wages, equipment, expendable supplies, services, travel, subcontracts, other direct costs and overhead

☐ Names of any other federal agencies receiving the unsolicited proposal and/or funding the proposed effort or activity

☐ Brief description of the offeror's facilities, particularly those that would be used in the proposed effort or activity

☐ Brief outline of the offeror's previous work and experience in the field

☐ Period for which the proposal is valid

☐ Names and telephone numbers of offeror's primary business and technical personnel whom the agency may contact during evaluation or negotiations

☐ Identification of proprietary data that the offeror intends to be used by the agency for evaluation purposes only

☐ Signature of a responsible official of the proposing organization or a person authorized to obligate the organization contractually

☐ Other statements, if applicable, about organizational conflicts of interest, security clearances, and environmental impacts

F.1. Receipt and Initial Review of Unsolicited Proposals

The Head of the Contracting Activity (HCA) is responsible for establishing procedures for controlling the receipt, evaluation, and timely disposition of unsolicited proposals. The HCA or his/her designee shall be the point of contact for coordinating the receipt and handling of unsolicited proposals. Before initiating a comprehensive evaluation, the agency contact point shall determine if the proposal:

Is a valid unsolicited proposal, meeting the required information and certification stated above;

☐ Is suitable for submission in response to an existing agency requirement;

☐ Is related to the agency mission;

☐ Contains sufficient technical and cost information for evaluation;

☐ Has been approved by a responsible official or other representative authorized to obligate the offeror contractually; and complies with the marking requirements for limited use of data.

If the proposal meets the above requirements, the contact point shall promptly acknowledge receipt and process the proposal. If a proposal is rejected because the proposal does not meet the requirements in the initial comprehensive evaluation above, the agency point of contact shall promptly inform the offeror of the reasons for rejection in writing and of the proposed disposition of the unsolicited proposal.

F.2. Evaluation of Unsolicited Proposals

Comprehensive evaluations must be coordinated by the agency contact point, who shall attach or imprint on each unsolicited proposal, circulated for evaluation, the legend for "Use and Disclosure of Data" for data that the offeror does not want disclosed to the public or the government except for evaluation purposes. When performing a comprehensive evaluation of

an unsolicited proposal, evaluators shall consider the following factors, in addition to any other appropriate factor for the particular proposal:

Unique, innovative, and meritorious methods, approaches, or concepts demonstrated by the proposal;

Overall scientific, technical, or socioeconomic merits of the proposal;

Potential contribution of the effort to the agency's specific mission;

The offeror's capabilities, related experience, facilities, techniques, or unique combinations of these that are integral factors for achieving the proposal objectives; The qualifications, capabilities, and experience of the proposed principal investigator, team leader, or key personnel critical to achieving the proposal objectives; and

The realism of the proposed cost.

When the evaluation is completed, the evaluators must notify the agency point of contact of their recommendations.

G. Monitoring the subsequent effort

To provide the "forest through the trees" of the phases and steps of contract administration that the COTR will interface, the following the chart so demonstrates:

CONTRACT ADMINISTRATION PHASES AND STEPS

Phases	Steps
1. Start Up	Administration Planning
	Appointment of Technical Reps.
	Post-award Orientation
	Performance Planning
	Establish Project Management File
	Form Relationships
2. Creating Task Orders	Process of Ordering
	Writing the PWS
	Creating the GCE
	Negotiating the Proposal

Phases	Steps
3. Monitoring and Problem Solving	Technical Direction
	Baseline Management
	Meeting Records
	Key Personnel
	Tracking Deliverables
	Periodic Reviews
	Risk Assessment
4. Inspection and Acceptance	Quality Definitions
	Mutual Responsibilities
	Inspection
	Nonconformance
	Acceptance
	Post-acceptance Rights
5. Cost Control and Payment	Periodic Cost Reviews
	Analysis of Invoices
	Correction of Cost Problems
6. Improving Performance	Effective Communication
	Recognize Trouble Indications
	Identify Actions
	Resolve Performance Issues
	Handle Disagreements
7. Closeout	Responsibilities
	Overall Evaluation Report
	Release of Monitoring File
8. Changes	Recognizing the Need
	Gathering Substantiating Information
	Justifying the Change
	Negotiating Proposal and Reaching Agreement
	Gaining Approval
	Implementing the Change

Phases	Steps
9. Claims	Understand Origin of Disagreement
	Take Informal Steps toward Resolution
	Take Formal Steps toward Resolution
10. Termination	Gather Supporting Evidence
	Determine Type of Termination
	Prematurely end Task Order or Contract
	Negotiate and Recover based on Settlement Reached

NOTE: The "watchword" of this table is: if the requirement is well defined and Steps 1-7 are well executed, there will be less instance or cause for Steps 8-10 to occur.

G.1. Post-award Goals

Expanding on the information provided in Steps Two and Three, contract administration involves ensuring that the contract is performed, as written, by both the contractor and the government. No matter what type of contract is involved, a breakdown in administration can undo all previous achievements discussed in the other sections of this handbook. The COTR must monitor a contractor's progress closely and make known to the CO potential problems that threaten performance so that remedial measures may be taken. Planning for effective contract monitoring begins in the acquisition planning stage.

The administration of a contract begins after contract award. It ends at closeout of the contract when performance is complete and accepted by the government, and the contractor has received its final payment. Therefore, contract administration includes all the functions and duties relating to such tasks as:

Monitoring the contractor's technical progress;

Reviewing invoices for payment in accordance with contractual terms;

Reviewing and directing the correction of the contractor's property control system controlling government property;

Consenting to subcontracts;

Reviewing task orders;

Overseeing contract modifications and terminations where authorized; and

Performing other administrative tasks required by the contract.

Contract administration can be simple or complex and time consuming, depending on the type of contract, contractor performance, and the nature of the work. For example, a fixed-price contract for commercial items requires relatively little post-award administration. In contrast, a cost-type contract requires careful technical surveillance and auditing of costs and imposes an administrative burden on both the government and the contractor. No matter what type of contract is involved, however, it will be closely monitored. If technical or business problems are not solved before they disrupt the contractor's scheduled performance, the government may find itself in a situation with either a pending termination or a forced contract modification. Either is a poor remedy, considering the lost time or unnecessary costs that could have been avoided if the government had administered the contract properly.

G.1.a. Limitations of the COTR

The CO is responsible for contract administration. The CO is the only person who may modify the contract, or take any action to enter or change a contractual commitment on behalf of the government. The legal responsibility for the contract rests with the CO. He or she delegates certain authority to the COTR and holds the COTR accountable for exercising that authority properly. In most cases, the CO authorizes the COTR to perform the following functions in administering the technical aspects of the contract:

Correspond directly with the contractor. Copies of all correspondence must be sent to the CO. In situations where the COTR is not clear about the effect of the correspondence on contractual provisions, the correspondence will be cleared with the CO in advance;

☐ Hold conferences with the contractor;

☐ Conduct onsite visits;

☐ Approve all technical data submitted by the contractor;

☐ Provide technical monitoring during contract performance; and

☐ Issue letters to the contractor and CO relating to delivery, acceptance, or rejection in accordance with the terms and conditions of the contract.

In addition to exercising delegated authorities, the COTR is expected to:

Maintain a file documenting significant actions and containing copies of trip reports, correspondence, and reports and deliverables received under the contract; and

Advise and assist the CO, as necessary, in administering the business aspects of the contract, reviewing vouchers, invoices, reports, and deliverables; coordinating program office

decisions as they bear on the contract; preparing final summary statements for contract closeout; and preparing contractor performance evaluations.

The COTR is not authorized to issue or approve changes in the contract or to enter into any agreement, contract modification, or any other matter changing the cost or terms and conditions of the contract.

G.1.b. Communicating with the Contracting Officer

The COTR functions only as the technical representative of the CO. The CO delegates certain contract administration functions to the COTR, but the legal responsibility for the contract remains with the CO. The COTR functions as the "eyes and ears" of the CO by monitoring technical performance, and reporting any potential or actual problems to the CO. It is imperative that the COTR stays in close communication with the CO, relaying any information that may affect contractual commitments and requirements.

The balance of this section discusses the myriad functions that contract administration entails, with special emphasis on the communication between the COTR and the CO.

G.2. Contract Start-up

Once a contract has been awarded, the COTR will be given a copy of the contract. The COTR's first responsibility is to read and understand the contract. Government contracts are subject to essentially the same common-law rules of interpretation applied to other contracts. Several of these basic rules are:

The intent of the parties must be gathered from the whole contract.

The provisions of a contract will not be interpreted so as to render one or more meaningless, unless otherwise impossible, and the interpretation that gives reasonable meaning to the whole document is preferred.

The dominant purpose and the interpretation adopted by the parties will be used to ascertain the meaning of the contract provisions.

Specific provisions prevail over general provisions when in conflict.

A standard clause entitled "Order of Precedence" resolves inconsistencies within the contract provisions by assigning precedence in a specified order within the contract parts.

An ambiguous provision susceptible to more than one interpretation will be interpreted against the party responsible for creating it — in government contracts this is almost always the government, as the contract provisions are normally prepared by the government.

Equally important to the performance of government contracts, or more aptly the risk thereof, is the list of specifications or SOW that the contractor must meet. Contract specifications dictate the nature and degree of performance to be undertaken by a contractor. When the specifications are accurate, complete, and realistic the only issue is contractor performance or, more properly, attributing the responsibility for a performance failure to either the government or the contractor.

On the other hand, where specifications are shown to be defective, or are such that performance is impossible, the contractor may either be excused for lack of performance or may be entitled to additional compensation if the cost of performance is increased.

Similarly, a mutual mistake of fact may result in an adjustment to the contract price. In this situation, there must be a mistaken concept by both parties as to a material fact that results in performance being more costly. In order for the contractor to recover the extra cost of performance, the contractor must show that the contract did not allocate to it the risk of such a mistake. In addition, contractor must show that the government received a benefit from the extra work for which it would have been willing to contract had the true facts been known. As the contracted effort begins, it is an excellent idea for the COTR to have drawn up a Work Plan to guide the subsequent contract efforts (see Attachment Seven, http://www.governmenttraininginc.com/The-COTR-Handbook.asp).

G.2.a. Post-award Orientation

COTRs play a key role in the post-award orientation. Generally, the COTR performs the following tasks to ensure successful post-award orientation:

- ☐ Develop a discussion paper for the CO's preliminary briefing.
- ☐ Participate in the preliminary briefing.
- ☐ Participate in the orientation.
- ☐ Review the report of the post-award orientation.
- ☐ Complete assigned action items.
- ☐ What will be their qualifications?
- ☐ What will be the qualifications/experience of the contractor?

Methodology

- ☐ What is the appropriate methodology?
- ☐ Are there different possible methodologies?
- ☐ What stages/phases can the project be broken into?

Schedule

☐ When are the results of the project needed?

☐ How long will the project take?

What is the schedule for the deliverables?

Location

☐ Where will the project take place?

☐ Will travel be required?

Once all of the requirements have been listed, they can be arranged into a logical sequence.

During the process of listing the requirements, it may be helpful to do some background reading. Collect and analyze previous documents and contract deliverables that bear on the requirements, including:

☐ Documents that discuss overall program goals and objectives;

☐ Reports, manuals, or other deliverables produced in the past; and

☐ SOWs developed for similar projects.

Review government-wide or departmental regulations, policy directives, or administrative memoranda that apply to the type of acquisition under consideration. Consult with other program personnel to elicit views on the project, its objectives and requirements. At this stage, it is important to decide if the complexity of the project requires advice from technical specialists or help from additional writers. If so, identify the personnel needed and specify the areas that each will address.

G.2.b. Participate in the Orientation

The CO usually chairs the orientation. Any presentation that the COTR makes must be consistent with the terms and conditions of the contract. Discussions at the orientation can establish procedures or processes to ensure compliance with contract terms, but the COTR must be careful that these discussions do not alter the contract terms. Handouts are permitted at the orientation. Some handouts are required, such as Department of Labor posters and notices. Other handouts are developed specifically for the post-award orientation. The COTR must ensure that any information in the handout complies with the contract terms.

Adverse past-performance information could result in the contractor not receiving future contracts. At the orientation, any presentation on past performance must include a discussion

of the contractor's rebuttal rights. If the COTR will prepare information for the past performance file, he or she will make the presentation at the orientation.

Issues that cannot be resolved at the orientation must be identified and recorded. When possible, a date is established for resolution. All participants are made aware at the orientation of any specific follow-up actions they personally must handle. For milestones that require contractor input, it is best to agree on milestones at the orientation. The CO incorporates action items and due dates in the post-award orientation report.

Post-award Orientation Checklist

PART I - GENERAL			
1. Contract No.	2. Total Amount	3. Type of Contract	4. Date of Conference
5. Pre-award Survey? __ YES __ NO	6. Contractor Name	7. Contractor Address	
PART II - CONFEREES			
1. Government		2. Contractor	

PART III - CONFERENCE PROGRAM			
Subject	Check if Applicable	Clause No. if Applicable	Significant conclusions, further action to be taken (attach additional sheets if necessary)
A. GENERAL 1. Function and authority of assigned personnel			
2. Routing of correspondence			
3. Omissions or conflicting provisions			
4. Other (specify)			
B. REPORTS: PREPARATION AND SUBMITTAL 1. Work progress			
2. Financial			
3. Other (specify)			
C. SUBCONTRACTS 1. Consent to placement			
2. Prime's responsibility for administration			
3. Cost or pricing data			

PART III - CONFERENCE PROGRAM

Subject	Check if Applicable	Clause No. if Applicable	Significant conclusions, further action to be taken (attach additional sheets if necessary)
4. Source inspection			
5. Other (specify)			
D. SB, SDB, SDVOSB, and WOSB Subcontracting 1. Contractual requirements			
2. Program to facilitate			
E. CONTRACT MODIFICATIONS			
F. GOVERNMENT PROPERTY 1. Use of facilities and tooling			
2. Maintenance and preservation			
3. Property procedure approval			
4. Property disposal procedures			
5. Other (specify)			
G. SPECIAL CLAUSES 1. Issuing task orders			
2. Liquidated damages			
3. Government financing			
4. Special tooling			
5. Overtime			
6. Bill of materials			
7. Data/copyrights			
8. Warranties			
9. Work performed at government installations			
10. Other (specify)			
H. GENERAL CLAUSES 1. Limitation of cost			
2. Allowability of cost			
3. Other (specify)			
I. DELIVERY/PERFORMANCE SCHEDULES			
J. TRANSPORTATION			

PART III - CONFERENCE PROGRAM

Subject	Check if Applicable	Clause No. if Applicable	Significant conclusions, further action to be taken (attach additional sheets if necessary)
K. INVOICING AND BILLING INSTRUCTIONS			
L. PROCESSING OF COST AND PRICE PROPOSALS			
M. LABOR 1. Actual and potential labor disputes			
2. Davis-Bacon Act			
3. Work Hours Act			
4. Walsh-Healey Act			
5. Copeland Anti-Kickback Act			
6. DOL Posters and Notices			
N. QUALITY ASSURANCE AND ENGINEERING			
1. Quality control system			
2. Waivers and deviations			
3. Drawing/design approval			
4. Manuals			
5. Pre-production sample			
6. Qualifications and environmental tests			
7. Inspection and acceptance			
8. Specification interpretation			
9. Laboratory facilities			
10. Value engineering clause			
11. Other (specify)			
O. PRODUCTION 1. Production planning			
2. Milestones and other monitoring devices			
3. Production surveillance			
4. Safety			

(Additional Notes)

G.2.c. Review the Post-award Orientation Report

An orientation report contains all information necessary to document the events of the meeting. All participants will receive copies for review. Any omissions, deficiencies, or disagreements are thoroughly documented and submitted to the CO. Key elements of a Post-award Orientation Report include:

☐ The names and affiliations of all participants

☐ The main discussion points and all agreements

☐ Areas requiring resolution

☐ Participants assigned responsibility for further action and completion dates for actions

G.2.d. Complete Assigned Action Items

The COTR will resolve each action item or issue in a fair and equitable manner, and as quickly as possible. Although not always practicable, it is best to resolve all problems before the contractor begins work. If a contract change is necessary, the COTR must clearly define the extent of the change and promptly submit it to the CO. The contract file will include the conference report and other material, correspondence, or actions developed or acquired from the post-award orientation. A well-documented contract file will identify and verify the government's initial position on any performance problems that were anticipated during the orientation or in the early implementation of the contract.

G.2.e. Standard Contract Clauses

Federal agency contracts contain clauses applicable to that particular agency that are incorporated by reference. The COTR will understand what these clauses require. They can be found in either the FAR Part 52 or the agency's regulation.

Subcontracts

Subcontracting means any contract entered into by a subcontractor to furnish supplies or services for performance of a prime contract or a subcontract. In the case of a prime contract, the government is the buyer and the contractor is the seller. However, when the contractor lets subcontracts, the contractor becomes the buyer, while the subcontractor becomes the seller. The prime contractor and the government have a direct legal relationship. No such direct legal relationship exists between the government and the subcontractor. Even in acquisitions where the contract specifies that the government has a right to review and approve subcontracts, no direct relationship between the government and the subcontractor is established.

Administration of Subcontracts

The prime contractor, not the government, is responsible for administering subcontracts. When the government buys the services of a contractor it is buying, among other services, its management services. It is the responsibility of the prime contractor in an acquisition to ensure the performance of the

subcontractor. Nevertheless, a COTR can perform a number of monitoring and contract administration functions to promote effective subcontract operations.

Action Prior To Award

The COTR has the opportunity to begin monitoring the sub-acquisition process prior to award. When the COTR reviews proposed subcontracts before forwarding them to the CO for approval, the FAR suggests that the following questions be asked:

Is the decision to subcontract consistent with the contractor's approved make-or-buy program, if any? (See FAR Subpart 15.407-2.)

Is the subcontract for special test equipment or facilities that are available from government sources? (See FAR Part 45.3.)

Is the selection of the particular supplies, equipment, or services technically justified?

Has the contractor complied with the prime contract requirements regarding small business subcontracting, including, if applicable, its plan for subcontracting with small business, small disadvantaged business, and women-owned small business concerns? (See FAR Part 19.)

Was adequate price competition obtained or its absence properly justified?

Does the contractor have a sound basis for selecting and determining the responsibility of the particular subcontractor?

Has the contractor performed adequate cost or price analysis or price comparisons and obtained accurate, complete, and current cost or pricing data, including any required certifications?

Has adequate consideration been obtained for any proposed subcontract that will involve the use of government-furnished facilities?

Has the contractor adequately and reasonably translated prime contract technical requirements into subcontract requirements?

In reviewing the proposed subcontract, the COTR will be especially careful if:

The prime contractor has had previous subcontracting problems;

There has been little or no competition for the supplies or services;

There is a close relationship between the prime contractor and the proposed subcontractor; and

The subcontract is to be placed on a time and material, cost-reimbursement, labor hour, fixed-price incentive, or fixed-price redeterminable basis.

Action after Award

After the subcontract has been let, it is the prime contractor's responsibility to manage it. But here again, the COTR has certain responsibilities to ensure that the prime contractor is managing it adequately. The COTR can review the effectiveness of the contractor's subcontract administration function. Observations can be made of such things as the support, direction, and timeliness of actions provided by the contractor to subcontractors. An important area to be covered in any review of subcontract administration is the contractor's system for making subcontract changes. Procedures must provide not only for timely processing of changes but also for prompt notification of all parties concerned, including the government.

G.2.f. Monitor Statutory Compliance

The CO may delegate some monitoring of statutory or regulatory compliance to the COTR. The COTR must notify the CO should any actual or potential noncompliance issues arise; only the CO can resolve noncompliance issues related to law or regulation. Steps involved in monitoring statutory and regulatory requirements include:

Identify contract clauses involving statutory or regulatory compliance, such as those involving:

☐ Labor law

☐ Privacy Act

☐ Drug-Free Workplace

☐ Hazardous or recovered material, safety, and environmental requirements

☐ Non-domestic materials

☐ Monitor compliance and respond to notices involving compliance

☐ Identify any insurance or bonding issues

☐ Monitor intellectual property issues

☐ Monitor compliance with the subcontracting plan

☐ Continue actions as needed to enforce statutory compliance, and keep others informed

G.2.g. Develop and Follow a COTR Work Plan

COTRs will develop and follow a cost-effective work plan for monitoring contract performance and performing other delegated responsibilities. The COTR work plan serves as a baseline for project management and scheduling, and tracking contractor performance. The plan will be drawn from lists of deliverables, reporting requirements, government-furnished property clauses, etc. When preparing a work plan, the COTR will include:

☐ Administrative information

☐ Contract title

☐ Identity of the contractor and key contractor personnel

☐ Location of files about the contract and the contractor

☐ Brief description of the work to be performed

☐ Place of performance and delivery points

☐ Assigned tasks and milestones for each task and function, such as:

☐ Monitoring the contractor quality assurance program

☐ Furnishing government property and monitoring its use

☐ Reviewing and responding to contractor reports and requests

☐ Receiving, inspecting, and accepting work

☐ Certifying costs incurred or physical progress for payment

☐ Monitoring compliance with the small business subcontracting plan

☐ Consider historical factors

☐ Determine the technique to be used for monitoring the contract

☐ Determine how to document performance under the contract

☐ Identify areas of concern or conflict

G.2.h. Consider Historical Factors

To help determine the level of commitment involved, the COTR will consider historical factors and the contractor's performance history. Historical factors include:

Type of Contract	■ What type of contract is this?
	■ If there was a previous procurement, did the type of contract change?
Past experiences with this type of requirement	■ Has this requirement ever been purchased before?
	■ What are current problems associated with this product or service?
Past experience with the previous contractor	■ Did the previous contractor deliver on time?
	■ Did the contractor perform as expected?
Type of requirement	■ Does this type of requirement - service or supply - necessitate extensive monitoring to ensure compliance?
Urgency of the requirement	■ How soon is this requirement needed and what would happen if delivery is delayed?
	■ Were there any previous problems with contractors meeting the delivery terms?
	■ Has this contractor established that it can expedite delivery, if needed?

Government databases, such as National Institute of Health's Contractor Performance System (online at: cps.od.nih.gov) contain information about a contractor's performance history. The COTR will review contractor past performance for the last three years, to help determine the level of attention needed for monitoring the current contract.

G.2.i. Notify the CO of Problems

The COTR will contact the CO to resolve any areas of concern as soon as possible, particularly if it may result in a contract modification (only the CO has authority to modify the contract).

COTR Duties

The COTR often helps the CO monitor government property under the contract. In fulfilling this duty the COTR:

☐ Supervises initial transfer of government property

☐ Monitors contractor use of government property

☐ Monitors disposition of government property

☐ Supervise Initial Transfer of Government Property

☐ Monitor Delivery of Government Property

The COTR reviews the contract to determine if any government data, equipment, or other property will be furnished to the contractor. When monitoring delivery of government property to the contractor, the COTR:

☐ Establishes an inventory list of the property

☐ Sets up control requirements

☐ Prepares site facilities

☐ Coordinates agency procedures

☐ Prepares an inspection report

The COTR examines the contract and discusses the following with the contractor:

Contract date for delivering property to the contractor

If no contract date is specified, date when the contractor needs the property so as not to impact the contract completion date

Location of the property

Condition of the property and any repair, correction, or other action necessary to avoid delaying contract completion

Any special instructions or limitations regarding use of the property

The COTR must ensure any problems with the property are remediable. Contractor claims related to government property could arise when the property:

Is not delivered by the date in the contract, or, if no such time was specified, by a sufficiently early date to permit the contractor to finish contract work by the completion date

Is not delivered in a condition suitable for the intended use (e.g., poor copies or illegible data)

Is delivered without crucial information concerning techniques or conditions of the property's use, and the contractor is unable to use the property effectively or for its intended use

The COTR will advise the contractor to submit written notice about problems with delivery or condition of government property to the CO.

Monitor Contractor's Property Control System

The CO may request the COTR to review the contractor's property control system to ensure compliance with the government property clause of the contract. Once the contractor takes possession of government property, the COTR will:

Prepare a report on the contractor's property control system

Perform periodic property audits

Record any contractor notification that property is not in working order

Submit a written report of any shortages, losses, damage, destruction, or misuse

After reviewing the contractor's property control system, the COTR will ensure the contractor:

Maintains the approved system

Obtains all required approvals for use of the property

Uses the property only for those purposes authorized in the contract

Segregates government property from contractor property

Maintains, protects, and preserves the property

Discloses the need for major repair, replacement, or other capital rehabilitation work

Resolve Deficiencies in the Contractor's Government Property Control System

If the property control system does not adequately maintain and monitor government property under the contract, the COTR will notify the CO and:

Notify the contractor of deficiencies in the system

Specify, in writing, required corrections and establish a schedule for completion of actions

Monitor compliance with the schedule of corrective actions

The COTR will notify the CO if the contractor fails to correct any deficiency.

G.3. Special Topic: Monitor Contractor Use of Government Property

The COTR monitors contractor use of government property by conducting physical inventories at the contractor's site, and by reviewing the contractor's preventive maintenance program. To ensure contractor use of property complies with the contract clause for government property and is in accordance with sound industrial practices, the CO may require the COTR to investigate and resolve the following:

Reported Loss, Damage, or Destruction of Government Property

Identify the extent to which the contractor is liable.

Prepare written reports on the extent and value of the property which covers:

☐ Proposals from the contractor to repair, replace, or otherwise mitigate damage

☐ Government estimates and/or audit reports

☐ Government position on a remedy

☐ An opportunity for the contractor to present additional facts

Prepare information to support the CO's written demand for payment or make any equitable adjustment for the repair of property when the government has assumed the risk for property.

Unauthorized Use of Government Property

Determine whether there has been unauthorized use.

Evaluate and document any evidence.

Provide the contractor with an opportunity to present additional facts.

Assess the contractor for the contract clause amount if a finding of unauthorized use is determined.

Normally, government property is kept physically separate from contractor-owned property. When advantageous to the government and the contractor agrees, government

property may be commingled with contractor property. The COTR will verify with the CO or the FAA property management organization to determine when commingling is permitted.

Monitor Disposition of Government Property

When property is no longer needed, the COTR ensures the contractor:

Discloses excess inventory

Prepares and documents inventory schedules

Corrects inventory schedules that are not accurate or complete

When the contract is completed, the COTR may:

Request the contractor to return government property to the government

Request the contractor to deliver government property to another government contractor

Dispose of the property

When disposing of property, the COTR may, in the following priority:

Allow the contractor to purchase or retain government property at cost

Return the property to supplier.

Use within the government

Donate to eligible organizations (i.e., schools, charitable groups)

Sell the property

Donate to other public agencies (i.e., state and local governments)

Abandon the property

Once the method of disposition is determined, the CO may request COTR assistance in:

Preparing funding requirements for disposition, if applicable

Providing information to support the disposition modification, if necessary

Resolving property disposal problems

G.4. Determine Techniques for Monitoring the Contract

(See Attachment Eight, http://www.governmenttraininginc.com/The-COTR-Handbook.asp)

The appropriate monitoring technique depends on the nature, scope, and type of contract, and on contract requirements for monitoring, inspection, and acceptance. Selecting techniques for monitoring also depends on what will be monitored, such as contractor technical performance, schedule, or cost. Techniques for monitoring include:

I. Process: Baseline Management

    A. Establish baseline - technical, schedule, cost and quality

    B. Monitor performance - if deviations to baseline occur, need to decide whether they can be fixed or changes are needed

    C. Timely and frequent contractor interaction will give heads-up to resolving deviations prior to modifying a task order

II. Records: are necessary to –

    A. Commit to writing all interactions with the contractor

    B. Document actual performance

    C. Provide basis for problem identification and resolution

    D. Notify the contractor in writing (via the COTR) of any significant actions

    E. Indicate actions to get performance back on track

    F. Provide evidence for contracts office to take actions in resolving legal concerns

III. Correspondence

    A. Check to see how it relates to deliverables

    B. Verify that it is requested by the CO

    C. Validate necessity, and potential performance impact

    D. Mark your file with notation and/or comments about correspondence, next actions and contractor interface

IV. Meetings

    A. Can be scheduled or unscheduled; informal or formal; critical or noncritical; in-person or otherwise; long or short; or one-time or regular

    B. Having a game plan for conducting and achieving certain meeting outcomes is key to ensuring that progress is really happening

V. Other

Make onsite visits and other personal observations

Contact other government officials for input

Make telephone calls to the contractor and other government officials

Review contractor requests and other correspondence

Review contractor progress or status reports

Review tracking and management systems

Respond to Requests from the Contractor

The COTR reviews, approves, or takes other action on contractor requests based on contractual requirements. Contract terms and conditions guide government responses to contractor requests. The COTR will consider:

☐ A contractor's right to request government action

☐ Government responsibilities

☐ The impact for not complying with a request

☐ Contract terms generally specify if the contractor is required to:

☐ Respond in writing

☐ Respond within a pre-established timeframe

☐ Notify other government personnel

☐ Stop work

Depending on the contractual requirement, the COTR will either respond within the timeframe set by the contract term; or forward any request outside the scope of delegated authority to the CO in sufficient time to permit a timely response or other action. When there is no specified timeframe for responding to a contractor's request, the COTR will reply within a reasonable time that does not delay the contractor's performance. An untimely government response may have major consequences. The contractor may legitimately point to the government's inability to act on its request as a reason for not meeting a delivery or performance requirements. Knowing in advance when and what a contractor will be requesting helps the COTR monitor contractor performance. The COTR will identify:

☐ Contractual terms that allow contractor request

☐ Government need to respond to those requests

☐ Contractor's obligation and government responsibilities for responding

G.4.a. Monitor Contractor Technical and Schedule Compliance

The COTR closely monitors contract performance to ensure desired end items or services are as intended and are delivered on time. Among other things, monitoring technical compliance will:

☐ Identify potential delinquencies

☐ Isolate specific problems with quality

☐ Support contractor requests

☐ Point out the need for government assistance

☐ Reveal actual or anticipated default

Technical compliance is monitored through various techniques, such as site visits, testing, visual inspections, or analyzing data and reports. Monitoring schedule progress for some contracts is done through review of graphical charts that display progress, such as a network, PERT, or GANTT charts. Contracts for commercial items generally rely on a contractor's quality assurance system as a substitute for government monitoring, inspection, and testing. Customary market practices may permit buyer in-process monitoring and inspection. Any government in-process inspection must be conducted in a manner consistent with commercial practice.

Techniques Used for Monitoring

Monitoring contractor performance may be guided by the contract terms, but in general there are no set rules for techniques. The COTR will probably use a combination of monitoring methods, such as:

Sample Work Plan

February

1   Progress Report due

3   Meeting with CO to discuss Progress Report

9   Meeting with contractor to discuss Progress Report (if necessary)

15 Data Delivery

20 Site Visit

28 Provide feedback on Data Delivery (coordination with staff experts required)

March

1 Progress Report due

3 Meeting with CO to discuss Progress Report

9 Meeting with contractor to discuss Progress Report (if necessary)

18 Status Meeting on Task X

22 Line Item Delivery: Formal inspection and acceptance required

27 Inspection Report completed and deliverable accepted or rejected

Note: Items for Work Plan will be drawn from the contract — PWS and QASP mostly — and will be different in each situation. The sample merely gives you a scenario of events that might be included and a simple format for drafting the Work Plan.

Meetings

Periodic meetings with the requiring activity and end users allow the COTR to obtain and provide pertinent information on contract status. Meetings will be kept to a minimum and focus on problem resolution, because unscheduled meetings cost the contractor time and money. In cost-type contracts, the government will pay the costs associated with meetings. In fixed-price contracts, the contractor may be concerned about meetings that are not accounted for in the contract price.

Onsite Visits

Periodic onsite visits with the contractor allow the COTR to monitor through observation. Onsite meetings also provide an opportunity to identify and resolve problems at the working level. Rules of etiquette for scheduling onsite meetings include:

Providing names, official positions, and security clearance information for all visitors

Identifying date and duration of the visit

Identifying name and address of contractor facilities and personnel you wish to contact

Identifying contract number, any overall program involvement, and the purpose of the visit

Identifying data you may wish to obtain in conjunction with this visit

Notifying the CO and request that he or she attends

Telephone Contact

Telephone contact with the contractor may be used to check on contract progress, identify performance problems, and determine if the government is causing any problems. The COTR will document these communications with date, time, synopsis of the conversation, and any action items.

Contactor Status Reports

Progress reports, status reports, daily logs, and other monitoring reports are normally provided by the contractor in addition to any scientific and technical reports required under the contract. Contractor reports provide indicators of potential changes, delays, or other issues, such as failed tests, rejections, etc. COTRs will review status reports to identify any potential or actual delays or other problems with contractor performance. If problems are identified, the COTR will notify the CO in sufficient time to resolve any performance issues. A Sample Progress Report is provided here:

CONTRACTOR'S PROGRESS REPORT SAMPLE FORMAT

To: Contracting Officer/Contract Administrator

FROM: Contracting Officer's Technical Representative

SUBJECT: Contract No. _____ (Completion Data)

    Report Frequency [ ] Quarterly [ ] Final

1. HOW WOULD YOU DESCRIBE THE CONTRACTOR'S PERFORMANCE TO DATE?

[ ] A-Satisfactory [ ] B-Marginal [ ] C-Unsatisfactory

If "B" or "C" is checked in item 1 above, give a brief description of your findings:

2. WERE DELIVERABLES RECEIVED ON TIME AND IN GOOD CONDITION?

[ ] Yes [ ] No-Give a brief description of facts:

3. WERE THE CONTRACTOR'S SERVICES/PRODUCTS IN ACCORDANCE WITH SCOPE OF WORK?

[ ] Yes [ ] No-Describe any deficiencies:

4. HAVE YOU, AS COTR, PROVIDED TECHNICAL ASSISTANCE TO THE CONTRACTOR?

[ ] Yes [ ] No-Describe why not:

5. STATE ANY OTHER SIGNIFICANT ISSUES THAT WILL BE BROUGHT TO THE CONTRACTING OFFICER'S ATTENTION.

NOTE: ATTACH COPIES OF ALL DOCUMENTATION OF CONTRACTOR AND

COTR DISCUSSIONS AND FORWARD WITH THIS REPORT.

SIGNATURE OF COTR _____ DATE _____.

G.4.b. Contact with Other Government Officials

COTRs will report to the CO any substantive communications between the contractor and other government officials. Meaningful communications include any discussions that might affect performance, price, schedule, quality, or other contract requirements. Contractors may misinterpret this communication as direction by other government officials to change the contract terms and conditions.

G.4.c. Review Tracking and Management Systems

Both the contractor and government use some method to track progress. For some contracts, the COTR may informally verify that these systems or processes are in place and followed by the contractor. The more complex the contract, the more sophisticated the tracking system, such as an earned value management system. An earned value management system provides planned and actual cost and schedule data; the COTR will review this data to track actual work accomplished versus that which the contractor planned.

G.4.d. Determine How to Document Monitoring Actions

The COTR documents both contractor performance and government actions under the contract. Copies of documentation may be sent to the CO as notification of a problem or other issue, or to include as part of the contract administration file. Documentation related to monitoring contractor performance includes:

Memorandum to the file – this can be prepared at any time for any reason and is useful for documenting a contract problem.

Trip report – this documents visits to a contractor facility. A trip report can be used to record contract status or issues that need attention.

Contact records – this documents discussions with a contractor and other government officials to preserve the conversation for the file. There may be action items and recommendations based on the conversation.

Reports – this documents a contractual issue or situation. Reports can convey contract status, identify problems, provide background information, justify actions taken, or request assistance or resources.

Minutes – this documents contract-related meetings and is another way to document contract performance. Minutes will be provided to all attendees.

Correspondence – this can be used by the contractor and government to formally notify each other of performance issues or other matters that need attention.

Technical analysis — this may provide the basis for contract modifications, payment, and future work.

G.4.e. Identify Areas of Concern

There may be contract requirements that the COTR identifies as potential problems. These areas and possible solutions may be addressed in the COTR work plan; examples might include:

☐ Delivery time indicated in the contract is after normal business hours.

☐ Government-furnished property may not exist or may be defective.

☐ Technical review cannot be accomplished within the allotted timeframe.

Potential Risk Worksheet

#	Describe Issue	Will the contract price need to be revised?	Will this create a change in the performance delivery schedule?	Will technical requirements have to be modified?	Do other resources need to be added?	Impact of problem: -High -Moderate -Low
1						
2						
3						

The risks and possible mitigation will be addressed by the government team before meeting with the contractor.

G.4.f. Monitor Reports and Other Deliverables
G.4.f. i. Technical Progress Reports

Progress reports will include all relevant details to provide COTRs with most of their information on the progress of the work. However, they will not become too burdensome to prepare. Technical progress reports may be submitted in letter format. The letter may include the number and names of persons working on the project; the facilities devoted to the work; the number of person-days expended; the direction of the work; and the latest observations, problems encountered, predictions, and plans for the next reporting period.

Contractors will be encouraged to furnish preliminary technical information in these status reports, even though it is tentative and not ready for widespread distribution. Researchers are often reluctant to commit themselves to premature technical conclusions, and it may be necessary to assure the contractor that the department will treat its technical progress information as privileged communications.

In addition to keeping the COTR informed of progress, the technical progress report gives the contractor an opportunity to stop periodically and evaluate its efforts in terms of the intent and specifications of the contract. The necessity for writing and analyzing progress reports forces both the contractor and the COTR to periodically evaluate the work in relation to all contractual requirements.

G.4.f. ii. Deliverables

As stated above, the COTR is responsible for determining whether supplies or services delivered by the contractor conform to the contract quality requirements. In discharging this responsibility, the COTR will keep in mind that, once a contractor's work has been accepted, the contractor is excused from further performance or correction should it prove to be unsatisfactory.

In many agency contracts, the end result or deliverable is a report or an instrument, such as a survey. The COTR is responsible for conducting a technical review of the report, comparing it to the requirements set forth in the contract SOW and applicable specifications. Where appropriate, the COTR will solicit the comments and concurrence of other appropriate technical experts and/or from other affected POs. Any required revisions must be transmitted to the contractor over the signature of the CO.

In the event that the work is termed unsatisfactory, the COTR and the CO must determine what further actions are required, asking the advice of legal counsel if necessary. The COTR will provide written notification to the CO when the contract work has been judged complete and technically acceptable, so that the CO can communicate acceptance to the contractor.

G.4.f.iii. Site Visits

Site visits may be unnecessary for small, straightforward contracts, but when a contract is large and complex, they are indispensable.

Strictly speaking, site visits will be conducted jointly by the CO and the COTR, but as a practical matter site visits are often delegated to the COTR. However, the CO will clear site visits, whether or not a representative from the contracting office is making the site visit. A site visit is usually arranged in advance with the contractor. In rare cases, there may be a reason to make an unannounced visit, but these situations require careful consideration and will have the explicit approval of the CO.

The purpose of a site visit is to check the contractor's performance. Reasons for making a site visit include:

Checking actual contract performance against scheduled and reported performance;

Seeing if the facilities and working conditions are adequate; and

Verifying that the number of employees charged to a cost-reimbursement contract is the number of people actually performing work under the contract. For example, if the voucher shows 10 people assigned to the contract full-time, the government representative making a site visit will verify that these individuals are actually working on the contract.

G.5. Task Order Management

A very popular form of contracting that requires special administrative procedures is task order contracting. Under a task order contract, which may be awarded to one vendor or to multiple vendors, the work statement for the contract is often very general, requiring the specifics of each job to be written into specific task orders. This structure, while providing maximum flexibility, puts something of an administrative burden on the COTR, since a work statement must be developed for each task order situation, and frequently the price of the task orders must be individually negotiated, and, of course, the administration of each task order is separate from the administration of every other task order.

The best way to understand task orders is to conceptualize them as separate "mini-contracts" written within the broad "umbrella" of the "mother contract." The flexibility that these contracts provide to the agency is that many groups within the agency may be able to take advantage of the task order contract, write unique task statements, and administer their task orders individually.

Task order contracts are usually limited in three ways. One limitation is on the type of work that is included in the work statement, which may be restricted to certain work skills or may be so broad as to encompass any activity supporting a program area. The second limitation is a level of effort, usually stated in person-hours terms or in overall dollar amounts. Third, the duration of the contract, including options, is normally limited to five years. As a task order manager, each COTR may be able to experience the entire acquisition cycle as the developer of a task statement, a key advisor to the CO in negotiating the terms and price of the task order, and in administering the task order to successful completion.

G.6. Monitor Costs

Various procedures and techniques can be used to monitor and verify appropriateness of costs. Under cost-reimbursement contracts, payments based on incurred expenses; payments include costs for labor, materials, other direct costs, overhead, and other indirect costs. For payments to be proper and allowable under the contract, costs must be:

☐ Reasonable - not exceeding that which would be incurred by a prudent person conducting competitive business.

☐ Allocable - properly assigned to one or more cost objectives under the contract.

☐ Consistent with applicable cost accounting standards and prohibitions on the allowability of certain costs.

Cost monitoring techniques include:

☐ Relying on the contractor's financial system.

☐ Analyzing voucher backup information

☐ Periodically analyzing data obtained from the contractor, Government reports, and Government site visits.

☐ Scheduled audits.

☐ Specific audit requests.

Cost monitoring involves tracking and analyzing the rate of contract expenditures to detect variances in planned or budgeted costs versus progress made to determine whether the contract will be completed within budget. When incurred costs are considered too high, contract funds may be insufficient to complete the work. Alternatively, performance may be behind schedule when incurred expenses are too low.

Achieving full performance consists of technical and schedule excellence. It also means providing the needed product or service at the costs agreed to. Therefore, to ensure that the costs spent reflect the contractually mandated work and deliverables, cost monitoring is appropriate in either cost reimbursement or fixed price situations.

	Risk	Monitoring
Cost Reimbursement	Government bears the risk of the funds running out before the work is completed.	The Government must guard against paying for costs that are excessive, improper, or incurred for work not related to the contract. The Government is responsible for overall planned expenditures.
Fixed Price	Contractor bears the risks of delivering a product or service as required by the contract, and within a specified price.	The contractor must monitor its own cost to ensure there are sufficient funds to deliver the product or perform the service. Government monitoring focuses on ensuring product or service conforms to all facets of the contract requirements: technical, schedule, quality and cost.

G.6.a. Monitor Financial Condition of a Contractor

Financial monitoring means detecting and acting on changes in a contractor's financial condition that have potential for endangering contract performance. The decision to monitor a contractor's financial condition will consider:

An indication is received that the contractor is in financial trouble;

☐ A determination is made that the government would be harmed by contractor financial difficulties; and

☐ A determination is made the government could take positive steps to protect its interests.

☐ The government's interest is not always in jeopardy because of failing contractor financial condition. Steps in monitoring financial condition include:

☐ When alerted, monitor financial circumstances that might endanger government's interests.

☐ Protect the government interest if a lien is placed against contractor inventory.

☐ Protect the government interest if the contractor is facing bankruptcy.

☐ Furnish information to interested parties upon request.

The CO will be notified when conditions may warrant intervention by the government.

Financial Warning Signs

Occasionally there may be evidence or rumors that a contractor is in "financial trouble." Warnings of an impending bankruptcy or financial difficulties sometimes go hand-in-hand with a delinquent contract when:

* A contractor fails to pay subcontractors on time.

* Deliveries of materials to the job site are late and usually brought in on a C.O.D. basis.

* A contractor is falling behind the schedule.

* Complaints occur by laborers on the job.

* Telephone calls go unanswered.

* Sloppy performance and workmanship is evident.

Financial Status Reports

Financial reports are an important element in contract administration, especially in cost-reimbursement type contracts. They reveal the financial status of the contract and provide information that is helpful in avoiding or anticipating cost overruns. Financial reports provide both the COTR and the CO with a

means of checking the contractor's expenditures based on the negotiated cost elements and enable them to match the costs incurred with the technical results achieved.

The amount of detailed financial information required will vary, depending on the type of contract involved, the nature of the work or services being procured, and the method of payment. Under a cost-reimbursement contract, the contractor is entitled to full and prompt payment for all incurred allocable and allowable costs, without any holdback by the government pending completion of performance. Therefore, cost-reimbursement contracts require close monitoring by the COTR so that the government does not pay excess costs for the end product either because of a contractor's inefficiency (e.g., missed schedules, unacceptable reports, etc.), or as a result of unforeseen problems which, if promptly addressed, could have prevented excess costs.

G.6.b. Payment

(Also see Attachment Twelve, http://www.governmenttraininginc.com/The-COTR-Handbook.asp)

In assisting the CO with determining and authorizing payment, the COTR will:

☐ Accept the payment document for processing

☐ Calculate payment amount

☐ Notify the contractor of the final amount calculated to be paid

☐ Submit the correct invoice to the paying office

G.6.b.i. Accept the Payment Document for Processing

Determine if Payment can be Processed

Before processing any payments, acceptance of the product or service must have occurred; or the contract must have been otherwise completed. The COTR may need to obtain documentation to make this determination. This may include:

Documentation to support successful delivery of products or completion of services, including inspection forms, receiving reports, commercial shipping documents, and packing lists

Documentation on suspension of performance

Documentation on remedies applied, such as liquidated damages or rejection of work

Adjustments to liquidation rates or reductions in progress payments

Interim or final adjustments to the contract price

Modifications to the contract

Termination settlements

Review the Payment Document for Completeness

Once a contractor submits an invoice for payment, the COTR may be required to:

Determine if the invoice is under a fixed-price or cost-type contract

Review submitted invoices

Determine if the invoice was complete

G.6.b.ii. Accept Invoice or Not

Once an invoice is received, the COTR evaluates the invoice and either accepts it or notifies the contractor and CO of any deficiency. Incomplete or incorrect invoices will be returned to the contractor before acceptance for payment. Contractors must be notified of the specific deficiency in writing and within seven calendar days after receipt of the invoice. The COTR will keep a record of the number of days of delay caused by contractor correcting a deficient or incomplete invoice.

G.6.b.iii. Calculate Payment Amount

Identify Terms and Conditions of the Contract

The COTR will identify applicable contract terms and conditions for payment, such as:

☐ Price

☐ Type of contract

☐ Payment provisions (in-full, partial, performance, or progress)

☐ Period for acceptance

☐ Discounts

☐ Liquidated damages

Obtain Documents and Determinations

Supporting information and data for invoices and vouchers are essential to verify contractor billing for:

Work that has been completed

Work in process

Costs incurred for a specified period of time

The extent of such information and data may vary considerably under different types of contractual arrangements, but the contractor must support the amount claimed on the invoice or voucher.

G.6.b.iv. Voucher Documentation Required

Vouchers submitted by the contractor will list corroborating information or data concerning all incurred costs. These may include:

☐ Vendor, subcontractor, or supplier billings

☐ Contractor internal cost sheets or displays

☐ Referenced cost-expenditure files where detailed information or data are stored

☐ Invoice Documentation

☐ Supporting information and data for invoice payments may include the following:

☐ Inspection or receiving reports

☐ Commercial or government shipping documents

☐ Determinations on billing rates

☐ Reports on contractor indebtedness

☐ Determinations for reductions in progress payments

☐ Determinations for the adjustment of liquidation rates for progress payments

G.6.b.v. Identify Amounts That Will Not be Paid

The COTR will determine when billed amounts cannot be paid. Reasons for nonpayment include:

Withholdings and Deductions in Fixed-Price Contracts

A withholding is a subtracted amount that may be paid at a later date.

A deduction is an amount that is permanently subtracted, unless a contractor provides appropriate supporting evidence for the reinstatement of any deducted amount. For example, some contracts specify deductions for defects of a service or product that do not meet an "acceptable" quality level.

Unallowable Costs in Cost-Type Contracts

In a cost-type contract, the COTR will examine each cost element (direct or indirect) vouchered to determine if the cost will be allowed under the contract. Voucher documentation must support whether or not costs are allowable. These costs are subject to a determination of allowability by audit. Factors for determining whether a cost is allowable include:

Reasonableness; A cost is reasonable if, in its nature and amount, it does not exceed that which would be incurred by a prudent person in the conduct of competitive business.

Allocable; A cost is allocable if it is assignable or chargeable to one or more cost objectives on the basis of relative benefits received or other equitable relationship.

Standards promulgated by the Cost Accounting Standards Board, if applicable, otherwise generally accepted accounting principles and practices appropriate to the particular circumstances.

Terms of the contract.

Any other cost limitations as set forth in government guidelines for cost principles.

G.6.b.vi. Determine the Total Amount Owed to the Contractor

Once all appropriate withholdings and deductions are identified, the COTR determines the amount due to the contractor. Depending upon the contractual situation, the contractor will then be issued:

Payment in full

Partial payment

Performance-based payment

When the COTR recommends payment in full or issues a partial payment, the amount owed the contractor is clearly known. When payment is performance-based, the amount due must be liquidated by deducting a percentage or a designated dollar amount from delivery payments, and the CO must specify the liquidation rate or designated dollar amount in the contract. Whatever the method of liquidation, it must ensure complete liquidation no later than final payment under a contract. The COTR may use the following methods of liquidation:

For payments established on a total contract amount, liquidation must be by pre-designated liquidation amounts or liquidation percentages.

For payments established on a partial delivery basis, the liquidation amount for each line-item must be the percent of that delivery item price that was previously paid or the specific dollar amount as stated in the contract.

G.6.b.vii. Notify the Contractor of Final Amount to be Paid

If there are differences between the amount of the invoice and the amount the government proposes to pay, the COTR notifies the CO and contractor. The government must accurately present all factual data that justifies the difference and the contractor will be

provided with an opportunity to present their position. Some reasons for the differences may include:

☐ Performance problems

☐ Allowable costs

☐ Defective products or inferior service

☐ Delivery problems

If a contractor disagrees with the calculated amount, the COTR will notify the CO who will make a final determination.

G.6.b.viii. Submit the Correct Invoice to the Paying Office

Once the amount is agreed by both the government and the contractor, the COTR submits approval of the correct invoice to the paying office for payment within the time specified in the contract.

G.7. Government Contract Quality Assurance

Before services or supplies furnished by the contractor can be accepted, the COTR must determine acceptability by review, test, evaluation, or inspection. He or she reports the results to the CO. Final acceptance by the CO of supplies tendered or services rendered concludes performance by the contractor, except for administrative details relating to contract closeout. After final acceptance, the contractor can no longer be held responsible for unsatisfactory effort, unless otherwise specified in the contract. Therefore, the COTR must ensure that the work performed under the contract is measured against the contract quality requirements. If performance does not meet contract quality requirements, it is incumbent upon the COTR to identify deficiencies and to advise the CO. This allows remedial action before final payment and contract closeout.

G.7.a. Quality Aspects
Concept of Quality

A.   Characteristics, attributes and functions of the desired outcome

B.   Government carries out quality assurance by doing three functions: inspection, handling nonconformance, and acceptance

C.   Contractor is equivalently responsible for sustaining quality through its own quality control program

Influence of Quality

A.   At the start of the task or contract

1. Government defines quality requirements in measurable terms as part of acceptance criteria in section E of contract and the relevant portion of the task order

2. Contractor presents quality control plan

3. Contractor demonstrates quality control program

B. During the task or contract

1. Contractor is timely and accurate with performance based on quality standards

2. Contractor uses quality controls to internally correct deficiencies before presenting them to the government

3. There is evidence of internal reviews and walkthroughs by the contractor

4. Record of quality outcomes without extensive rework and rejection is a key rating factor

Inspection and Handling Nonconformance

A. Inspection is the right of the government. It can be done anytime as long as the contractor's effort is not impeded. Effective strategy is to send a message of frequent quality checks.

B. Deliverables presented by the contractor must show evidence of quality controls at work.

C. The ultimate determinant of quality is what is stated in the order or the contract.

D. If the government discovers quality deficiencies, the contractor is given the first right to do the correction.

E. The contractor pays to correct deficiencies in fixed-price contracts; whereas, the government pays for corrections in cost-reimbursement contracts.

NOTE: Notify the CO of Acceptance or Rejection

Acceptance and Approval

A. Acceptance is the place and time when the item's ownership is transferred from the contractor to the government.

B. Acceptance acknowledges that the items conform to the task order requirements.

C. Approval says the item conforms but still belongs to the contractor.

G.7.b. Inspection and Acceptance

The COTR is often responsible for inspecting and recommending product acceptance or rejection to the CO. The COTR performs the following tasks to ensure acceptance/rejection is processed accurately:

☐ Inspect products or services

☐ Recommend acceptance

☐ Recommend rejection

☐ Assist the CO in evaluating a contractor reply to rejection notification

G.7.b.i. Inspect Products or Services

Inspection and acceptance is based on compliance with contractual terms and conditions. Inspections are conducted to identify nonconformance. When the government awards a contract, the contractor assumes responsibility for satisfactory performance, and timely and quality delivery of supplies or services. There are three steps in inspection and acceptance:

☐ Identify the inspection method required by the contract

☐ Determine if acceptance has occurred

☐ Perform inspections

G.7.b.ii. Identify the Inspection Method Required by the Contract

Before accepting the product or service, the COTR must assure the quality of the deliverable or performance of the work. Various inspection methods are incorporated by contract clause. The SOW may also provide further clarification of inspection and acceptance requirements. A quality assurance plan may have been developed specifically for monitoring and inspection requirements. Contract clauses for inspection may be as follows:

Contractor Inspection Requirements - The contractor is required to accomplish all inspection and testing needed to ensure supplies or services conform to contract quality requirements before payment is made. The government may test supplies or services in advance of acceptance when it has determined that contractor quality assurance processes are inadequate, or customary market practices for the commercial item being acquired include this type of inspection.

Standard Inspection Requirements Clauses (various clauses, based on the nature of the contract, e.g., supplies, services, fixed price, cost reimbursement) - Standard inspection clauses generally require the contractor to provide and maintain an inspection system acceptable to the government. They give the government the right to make inspections and perform tests while contractor work is in progress. They also require the contractor to keep and make available to the government complete records of its inspection work.

Higher-Level Contract Quality Requirement - This clause is appropriate in contracts for complex and critical items or when technical requirements of the contract require the government to maintain control of work operations, in-process controls, and inspection; and

concentrate its attention to organization, planning, work instructions, and document control. This clause also applies when the contractor must comply with a government-specified inspection system, quality control system, or quality program.

G.7.b.iii. Determine if Acceptance has Occurred

Before performing inspections and any testing, the COTR will determine if the government has the right to reject nonconforming supplies or services. This determination will resolve whether the work has been accepted by:

Acceptance notice

Acceptance made on receiving report, or letter indicating acceptance has been provided to the contractor

☐ Any evidence of implied acceptance

☐ Silence and the time allowed for rejection has passed

☐ Payment has been made

☐ Retention and use of delivered items or performed services

It is critical to determine if acceptance has occurred since acceptance is final except for limited situations, such as fraud or latent defect, and the government may not reject deliverables or services after acceptance.

G.7.c. Perform Inspections

The COTR will inspect contractor deliveries to determine if:

☐ Proper type or kind of supply or service was provided

☐ Correct quantity was provided

☐ Any damages exist

☐ Product operates as intended

☐ There are signs of spoilage or age deterioration

☐ The item is properly identified or marked

☐ Appropriate packaging was provided

Inspection Methods and Occurrences

Sensory and dimensional checks - sensory checks are examinations by an inspector using eyes, ears, and other senses to measure surface defects, missing pieces, noisy operations, or parts which may be out of alignment. Dimensional checks use gauges and micrometers to measure whether the dimensions of the items conform to contract specifications.

Performance or physical tests - These types of inspection result in actual performance data and indicate whether the product can perform as required by the contract. Requiring a motor to run or an operating system to perform at a certain level for a specified period of time are examples of performance testing. Determining hardness of an item's chemical composition is an example of a physical test.

Interim Inspections

The government has the right to inspect all materials and workmanship in a manner that will not unduly delay the work. Interim government inspections may be used to determine if:

On-schedule performance can be expected.

Cost will be within the initial estimate for cost-reimbursement contracts or fixed-price contracts with progress payments.

Resources are being applied at originally predicted levels.

Quality of end products will be consistent with the specification.

Progress payments are warranted.

New components need to be incorporated in major systems.

A contractor's own inspection system is adequate.

Sample of an Inspection Report

INSPECTION, ACCEPTANCE AND RECEIVING REPORT SAMPLE FORMAT

DATE:

CONTRACT NUMBER:

MODIFICATION NUMBER:

CONTRACTOR'S NAME:

ORDER NUMBER:

DATE ITEMS RECEIVED OR DATE RECURRING PAYMENT DUE:

LOCATION WHERE ITEMS WERE DELIVERED OR CONTRACTOR'S PERFORMANCE:

ALL THE REQUIREMENTS HAVE BEEN INSPECTED, RECEIVED AND ACCEPTED BY ME AND MEET THE TERMS OF THE CONTRACT EXCEPT AS NOTED BELOW:

LIST THE REQUIREMENTS THAT WERE NOT ACCEPTED AND/OR THE DEDUCTIONS MADE AND STATE THE REASON WHY:

TOTAL AMOUNT OF DEDUCTIONS:

TITLE OF AUTHORIZED GOVERNMENT REPRESENTATIVE:

SIGNATURE OF AUTHORIZED GOVERNMENT REPRESENTATIVE

DATE SIGNED

Improper Inspections

The government has certain rights in the application of inspection procedures. Tests are considered improperly applied when they:

Impose a stricter standard of performance than is otherwise prescribed;

Do not reasonably measure if the contract conforms to specified requirements;

Are inconsistent with prior inspections;

Result in unnecessary delays due to unreasonable time and place inspections.

Unusual or Incompetent Inspections

Any test to overturn the results of another test is considered an unusual test. The CO must be involved in these cases. Inspections made by incompetent inspectors may result in the government being negligent. If the negligence of a government agent causes damage to a contractor, then in all likelihood the government will be held liable for those damages.

Documenting Inspections

The format to be used and the results of inspections that need to be documented are specified by the contract, quality assurance plan and/or FAA quality assurance policy and guidance.

G.7.d. Nonconformance

Nonconforming supplies or services can be usually accepted when it does not adversely affect one or more of the following:

Safety or health

Reliability, durability, or performance

Interchangeability of parts or assemblies

Any other basic objective of the contract

Minor nonconformance may be accepted without modifying the contract. Written documentation to support the decision to accept minor nonconformance will be placed in the contract administration file. Accepting a nonconformance on one contract does not provide

relief for correcting similar defects on pending or future work. Acceptance of critical or major nonconforming supplies or services requires modification to the contract, and obtaining an equitable reduction in price or some other consideration.

Preparing Written Rejection of Nonconforming Supplies or Services

The rejection of nonconforming supplies and services must clearly demonstrate the reason the supply or service did not conform to the specification or SOW. COTRs need to provide supporting documentation, identifying which part of the contract the contractor did not perform and why. Inspection and acceptance clauses in the contract provide the basis for rejecting supplies and services.

When the nonconformity seriously affects the requirement, the item will be rejected. The COTR will discuss the rejection with the contractor before issuing any written notification since the contractor may have additional information concerning the deliverable. Before rejecting the product or service, the COTR will determine whether any contract requirement may have been changed. COTRs, when authorized by the CO to perform inspection and determine acceptance, may also be required to notify the contractor of the rejection. The notification must be in writing if:

The rejection took place at a location other than the contractor plant.

The contractor persists in providing minor nonconforming items or services.

Late supplies are being rejected and no excusable delay factors were involved in the delinquency.

Written notification will:

- Provide the reason for rejection.
- Allow a time period for the contractor to reply.
- Be furnished promptly.
- COTRs need to consider the following when issuing rejection notices:
- The contractor's acknowledgment of delivery.
- The context of the supplies or services that were rejected.

A rejection notice does not extend the delivery period.

G.7.e. Recommend Acceptance

Supplies or services will be accepted when they conform to contract requirements.

Time of Acceptance

After delivery is made, a reasonable period of time is allowed for government acceptance or rejection. Although the government may not have formally accepted items, acceptance may be implied by government conduct or government delay.

Point of Acceptance

The contract controls where items will be accepted. The point of acceptance may be:

At the contractor plant when the contract requires government quality assurance actions

A prescribed destination point when quality assurance actions are performed at the destination

Anywhere else that is mutually agreeable

Transfer of Ownership

Ownership (title) transfers to the government upon formal acceptance. The time of title transfer is significant if damage or loss occurs. The government becomes liable for damage or loss based on when and where acceptance occurs; it may be when the contractor delivers conforming supplies to a carrier (FOB Origin) for shipment or after shipment and at the final government destination (FOB Destination).

Evidence of Final Inspection or Acceptance

Evidence of final inspection or acceptance may entail one or more of the following documents:

Receiving Report - the COTR, as the official authorized to accept supplies or services for the government, signs the receiving report. This report is usually written evidence of final acceptance.

Copy of an Invoice (or Voucher) - this instrument, signed by an authorized official, can serve as an acceptance document if permitted by a contract.

Contractor's Bill of Lading (CBL) - under a CBL, the transportation carrier is responsible to the contractor for any damage or loss, and the contractor, in turn, is responsible to the government. Under contract terms, a CBL usually means the government is responsible for freight payments.

Certificate of Conformance - acceptance on the basis of a contractor Certificate of Conformance is in the government's interest; small losses would be incurred in the event of a defect; or contractor past-performance reputation makes it likely deliverables will be acceptable and any defective work will be replaced or corrected without contest. The government still retains the right to inspect the deliverables.

Finality of Acceptance

The acceptance procedure is important because at the time and place of formal acceptance title passes from the contractor to the government. Acceptance is final except for latent defects, fraud, or gross mistakes that amount to fraud.

Recommend Rejection

Notification to reject will include sufficient data to support a written rejection notice of nonconforming supplies or services.

Notices of Rejection

Notices of rejection must be furnished promptly to the contractor and include the reasons for rejection, and a stated time-period for the contractor to reply.

A notice of rejection must be in writing if:

Supplies or services have been rejected at a place other than the contractor plant.

The contractor persists in offering nonconforming supplies or services for acceptance.

Delivery or performance was late without an excusable delay.

A written notice of rejection requires a written receipt from the contractor.

Timeliness of Notices - Delivery Schedule

A notice of rejection does not extend the specified delivery schedule, and the contractor remains obligated to provide supplies or services that conform to the contract within that delivery schedule.

Notifying the CO

The CO will be provided with documentation reflecting:

The nature of government contract quality assurance actions, including:

☐ Number of observations made

☐ Actions taken to notify the contractor

Decisions regarding the acceptability of the products, processes, or other requirements, including:

☐ Number and type of defects

☐ Impact on the government

☐ Any actions taken by the contractor to correct defects

Assist the CO in Evaluating the Contractor's Reply to Rejection Notification

Advise the CO on the acceptability of non-monetary consideration, acceptance of nonconforming supplies, or impact of contractor refusal to repair the work. A contractor may reply to a notice of rejection by:

Submitting a proposal to repair or correct the work

Submitting a proposal to provide a downward adjustment in price or cost as a basis for acceptance

Refusing to repair or correct the work or to offer any consideration

A COTR can assist the CO in evaluating the contractor proposal by:

Providing advice concerning safety and performance

Evaluating whether acceptance of the supplies or services would be in the government's best interest after repair, correction, or price adjustment

Providing supporting rationale for rejecting or accepting the contractor proposal

Attending any negotiations to respond to contractor positions

G.7.f. Determining Warranty Provisions

The CO may request the COTR to assist in identifying some of the following information:

A summary of warranties that apply to a specific product or service.

Specific components to which a warranty applies, if all components are not included.

Who has government responsibility to report warranty incidents and the authority to implement warranty clauses.

Duration of the warranty.

Documentation and other warranty requirements.

Packaging and transportation requirements.

COTRs may also be asked to verify that a warranty clause applies to a specific failure by:

Confirming the government has officially accepted the items or services.

Examining the written terms and conditions of the warranty. This examination will reveal duration of the warranty, and coverage for specific defects.

Determining if any government obligations under the warranty were met or providing assurance they will be met.

Confirming that facts support invoking the warranty.

G.8. Contract Closeout

A contract is completed when all services have been rendered; all articles, material, report data, exhibits, etc., have been delivered and accepted; all administrative actions accomplished; and final payment made to the contractor. Contract closeout actions are primarily the responsibility of the CO, but the assistance of the COTR will be required to certify that all services have been rendered in a satisfactory manner and all deliverables are complete and acceptable. The COTR also will play an important role in evaluating the contractor's performance under the contract. The COTR's assistance is indispensable when disputes, litigation, patent and copyright problems, etc., are involved. Upon completion of the contract, the CO must ensure or determine, as applicable that:

All services have been rendered;

All supplies have been tendered and accepted;

All payments and collections have been made;

Release from liabilities, obligations, and claims have been obtained from the contractor;

Contractor performance has been appraised as provided for by the terms of the contract.

Assignment of refunds, credits, etc., have been executed by the contractor;

All administrative actions have been accomplished, including the settlement of disputes, protests, and litigation; determination of final overhead rates; release of funds; and disposal of property; and

The file is properly documented.

The file must include all inspection and acceptance documents or a statement from the COTR that all services and deliveries required by the contract have been performed or delivered in accordance with the terms of the contract and are acceptable to the government. All discrepancies in actual performance or delivery with contract requirements must be reconciled before the contract file is closed.

All public vouchers and contractor invoices that support advance, partial, progress, and final payments must be included. The contract file must also include written documentation

related to settlement of any questions of disallowed or suspended costs. In addition, any discrepancies between payments and deliveries or performance and between billings and payments require documentation.

If there was a subcontract, the file must contain subcontract approvals, including the letter or document of approval and the subcontract review memorandum. If approval of individual subcontracts is waived by approval of the contractor's purchasing system, approval must be included in the contract file. The file must also contain documentation of the resolution of disputes between prime and subcontractors, unless the prime contractor releases the government from any obligation relating to the subcontractor's claim.

Contract modifications that result from additions or changes to the terms and conditions must be included, as must inventory and records of disposition of government-owned property. All clearance and reports relating to inventories, patents, royalties, copyrights, publications, tax exemptions, etc., will go into the file. Also the file must contain copies of inquiries and answers and reports to and from sources, such as the Congress, the General Accounting Office, audit activities, etc.

G.8.a. Documentation for past-performance

☐ Quality of product or service

☐ Timeliness of performance

☐ Cost control

☐ Business practices

☐ Customer satisfaction

☐ Quality awards

G.8.b. Contract Completion Statement

The contract completion statement will provide information about:

☐ Contracting office name and address.

☐ Contract number.

☐ Name and address of contractor

☐ Date of physical completion

☐ Last modification number, if any.

☐ Last call or order number, if any.

☐ Disposition of classified or sensitive material

☐ Final patent and royalty reports

☐ Settlement of value engineering change proposals

☐ Plant and property clearance reports

☐ Settlement of interim, disallowed costs, and prior year overhead rates

☐ Final close-out audit report

☐ Completion of any price revisions

☐ Settlement of subcontracts by prime contractor

☐ Final subcontracting plan

☐ Completion of termination docket

☐ Dollar amount of excess funds to be deobligated, if any.

☐ Security badges and keys returned

☐ Termination of access for contractor personnel to contract-specific systems

☐ Invoice or voucher number and date, if final payment has been made.

Generally closed official contract are transferred to the Federal Records Center after final payment. These records are then destroyed after six years and three months.

G.9. Contract Modifications

Various contract terms and provisions provide for modifications to a contract if certain conditions arise or if information not known at the time of contract award becomes available. For example, the Government-furnished Property clause provides for equitable adjustment of the contract estimated cost and performance dates in the event the property furnished by the government is not suitable for the intended use. The Limitation of Cost clause used in cost-reimbursement contracts permits funding of cost overruns, when authorized.

G.9.a. Change Orders

The contract clause entitled Changes distinguishes government contracts from other contracts by the control over performance vested in one of the contracting parties — the government. Unlike contracts in the private sector where performance must conform to pre-agreed terms in the absence of a modification issued by both parties, the Changes clause in a government contract allows the government to alter the work to be performed without the consent of the contractor.

The clause provides, in essence, that the CO may by written order make any change in the work within the general scope of the contract. Such changes may result also in an appropriate upward or downward equitable adjustment in the contract price, delivery schedule,

or time for performance. Additionally, the clause provides that a dispute over the equitable adjustment is a question of fact under the "Disputes" clause, and that nothing in the Changes clause excuses the contractor from proceeding with the contract as changed. This power, unique to government procurement, allows the CO to alter performance without unnecessary interruption and to subsequently determine the appropriate contract price adjustment. The Changes clause imposes certain requirements for issuing a valid change order. The clause states that the change must be ordered by the CO and must be made by written order. One of the more important requirements is that the change ordered must come within the general scope of the contract.

G.9.b. Supplemental Agreement

A supplemental agreement is a bilateral modification of the contract that either adds work or revises the existing terms of the contract. Such agreements may have cost implications. Supplemental agreements are generally used under the following circumstances:

To provide an equitable adjustment when a change order has been issued pursuant to the Changes clause, Government-furnished Property clause, and other clauses or special provisions of the contract;

When it is necessary to change the contract price, delivery schedule, quantity, or other terms of the contract;

When the government wishes to modify a contract and the proposed modification is for work that is an inseparable part of the original procurement;

To finalize the settlement agreement when a contract has been terminated for convenience of the government; and

To permit a contractor to complete a contract after a non-excusable delay when the contractor assumes liability for actual damages.

G.9.c. Modifications Involving New Acquisition Actions

Before initiating a modification, it is necessary to determine that it is within the scope of the existing contract rather than a "new procurement" outside the scope of the contract. A "new procurement" must be conducted as a separate procurement action. If a new procurement is involved and the government decides to contract with a contractor who is already providing the desired services (under an existing contract), the new requirement may be covered by a new contract or by a modification to the existing one. Regardless, this new (or continuing) requirement must be treated as a new procurement and processed as such. This means that a synopsis must be published in the government-wide Point of Entry. The

solicitation may not be issued until 15 days after it has been published, and the proposal deadline may not be less than 30 days after that. When a new procurement is contemplated, it will be subject to competition; it cannot be awarded automatically to a contractor simply because the contractor has a current contract with the agency. If the new procurement is to be awarded noncompetitively, it must be justified as a noncompetitive procurement.

G.9.d. Consideration for Contract Modification

Generally there must be consideration whenever a contract is modified. "Consideration" is the benefit each party confers upon the other for the modification. Although contract modifications usually result in price/cost increases, they may sometimes result in price/cost reductions. The requirement for consideration, as set forth in various decisions of the Comptroller General, is that no officer or employee of the government may alter a contract to the prejudice of the government unless the government receives corresponding, tangible, contractual benefits. Thus, there is no such thing as a "no cost" extension to the period of performance of a contract. If the government allows a longer period of time for delivery, the "cost" to the government is its right to delivery of the product or service by the date agreed upon. The law requires the contractor to provide some form of consideration for the government giving up of that right.

Certain administrative changes may be made without consideration provided the contractor's rights are not affected; e.g., change in the appropriation data or a change in the paying office, etc. Once a valid contract is executed, no adjustment can be made to contract terms merely because it may appear, in retrospect, that either the contractor or the government has made a "bad bargain."

G.9.e. Processing Contract Modification

Requests for unilateral modifications are initiated by the government. Unilateral modifications (such as administrative changes or exercise of the provisions of the Changes clause) are within the authority of the CO, without agreement from the contractor. Modifications resulting from bilateral modifications can be initiated by a written request from either the government or the contractor. For these bilateral modifications the COTR must prepare a supporting memorandum to document the need for the modification and to provide other appropriate information necessary to process it. The memorandum will contain the following information.

☐ The number of the contract being modified and the modification number

☐ The contract title (project identification)

☐ The complete name and address of the contractor

☐ The names, mailing addresses, and telephone numbers of the project and alternate POs

☐ The type of modification recommended

☐ The basis for the modification (Explain the circumstances; e.g., who, what, when, where, and why that resulted in the need for the modification and the reasons why a modification will be made.)

☐ A brief description of the contractor's performance, as well as the identification of any known problem areas

☐ An independent government estimate of cost for the modification

☐ The estimated total time necessary to accomplish the required services

☐ A complete description of the work to be changed or modified

Contract modification concurrence must be obtained to the extent that such modifications result in new or additional requirements that are subject to a concurrence. For example, a new report format used by 10 or more respondents would require OMB approval. The CO must advise COTRs of the need for such concurrence.

The CO may delegate to the COTR the following responsibilities related to contract modifications:

Identify the need to change the contract

Prepare the technical analysis

Assist in negotiations

G.9.e.i. Identify the Need to Change the Contract

Some circumstances that can prompt a change to the contract include:

☐ A change in agency need

☐ Inadequate specifications

☐ A need to increase or decrease funds

☐ A need for extensions to provide additional time

☐ Suspension of work

☐ Required revisions to the original terms and conditions in the contract

☐ A change in performance requirements

☐ Development of contingencies that need resolution

Some circumstances that will NOT prompt a change to the contract include those:

☐ Already covered by terms and conditions of the contract

☐ Outside the scope of the contract

G.9.e.ii. Prepare a Technical Analysis

The COTR performs the following when preparing a technical analysis for a modification:

☐ Gather information for a change request

☐ Prepare written documentation to support the proposed change

☐ Notify the CO of a pending change

G.9.e.iii. Gather Information for a Change Request

A COTR will obtain necessary documentation from the contractor. This may include:

☐ Description of the change

☐ Chronology of events

☐ Justification for change

☐ Pricing information

The COTR will also obtain input from the requiring activity and other support personnel. This may include:

Statement of facts

Correspondence with the contractor

Reaction to the request

Impact of the change request on its mission

Prepare Written Documentation to Support the Proposed Change

Before issuing a contract modification, the COTR will determine the impact a change will have on contract price or cost, delivery, and performance. The documentation will address:

☐ Background of the issue and reason for the change

☐ Whether the issue is already covered by the technical requirements of the contract

☐ Whether the change is within the scope of the contract

☐ Impact on the requirement in terms of quality, quantity, or delivery

☐ Impact on cost or price

☐ Consequences if the change is not made

☐ Available alternatives

☐ Proposed recommendation for a solution

☐ Any attachments supporting the technical analysis

G.9.e.iv. Within the Scope of Contract

Consider whether any change, initiated by either the government or the contractor, is within the scope of the contract. Adding work under an existing contract avoids the costs and disruption associated with issuing a new procurement. But there are definite limits to additional work. A proposed contract change within the scope of the contract encompasses the following:

Factors indicating "within scope" changes –

☐ The function of the item or service has not changed.

☐ The basic contract purpose has not changed.

☐ The dollar magnitude is proportionate to the price of the original contract.

☐ Competitive factors of the original solicitation are the same.

☐ Changes to the specification or SOW are not extensive.

Questions to consider when deciding whether a change is outside the scope of the contract include:

Does the changed work represent what both parties reasonably contemplated at the time of award?

Is the changed work essentially the same as was bargained for?

Is the nature of the requirement altered by the change?

Would this type of change normally be expected for this kind of requirement (sophisticated, complex requirements)?

Was the specification defective, requiring extensive redesign?

G.9.e.v. Cost and Price Documentation

Although the CO is the person ultimately responsible for all decisions on contract modifications, he or she relies on the COTR and other support personnel for technical and pricing decisions. Changes to basic contract requirements can be classified in three ways, according to the effect the change has on the resulting price adjustment. Usually a single change will embody elements of more than one type. These categories of change are:

Additive Changes - work added to the contract, resulting in more money to the contractor.

Deductive Changes - work a contractor has not yet performed deleted from the contract, resulting in a reduction of contract price.

Substitution Changes - added work substituted for deleted work, resulting in either no change in contract price or a change that is tempered by the monetary effect of the substitution involved.

The effects of the change on the original pricing and technical proposal will be considered and addressed. Pricing considerations will consider a history for similar requirements, or current market prices.

G.9.e.vi. Notify the CO of a Pending Change

The COTR will notify the CO within a timeframe that does not:

Jeopardize the government mission

Delay the contractor from performing under the contract

At a minimum, the COTR's recommendation will include items, such as:

Memorandum to the file, letters, or other documents (These are used to request, explain, and justify the contract modification request.)

Work statement changes that specify deliverables and due dates

A purchase request attached with the appropriate signatures if the change requires additional funds

G.9.e.vii. Assist in Negotiations

The CO will often solicit assistance from the COTR in researching information, preparing the pre-negotiation position, developing negotiation strategies, and conducting the negotiation. A COTR can assist in evaluating the contractor proposal by:

Providing advice concerning safety and performance

Providing guidance on whether acceptance of supplies or services would be in the government's best interest after repair, correction, or price adjustments

Providing supporting rationale for rejecting or accepting the contractor proposal

Attending any negotiations to respond to the contractor position

The CO makes a final decision at the conclusion of negotiations.

G.9.f. Contract Options

The COTR often advises the CO of the need to exercise options under the contract. To ensure options are processed accurately, the COTR must:

Identify available options

Determine the need for additional supplies, services, or time

Research the marketplace for the latest pricing information

Document the file and provide written data to the CO

Identify Available Options

The COTR will understand the requirement, pricing information, terms and conditions of the contract, and timeframe needed to exercise the option, and determine if it is in the government's best interest to exercise the option. The COTR will begin this step in sufficient time to make an informed decision and before the option expires. In supply-type contracts, options may be appropriate when:

Basic quantities are for learning or testing purposes; or

Competition for the options is not possible once the initial contract has been awarded.

The COTR will ensure that:

Funding is available;

The requirement covered by the option fulfills an existing government need;

Exercising the option is the most advantageous method of fulfilling the need.

Determine the Need for Additional Supplies, Services, or Time

The COTR submits to the CO a written determination that includes information about:

Government requirements supporting the need to exercise the option

Advantages of exercising the option

The technical impact and value of the option

Funding availability for the option

COTR documentation assists the CO in making a decision about the option. After review, the CO sends a written notice to the contractor advising of the government intent to exercise the option.

Research the Market Place for Latest Pricing Information

The COTR submits to the CO market research data which confirms:

The option price would be lower than prices likely to be offered by other vendors

The option otherwise represents the most advantageous offer

The following are factors taken into consideration:

Any economic price adjustment clause that affects the option price

The need for continuity of operations

Potential cost of disrupting operations

The COTR uses market research to obtain information on latest commercial market pricing and industry trends. Market research can include continuous market research. This research is ongoing and not related to a specific procurement. It can provide the COTR with knowledge involving:

☐ Changes, advances, and trends in technology

☐ Products of interest

☐ Industry capability

☐ Product availability

☐ Competitive market forces

☐ Alternative sources

Initial market research - Initial market research is related to a specific procurement and determines whether sources of commercial items are available to satisfy the specified need. The COTR can use this information to determine whether the government requirement could be modified (to a reasonable extent) to allow use of commercial items.

Subsequent market research - Subsequent market research is conducted before the solicitation of offerors. It helps the COTR determine whether the requirement fits market conditions by identifying the various standards and practices of commercial firms. The COTR notifies the CO when information is not available through market research.

Document the File and Provide Written Data to the CO

COTR written documentation will include:

☐ A rationale for exercising the option

☐ The option period as stated in the contract

☐ The technical evaluation that indicates the option meets the government requirement

☐ A funding document or form that certifies funds are available to exercise the option

G.10. Unauthorized Commitments and Ratifications

Only the CO has the authority to enter into, modify, and administer a contract. The authority of the COTR is limited to the responsibilities explicitly stated in the nomination letter. A COTR must not in any situation direct the contractor to take any action that would change the contract, such as the following:

* Total price or estimated cost
* Product deliverables
* SOW/PWS
* Delivery dates
* Total period of performance
* The administrative provisions of the contract

When a COTR exceeds his or her delegated authority, an unauthorized commitment (UAC) may result in a claim against the government. For example, suppose a COTR tells the contractor that the product would be better if the contractor used a different material. A UAC may result if the contractor takes the COTR's statement to be direction and substitutes the new material for the old. To avoid an unauthorized commitment, the COTR will first make it clear to the contractor that he or she does not have authority to give such direction, and will then submit a recommendation to the CO to modify the contract.

Another example of a potential UAC is when the government continues to conduct business as usual with the contractor after a contract lapses but has not been formally renewed or extended. In this case, the failure of the COTR to notify the CO in time to renew the contract or to promptly notify the contractor of the situation could be an unauthorized commitment. In general, the COTR must not take any of the following actions:

Make any commitments or promises relating to award of contracts or any representation that would be construed as such a commitment;

Issue instructions to the contractor to start or stop work;

Encourage the contractor by words, actions or a failure to act to undertake new work or an extension of existing work beyond the stated contract period;

Interfere with the contractor's management prerogatives with its employees, such as "supervising" or otherwise directing their work efforts of an employee;

Accept products or services not expressly required by the contract; and

Unless directed by the CO, authorize a contractor to:

- Obtain property for use under a contract; or
- Allow a contractor to use government property accountable under one contract in the performance of another contract.

In most cases, the CO will counsel a COTR that has exceeded his or her authority, or take other steps to ensure that the error is not repeated. However, in cases of gross abuse, the CO may revoke the COTR appointment immediately, without giving the COTR a second chance. UACs are very serious matters that may result in personal liability or other adverse consequences for the COTR.

G.10.a. Constructive Changes

A constructive change arises whenever, by informal action or inaction of the government, the situation of the contractor is so altered as to have the same effect as though an order had been issued under the Changes clause. The term is derived from the verb "to construe," not from "to construct." Thus, the constructive change is a situation that can be construed as having the effect of a change order.

There are several ways in which a constructive change occurs. The list provided is not all-inclusive. This is an area of equity or fairness   and fairness depends greatly on the situation. An action by the government may lead to a successful claim by a contractor under such principles, but in a very similar situation, the claim will be successfully defended by the government.

Common Causes of Constructive Changes

The following are the most common ways in which a constructive change can occur:

☐ Inadequate (latently defective) requirements documents

☐ Improperly interpreted specifications

☐ Overly strict inspection

☐ Failure to recognize delays caused by the government

☐ Technical defects in the change order process

☐ Improper technical direction

Resolve Constructive Changes

Identify actual changes to the contract

Prepare technical analysis and notify the CO

Assist the CO with negotiations

Identify Actual Changes to the Contract

When a COTR's technical direction to the contractor goes beyond the scope of his or her responsibility, the result is a change to the contract known as constructive change. The following table differentiates between technical direction, which is acceptable, and constructive change, which must be avoided.

Technical Direction	Constructive Change
A technical direction is guidance within the SOW. The need and ramifications of technical direction are different depending on whether the contract is fixed-price or cost-reimbursement. Work statements are normally more precise under fixed-price contracts than cost-reimbursement. When a work statement is precise, there is little or no need for technical direction. More technically complex contracts may require COTR direction.	A constructive change occurs when the CO or authorized representative changes the contract without the required legal formality of a contract modification. A constructive change can result from either an action or a failure to act. Examples are: • Errors of interpretation • Issuance of changes outside the scope of the contract • Failure to issue a change to correct a defective specification • Acceleration of performance

Prepare Technical Analysis of a Constructive Change and Notify the CO

Constructive changes may be identified by either the COTR or the contractor. The COTR must notify the CO that the contract may have had a constructive change. The notification will include sufficient information about the events that led to the possible constructive change. A contractor can use any method to notify the CO of the possibility of a constructive change. A contractor is not likely to perform extra work under a fixed-price contract without firm assurances of additional funding for the changed work. Such assurances are not needed under a cost-reimbursement contract because cost for the extra work is paid by the government. If the contract contains a "notification of changes" clause, the contractor must notify the CO using the format and timeframes specified in the clause. Upon notification, the CO determines if the event was proper under technical direction, or if the event resulted in a constructive change. No further action is required of the COTR if the CO determines the event was permitted under technical direction.

Assist the CO with Negotiations

The CO may require the COTR to participate in negotiations for contract adjustments related to constructive changes. The COTR may need to prepare a technical analysis of the circumstances and impact of the change. To avoid constructive change, it is very important for the COTR to keep proper records. For example, if, during an interim inspection, the

COTR tells the contractor that some aspect of performance is inadequate, the aspect will be explained in writing, with a copy transmitted to the contractor through the CO.

Documentation of final inspections is important. It is not sufficient to tell the contractor that the product is unacceptable. Specific problems will be identified in writing. Contractors can mistake a general comment about one way to correct a problem as specific direction that this is the only acceptable way. Good documentation can eliminate that sort of misunderstanding. Finally, the COTR must always act in good faith and must always follow government procedures. Do not try to get something for nothing. Do not try to get around the paperwork. The government loses claims, and the reasonable technical cooperation of its contractors, when the COTR circumvents the required procedures and principles.

G.10.b. Ratification of Unauthorized Commitments

Ratification means the act of approving an unauthorized commitment. An unauthorized commitment means an agreement that is not binding, solely because the government representative who made the agreement lacked the authority to do so. An unauthorized commitment can be approved (ratified) only by an official who has such approval authority.

The FAR makes it clear that unauthorized commitments will be precluded to the maximum extent possible and prescribes specific procedures and limitations relative to ratification.

Typically, unauthorized commitments are made by technical representatives, or project personnel in connection with their duties relative to a specific contract or contracts, or even when a contract does not exist. It seems that their actions are unintentional and occur because of a lack of understanding of their authority vis-à-vis that of the CO.

If ratification becomes necessary or desirable, the action shall generally be handled as follows:

The person who made the unauthorized contractual commitment must furnish the CO with all records and documents having to do with the action, as well as a written statement of the facts in the situation, including statements as to why the normal procurement process was not used; how the contractor was selected; the other sources considered; the work to be done or product to be supplied; the estimated or agreed price; the source of available funding; and, information as to whether the contractor has commenced performance. The CO will review the information supplied and forward it, with any additional information or comments, to the HCA or a designee for evaluation and approval or disapproval. If ratification is authorized, the HCA or the designee will return the file to the CO for the proper issuance of a contract

or contract modification, as well as the ratification notice. Agencies consider the problem of unauthorized commitments to be very grave, and the HCA must report all requests for ratification and ratification authorized to agency management.

G.11. Inadequate Contractor Performance

The COTR is often responsible for recommending a formal contract remedy to the CO. This involves two tasks:

- ☐ Notifying the CO of performance failures
- ☐ Providing technical assistance

G.11.a. Notify the CO of Performance Failures

During contract monitoring, the COTR may identify performance failures or other breach of contract situations. These may include:

- ☐ Anticipated or actual late delivery
- ☐ Failure to control costs
- ☐ Unsatisfactory performance
- ☐ Nonconforming supplies/services

Once a performance failure or breach is identified, the COTR must notify the CO. Because many remedies are time sensitive, delays in informing the CO may result in harm to the government. A remedy recommendation will best match the problem and include adequate and timely documentation that supports the decision.

G.11.b. Provide Technical Assistance

To provide the technical assistance, a COTR may need to prepare documentation and make appropriate recommendations to support the government position for:

- ☐ Any monetary or non-monetary consideration
- ☐ A new delivery schedule
- ☐ Modifying other terms and conditions of the contract
- ☐ Attending meetings with the contractor and providing technical advice as requested by the CO

The COTR can also assist in the contract remedy process by:

- ☐ Providing technical analysis for delinquency notice situations
- ☐ Calculating liquidated damages

☐ Preparing written rejection of nonconforming supplies and services

☐ Determining warranty provisions

☐ Providing technical review of contractor responses

G.11.c. Technical Analysis for Delinquency Notice Situations

COTRs may analyze critical performance problems that justify issuing a delinquency notice. In response to a cure notice, the COTR may be asked to determine the impact of the contractor's offer to:

☐ Correct the work

☐ "Cure" performance

☐ Provide a downward price adjustment for acceptance

☐ Provide substantial performance in exchange for relief from some terms or conditions in the contract

☐ Analyze and negotiate a revised delivery schedule for a conforming product with consideration

☐ Present a case for excusable delay

The COTR may be required to assist with reviewing a contractor's response to a "show cause" letter by evaluating:

☐ The impact of no reply or one with no offer of a justification

☐ A claim for a case of excusable delay

☐ An assertion that performance is impossible under the contract terms and conditions

☐ A claim that work is substantially complete

G.11.d. Calculating Liquidated Damages

When assessing liquidated damages is appropriate, the government withholds payments based on an accurate computation of the amount due. The actual computation will depend on the specific amount or formula in the contract, and also on actual events during contract performance.

Liquidated damages are calculated by the following means:

Identify all factors that control how these amounts are computed to reflect an accurate maximum amount authorized under a specific liquidated damages clause.

Subtract amounts of time that may have constituted an excusable delay from the period for liquidated damages. When subtracting time for excusable delay, also subtract calendar days

unless the performance is specifically described as "work" days. Holidays and weekends are not considered "work" days. The rate of assessment for liquidated damages may be in two or more increments, providing a declining rate of assessment as the delinquency continues.

Examine the contract for any restrictions. Generally, the contract will restrict the total amount withheld to the greatest amount that can be withheld under the authority of a single clause. Compute amounts that would be authorized under each clause.

To ensure the total liquidated damages amount is reasonable and not a penalty, there may be special contract terms limiting the overall dollar amount or period of time, or both, for liquidated damages. The courts and administrative boards will not uphold liquidated damages that are so excessive that they can be construed as a penalty.

G.11.e. Withholding Payment

All government contracts contain a clause allowing the government to withhold payments. A contractor's failure to either submit a report, or to perform or deliver services, or work when required by the contract, is to be considered default in performance. In either circumstance, the CO is directed to immediately issue a formal "cure notice." It includes a statement that contract payments will be withheld if the default is not "cured" or is not determined to be excusable. A "cure notice" is a formal notice from the CO pointing out a deficiency in contractor performance and directing that it be "cured" within a specified time — usually 10 days.

If the default is not determined to be excusable or a response is not received within the allotted time, the CO initiates withholding action on all contract payments and determines whether termination for default or other action would be in the best interest of the government. When determination is made that contract payments will be withheld, the CO will immediately notify the contractor, in writing, that payments have been suspended until the default or failure is cured.

G.12. Contract Delays

The COTR often performs the following tasks when advising the CO of delays:

☐ Identifies and verifies a delay in performance

☐ Notifies the CO of the technical impact of the delay

☐ Assists the CO in evaluating the contractor response

G.12.a. Identify and Verify a Delay in Performance

Every contract includes a delivery or performance schedule. To assist the CO, the COTR:

☐ Identifies the existence of a delay

☐ Verifies the delay

A delay occurs if the contractor fails to perform in accordance with the contract delivery or performance schedule; or the government causes the contractor to stop performing. Before identifying the reasons for a delay, the COTR reviews the contract for any applicable clauses and modifications to ensure the performance or delivery schedule was not previously extended by the CO. The COTR confirms the delay by:

Obtaining feedback from any other government personnel responsible for monitoring performance or delivery

Reviewing the notice and supporting documents from the contractor regarding the delay

Reviewing any contractor claim regarding the delay

Examples of Excusable Delays

Delays when neither the government nor the contractor is responsible:

☐ Acts of God

☐ Unusually severe weather

☐ Strikes and labor disputes

☐ Public enemy causes

☐ Causes beyond the control of subcontractors and suppliers

Delays caused by actions taken when a government official:

☐ Directs the contractor to stop work

☐ Makes a change to the contract

☐ Performs other acts within the government's sovereign capacity

Delays caused by government failure to act:

☐ Make the site available when required

☐ Process approvals

☐ Obtain funding

☐ Issue changes in a timely manner

☐ Respond to contractor requests

☐ Furnish government property when required

☐ Inspect or accept when required

G.12.b. Notify the CO of the Technical Impact of the Delay

Once a delay is confirmed, the COTR prepares documentation to assist the CO in developing the government position on the delay. Documentation will include facts and relevant information about the delay, such as:

List of persons with factual knowledge of the delay

Description of the delay

History of performance, indicating:

☐ When work under the contract began

☐ When work deviated from contract requirements

☐ When work stopped

Other issues, such as:

☐ Information that would support whether the delay was excusable

☐ Contractor progress to date and remaining obligations

☐ Estimate of a reasonable period of additional time to perform

☐ Potential alternatives and resolution

☐ Pros and cons of each alternative (price, quantity, and quality)

G.12.c. Contractor Delay Assessment

The following checklist will assist in evaluation of whether contractor delays are excusable. The CO relies on the COTR's knowledge of how the contract was executed and any additional information that may affect the determination. Before making a final determination, the COTR must be certain that the contractor: 1) had little or no control over the circumstances that caused the delay and 2) could not have taken any preemptive action to reduce the negative consequences of the delay. If the organization can prove these two assertions, then a "Yes" answer to any of the following questions means the delay was probably excusable.

#1. Was the delay caused by a labor strike? If NO, go to Question #2 If YES, did the contractor:	YES NO

File a charge with the appropriate labor relations board to seek injunctive relief in court?	Yes	No	N/A
Use other available government procedures or private boards or organizations in an attempt to settle or arbitrate disputes that caused the strike?	Yes	No	N/A
#2. Was the delay caused by government interference or disruption? If NO, go to Question #3 If YES, did the government:	YES	NO	
Delay in making payments due to the contractor?	Yes	No	N/A
Deliver government-furnished property late?	Yes	No	N/A
Fail to reply to a contractor request for clarification?	Yes	No	N/A
Fail to disclose all facts applicable to performance?	Yes	No	N/A
Cite or misrepresent conditions that were different from those portrayed?	Yes	No	N/A
Experience scarcity of supplies due to Defense Production Act priorities over commercial or non-rated orders?	Yes	No	N/A
Delay issuing a required notice to proceed?	Yes	No	N/A
Delay issuing changes?	Yes	No	N/A
Delay performance by other government contractors?	Yes	No	N/A
Experience delays because of an interested party protesting the contract award?	Yes	No	N/A
Delay making the site available?	Yes	No	N/A
Delay providing funding?	Yes	No	N/A
Delay inspection or acceptance?	Yes	No	N/A
Delay because of defective or ambiguous specifications?	Yes	No	N/A
Delay granting approvals?	Yes	No	N/A
#3. Was the delay caused by a subcontractor? If NO, go to Question #4 Note: The determination is «No» if either of the following occurred: YES NO			
Did a dispute between the subcontractor and prime cause the delay?	Yes	No	N/A
Were subcontracted products or services available from other sources in time for the prime to complete performance?	Yes	No	N/A

#4. Was the delay caused by any other occurrence specifically characterized in Default or Excusable Delays, (or other clauses), as generally excusable? If NO, go to Question #5 If YES, was the delay caused by: YES NO			
Acts of the government in either its sovereign or contractual capacity?	Yes	No	N/A
Acts of God or the public enemy?	Yes	No	N/A
Fire?	Yes	No	N/A
Flood?	Yes	No	N/A
Unusually severe weather?	Yes	No	N/A
Epidemics?	Yes	No	N/A
Quarantine restrictions?	Yes	No	N/A
Labor dispute resulting in strikes?	Yes	No	N/A
Freight embargoes?	Yes	No	N/A
Common carrier delays?	Yes	No	N/A
#5. Was the delay caused by other circumstances not previously mentioned? If YES, did the contractor: YES NO			
Not cause the delay?	Yes	No	N/A
Not have any control over the circumstances that caused delay?	Yes	No	N/A

G.12.d. Assist in Evaluating Contractor Response

COTRs may be asked to assist the CO in evaluating the contractor response. In their response, contractors may be asked to:

☐ Substantiate the evidence of the delay

☐ Substantiate the costs associated with the delay

☐ Demonstrate the delay was unreasonable

☐ Demonstrate the delay was void of any concurrent or commingled delays

Concurrent or commingled delays fall in a middle ground, being neither excusable nor non-excusable. A commingled delay occurs when both parties are at fault for one or more reasons contributing to the delay. A concurrent delay occurs when two or more delays happen at the same time. Before allowing a contractor to recover costs as a result of a delay, the contractor response must provide verifiable documentation of incurred expenses. The CO, with the assistance of the COTR, considers each expense and determines whether the

contractor will receive compensation. Compensation may be in the form of dollars or time extensions.

Examples of Recoverable Expenses

Possible Contractor Expenses	Government Verification Review
Idle time of facilities or equipment	Idleness of rental equipment is not normally a recoverable expense since the equipment can be returned to the rental agency. If the contractor can show it is less expensive to continue renting, these costs are recoverable.
Increase in material prices	The contractor will support these increases with supplier invoices or letters substantiating price increases.
Increase in wages	These costs can normally be verified by: Consulting local labor union officials Interviewing contractor personnel Examining payroll records in an audit
Loss of efficiency	When the contractor has been forced to work out of sequence, that is, in a poorly-organized, inefficient manner instead of in the originally scheduled sequence of work, learning-curve efficiencies will be lost. This is the most difficult expense to document, although it is also one of the most common delay and disruption costs.
Unusually severe weather conditions	To be recoverable, these conditions could not have had an effect on performance were it not for the change in time of performance due to the delay. Conditions of unusually adverse weather can be verified by National Weather Service reports for the affected period. These reports can be compared with those of the original period of performance to verify the degree or extent of unusual weather conditions that could have contributed to the delay.
Insurance and bond coverage	If the contractor extended this coverage for the period of the delay, and would not have otherwise done so, a notice from the bonding or insurance company for the amount of the increased premium will be provided.
Protection or storage of materials	These must be actual additional costs. Examples are re-handling and transportation charges that would not have been necessary if the work had proceeded without interruption.
Additional make-ready costs	If a production run is interrupted, there will be additional costs for restarting the production line.

Possible Contractor Expenses	Government Verification Review
Demobilizing and mobilizing the workforce	If the contractor lays off personnel during the delay, there may be administrative rehiring costs. If the delay is long and the contractor is unable to rehire part of the original workforce, recruitment advertising and employment fees to recruitment agencies may be included within these costs.
Interest	Interest on funds necessary to finance the extended performance time caused by the delay is recoverable.
Unabsorbed overhead expenses	Unabsorbed overhead, when it applies, can include both direct labor personnel underutilized because of the delay and general office overhead expenses directly attributable to or chargeable against the contract.

G.13. Stop Work

The COTR often advises the CO of the need to issue a stop work, or suspension of work, order. To ensure a work stoppage is processed accurately, the COTR:

Identifies potential conditions to stop work

Recommends a work stoppage to the CO

Assists in issuing a stop work order

Suspension of work is used under construction and architect-engineering contracts to halt all or part of the work.

G.13.a. Identify Potential Conditions to Stop Work

The government or contractor may request a stop work order. The COTR identifies conditions under which work stoppage might occur, which might include:

Government

When unable to furnish property or services per the contract schedule

When a request for a change to the contract has been received and a modification cannot be issued

When time is necessary to consider contract modifications that would substantially change the end product

Contractor

When a proposal has been submitted to materially change the technical requirement of the contract (i.e., value engineering change)

When conditions at a government work site make performance of work unsafe and not immediately correctable

G.13.b. Determine the Impact of a Work Stoppage

Work stoppages will only occur after the government has determined the impact, which may include:

Estimated cost for delaying the work

Potential effect on labor (loss of skilled labor, loss of efficiency, and so forth)

Potential damage to perishable goods

Estimated effect on overhead (inventory, indirect labor, etc.)

Any adverse effects of the potential delay on contract completion

The COTR will determine if there is a contract clause that allows the government to issue a stop work/suspension of work order. COTRs must avoid issuing oral or written instructions to a contractor to start or stop work. The CO is the official responsible for issuing stop work orders.

G.13.c. Document Recommendation

The COTR may be asked to document the stop work order. This documentation may include:

A description of the work to be suspended

Effective date and time

Timeframe to resume work

The contractor right to file a claim

Origin, purpose, and benefits of stopping the work

Any costs associated with the work stoppage

Alternatives to stopping the work (if any)

Nature or reason for stopping work

Nature or reason for number of days in the stop work order

G.13.d. Assist With Issuing Stop Work/Suspension of Work Order

The COTR may be requested to:

Select the method for issuing the stop work/suspension of work order

Assist in discussions with the contractor

Recommend when work can resume

The COTR may be asked to prepare information for the written stop work/suspension of work order. There are two methods for issuing stop/suspension of work orders:

Oral - Oral orders are issued for highly urgent reasons, such as life-threatening issues or safety violations. A CO issues oral orders only when the situation precludes waiting for a written one, and a timeframe for work stoppage needs to be conveyed. Oral orders will be confirmed in writing as soon as possible.

Written - Written orders include all details involving the stop work order and its requirements. Written orders are presented to the contractor in person or through a third-party messenger. Whatever method is used, a signature of a contractor employee acknowledging receipt must be obtained for the stop work order to become effective. The signature ensures the government is released from responsibility for paying any unnecessary costs incurred for contract work as a result of the stoppage.

G.13.e. Assist in Discussions with the Contractor

The COTR assists the CO to discuss the stop work order with the contractor. The following topics may be covered:

☐ Reasons for issuing the stop work order

☐ Factors for reaching specified timeframe and the probability of revisions

☐ Impact of possible timeframes for the work stoppage

Estimates of labor and other costs of the expected work stoppage

Alternatives for continuing the stop work order

Acceptance of a stop work order by the contractor

Types of costs that may or may not be allowed by the government

Daily communication, preferably in writing, is important since costs associated with the work stoppage are occurring daily. The CO, COTR, and the requiring organizations affected by the work stoppage will be included in any communication.

G.13.f. Recommend When Work Can Resume

Stop work orders are undesirable and will be discontinued as quickly as possible. The contractor will resume work when:

Written notice is received from the CO to resume work

The stop work order is cancelled

The stop work order expires and written notice is receive

The stop work order expires and no official government action is taken

G.14. Claims and Disputes

The COTR often analyzes a claim and recommends a settlement position to the CO. To complete this duty, the COTR:

Notifies the CO of potential disputes

Assists in responding to claims

Assists in resolving claims

G.14.a. Notify the CO of Potential Disputes

Disagreements between the government and a contractor can evolve into contract disputes. For instance:

Complex projects may create troublesome interrelationships.

Lengthy contractual documents with numerous revisions may lead to misinterpretations.

Unforeseen conditions may cause disagreements, e.g., changed weather conditions may disrupt schedules.

Well-intended actions can create out-of-scope changes.

A CO may be required to respond to different types of disagreements, such as:

Payment of invoices

Settlement of contract claims

Reinstatement of a previously terminated contract

Termination of a breached contract for default

Acceptance or rejection of nonconforming items

The COTR will be aware of warning signs of a potential dispute and will notify the CO as soon as it is identified. Disagreements not addressed early may turn into disputes. When possible, disputes will be avoided because of the time and cost involved in resolving them.

G.14.b. Warning Signs of a Potential Dispute

Warning signs include:

Lack of specific information from a contractor during a pre-proposal conference about how the job will be completed

Failure of a contractor to begin work within approximately 10 percent of the total contract period of performance

Repeated failure of a contractor to meet milestones on the critical path of a project schedule

Repeated safety violations or accidents, possibly indicating poor management

Repeated incidents of poor quality or rework

Complaints from site workers to government personnel about conditions

Refusal by a contractor to sign bilaterally negotiated contract modifications or agreements containing the required language necessary to release a modification

Letters from a contractor alluding to field problems without specific details regarding those problems

Numerous correspondences from a contractor requiring replies to very insignificant matters, creating a nightmare of paperwork

Persistent complaints from a contractor concerning the behavior, motives, or requirements of an inspector or contract administrator that are found to be without foundation

Receiving complaints from subcontractors concerning late payments or nonpayment

G.14.c. Assist in Responding to Claims

Prepare Supporting Documentation

When possible, the CO makes all reasonable efforts to informally resolve disagreements or controversies. The COTR submits supporting data to the CO that:

Describes the dispute

Refers to pertinent contract terms

States factual areas of agreement or disagreement

Determines if the contractor is indebted to the government

Makes a recommendation to reject, partially accept, or fully accept the claim

Includes background information covering:

☐ Facts in chronological order

☐ All separate issues or allegations

☐ Points of contact for discussion of the dispute

Methods used in developing supporting documentation include:

Discussions with the contractor

Personal observations at the work site

Discussions with other government personnel (e.g., audit personnel, quality assurance personnel, program office)

G.14.d. Submit a Detailed Analysis of the Claim

The analysis of a claim has five phases:

Identifying the issue(s)

Performing an impact analysis

Evaluating project documentation

Performing a price/cost analysis and damage apportionment

G.14.e. Preparing a Claim Report

The COTR provides information to assist the CO in a detailed analysis of the claim. A technical analysis will be submitted in writing and include:

Background information (including information used to support the dispute)

Contract number and date

Estimated contractor claim amount, the amount the contractor may be entitled to, and any differences between the two

Contractor labor and equipment usage and cost

Idle time, wasted time, or dragged-out time (including dates from monitoring reports)

Possible over-staffing of personnel or over-equipping

Contractor cost overage (or overrun) on materials, labor, equipment, and overhead

Contractor diligence and production efficiency (note the number of days or months the contractor is behind schedule)

Number of changes or change orders received and processed under the contract

The engineering approach employed by the contractor

The reasonableness of any additional time and person-hours expended

G.14.f. Assist in Resolving a Claim

Alternative Dispute Resolution (ADR) Procedures

ADR procedures are used at any time to resolve disagreements or controversial issues. ADR procedures are used when:

An issue exists

Both parties voluntarily participate with officials authorized to resolve the issue

Both parties agree on procedures and terms

Formal litigation will not be used

Participate in Formal Proceeding

The contractor may submit a contract dispute to the Contracting Officer. To prepare for a dispute proceeding, the Contracting Officer may request the COTR to assist with preparation or assembly of:

The contract specification and drawings, including all modifications

COTR correspondence files

Copies or documentation of any written or oral technical direction the COTR may have provided that may be pertinent to the claim

Modifications that include technical changes (Particularly important are originally approved changes, plus those added throughout the course of the contract.)

Inspection records including daily records, if applicable, and logs or reports by inspectors and contractor personnel

Memoranda of meetings pertinent to the claim

All progress charts and information, and all changes concerning progress

Copies of the post-award orientation meeting notes (These may establish expectations and understandings of both parties concerning a provision of the specification or anticipated problems.)

Copies of contract with relevant contract clauses

Copies of all photographs pertinent to the claim

Copies of pertinent logs, such as change-order logs or submittal approval logs

Copies of contractor interim and/or final performance evaluations of contractor performance

If the result of formal proceeding favors a contractor, the CO may request assistance from the COTR in negotiating any equitable adjustment. After negotiation, a contract modification formally reflects the equitable adjustment.

Resolving Disputes – Part I

No matter how carefully a contract is negotiated and written, disputes can and often do arise under government contracts. This is primarily due to the complex nature of the government acquisition process and the involved relationship between the contractor and the government. The Disputes clause included in all government contracts is designed to ensure that disagreements between the government and the contractor will not interfere with the scheduled performance of the contract. It also provides a channel through which disagreements and differences can be resolved by the persons directly involved.

The CO has wide powers to settle contractual matters. Some of the matters that may be settled by decision of the CO include making equitable adjustments pursuant to the Changes and Government-furnished Property clauses; reducing prices under the Inspection clause; and providing for reimbursement for extra work performed. If agreement can be reached between the two parties in regard to the

equitable adjustments, additional reimbursement, or refunds required under any contract clause, a bilateral agreement may be negotiated between the two parties.

If agreement cannot be reached, these issues as well as others involving disagreements are resolved under the procedures set out in the Disputes clause. The standard Disputes clause (FAR 52.233-1) included in all government contracts provides:

The contract is subject to the Contracts Disputes Act of 1978, as amended (41 USC 601-613).

For contractor claims of $100,000 or less, the CO must render a decision within 60 days. For contractor claims in excess of $100,000, the CO must decide the claim within 60 days or notify the contractor of the date when the decision will be made.

The CO's decision is final unless the contractor appeals or files a suit as provided in the Act.

The CO's authority under the Act does not extend to claims or disputes that by statute or regulation other agencies are expressly authorized to decide.

Interest on the amount found due on contractor claims is paid from the date the claim is received by the CO until the date of payment.

Except, as the parties may otherwise agree, pending final resolution of a claim by the contractor arising under the contract, the contractor must proceed diligently with the performance of the contract in accordance with the CO's decision.

Dispute resolution – Part II

Where appropriate, an alternative dispute resolution (ADR) technique known as "partnering" will be discussed with the contractor to help avoid future contract administration problems. Partnering is a technique to prevent disputes from occurring. It involves government and contractor management staff mutually developing a "plan for success," usually with the assistance of a neutral facilitator. The facilitator helps the parties establish a non-adversarial relationship, define mutual goals and identify the major obstacles to success for the project. Potential sources of conflict are identified, and the parties seek cooperative ways to resolve any disputes that may arise during contract performance. The process results in the parties developing a partnership charter, which serves as a roadmap for contract success. Many agencies have successfully used partnering on construction projects and are now beginning to apply these principles in the automated data processing/information resources management area.

G.15. Conflict Formulation and Resolution

G.15.a. Definition

A situation or action which blocks effective communication generally creating ill-will.

G.15.b. Causes of Conflict

A. Ambiguous roles – government representatives and/or contractor representatives not clear or confident what their responsibilities are.

B. Inconsistent or unachievable goals – that is, the project objectives and/or the task objectives are ill-defined or not coincident with other projects or tasks.

C. Communication barriers – inability to effectively transmit, receive, listen to, provide feedback for or change the medium through which messages happen.

D. Scheduling of resources – misunderstanding the complexities and/or mechanisms through which resources are defined and allocated.

E. Missing or incorrect information – through carelessness, misunderstanding, time delays, bureaucratic inertia, unavailable sources, and the like, information is not fully obtained.

F. Personality mismatch.

G. Unresolved similar past experience – incidents have occurred which have resulted in conflict, but they have not been resolved.

H. Resistance to Change – not being able to cope with changes in the organization, have engendered ill-feelings.

I. Uncertainty – fear of making a mistake, losing prestige or not conforming to group norms.

J. Not being prepared – the lack of effective planning and understanding of the situation before encountering the other side can lead to frustration and subsequent upset.

K. Pressures – personal or job-related problems that affect a person's attitude or demeanor.

L. Thwarted ability – frustration at personal inability to accomplish a goal.

M. Inappropriate conflict response – conflict avoidance, solving the wrong conflict or resolving poorly to the correct conflict.

G.15.c. Anatomy of a Conflict

Step One – Preconceived Notions

These are stated or unstated assumptions from either the government or the contractor about how others will behave.

Step Two – Past Experience

The preconceived notions are reinforced through everyday job experience, thus becoming expectations of how others will behave.

Step Three – Conflict "Spark"

The catalyst or incident which sets a conflict in motion can include any of the causes of conflict singularly or in combination.

Step Four – Conflict Inducement

Interaction occurs that enflames the spark. Attempt begins to thwart the activities.

Step Five – Conflict Mushroom

The tension and anxiety quickly become the focus of the interaction. Both parties argue and possibly break off communication.

Step Six – Stand-off

Both sides are in a state of mutual hostility.

G.15.d. Strategies for Resolving Conflicts

FIRST: Attempt to reach an understanding and settle concerns on your own. A way of doing so is as follows –

☐ One or both parties come to realization concerning tradeoffs between negative consequences of conflict versus positive gains of cooperation.

☐ This realization is subsequently communicated to the other side, either directly or indirectly.

☐ Response is to consider the message. Based on consideration, further response is to be willing to work together to discover a way out of conflict.

☐ Both sides brainstorm, analyze, and select alternatives to clear interaction of the conflict.

☐ Alternatives are implemented, monitored and feedback continues to prevent further occurrence.

SECOND: Use a third party to mediate the conflict by assisting both sides to find and agree on a solution(s).

THIRD: Use a third party to arbitrate conflict by giving an equitable settlement.

FOURTH: Use a third party to arbitrate conflict by imposing an equitable adjustment.

FIFTH: Use Alternate Dispute Resolution as a combination of strategies Two, Three and Four.

SIXTH: Seek resolution through litigation in the courts.

SEVENTH: Consensus decision is reached by a pre-agreed committee voting procedure.

EIGHTH: Give time to each party to consider separately resolution means.

NINTH: Positive reinforcement.

TENTH: Focus undivided attention on the issues at hand.

ELEVENTH: Prevent conflict from occurring through disagreeing diplomatically in order to reach agreement. That is:

A. Accept the other person's right to his or her opinion.

B. Listen carefully to understand fully what is said.

C. Clarify communication by requesting examples or summarizing.

D. Provide feedback by asking questions and giving previous insights that the receiver can act successfully upon it.

E. Acknowledge the other person's position without agreeing or disagreeing.

TWELFTH: Prevent more conflict by reaching consensus:

A. Ask if the other person is willing to listen to a different perspective.

B. Think through and plan your response so that it is listened to and understood.

C. Challenge without sounding negative or critical.

D. Reach toward consensus.

E. Identify agreement and next cooperative actions.

G.16. Termination

G.16.a. Circumstances Leading to Termination

In a delinquency or default situation, contractor performance is delayed, inadequate, or both. COTR must thoroughly understand the rights and responsibility of both the government and the contractor so that they will do nothing that might be considered prejudicial to either party. When unsatisfactory contract performance is identified, the COTR must notify the CO promptly so remedial steps can be taken. Silence on the part of the government could be interpreted by the contractor as government acceptance of performance, which may differ from that stated in the contract. Such situations could

adversely affect the government's right to withhold payments, terminate for default, or otherwise exercise certain rights under the contract.

Unsatisfactory performance can be considered in degrees. The government's actions can be oriented to correct the unsatisfactory performance or to protect the government's interest in the event of a contractor's default. Depending upon the CO's evaluation of the seriousness of the unsatisfactory performance he/she may:

By letter or through a meeting, bring the particular deficiency to the attention of the contractor and obtain a commitment for appropriate corrective action;

Extend the contract schedule if excusable delays in performance are involved;

Stop or suspend work in order to resolve problems before proceeding;

Withhold contract payments in cases where the contractor fails to comply with delivery or reporting provisions of the contract; or

Terminate the contract for default (all or part of the work).

After a complete review of the situation, the CO may send a notice of failure of performance to the contractor. This notice, which officially notifies the contractor of the delinquency, requires the contractor to inform the CO of the cause(s) of the delinquency so that a proper determination can be made concerning continuation or termination of the contract. Without express authority from the CO to the contrary, the COTR will have no contact with the contractor during this period. Any action that might encourage the contractor to continue performance may have the effect of waiving the government's rights under the contract.

G.16.b. Notify the Contracting Officer of Possible Contract Termination

The COTR will notify the CO when conditions indicate a contract may need to be terminated. The notification will include:

Clause(s) for the contract termination

Specific failure of the contractor and reasons provided by the contractor for such failure

Availability of supplies or services from other sources

Urgency of the need and the period of time that would be required for work by other sources as compared with the time in which completion could be obtained from the delinquent contractor

Degree of indispensability of the contractor, such as unique contractor capabilities

Impact the termination would have on availability of funds

Any other pertinent facts and circumstances

The COTR will suggest available alternatives to terminating a contract including pros and cons of each alternative. Alternatives may include:

Continuing the present contract, through such means as –

Permitting performance by the contractor, surety, or guarantor under a revised delivery schedule.

Permitting the contractor to subcontract with an acceptable third party or establish other business arrangements with such party.

A no-cost cancellation, such as –

☐ The government obtains the supply or service elsewhere.

☐ A no-cost settlement is acceptable to the contractor.

☐ Government property had not been furnished to the contractor.

☐ There are no outstanding payments, debts due the government, or other contractor obligations.

When performance monitoring leads to contract termination, the COTR will:

☐ Identify the event(s) that cause termination.

☐ Notify the CO of possible termination.

☐ Assist with termination proceedings.

☐ Identify the Event(s) that Cause Termination of a Contract

G.16.c. Triggering Events for Termination

The government might need to discontinue the contract and terminate for convenience when:

☐ There is no longer a need for the item or service under the contract.

☐ Funds are not available for continued contract performance.

☐ It is impossible for the contractor to perform as specified in the contract (specifications, acceptance, delivery, etc.).

☐ There has been a radical change in the requirement that goes beyond the contractor's expertise.

Triggering Events for Termination for Default (or Cause)

A termination for default (or cause) may be triggered by events that include:

The contractor has failed to perform as required by the contract.

A contractor response to the government cure or show-cause notice fails to show that the contract will be completed in accordance with its terms.

Terminations – Noncommercial Items (FAR Part 49)

Situations may arise when the work contracted for does not run to completion. Two standard contract clauses are designed to cover this eventuality: the "Termination for Convenience of the Government" clause and the "Default" clause. Both types of terminations can be either partial or complete (i.e., all or any part of the work can be subject to the termination). The portion of the contract that is not terminated must be completed by the contractor. The contractor has no contractual right to decide that the remaining work is insufficient to merit its attention and then opt not to continue with it. No matter what type of termination is issued, or the extent of the terminated portion of the work, the decision to terminate is a unilateral right of the government.

G.16.d. Termination for Convenience

The Termination for Convenience clause gives the government the right to cancel a contract when to do so is in the best interest of the government, notwithstanding the contractor's ability and readiness to perform. Termination for convenience requires that a financial settlement be made for the work that has been accomplished under the contract up to the effective date of the termination. Settlements may be reached by one, or a combination, of the following methods:

Negotiated agreement;

Determination of the CO; and

Costing out under invoices or vouchers (in the case of costs under cost-reimbursement contracts).

Following the termination, the government and the contractor may need to reach an agreement on an equitable settlement. The CO evaluates the contractor's settlement claim and establishes the government's position with respect to the various elements of cost or price included. A cost or price analysis must be performed and, in some cases, the contractor's

books and records must be audited. A memorandum documenting the negotiations must be placed in the contract file.

G.16.e. Termination for Default

The Termination for Default clause allows the government to terminate the contract when the contractor fails to make progress with the work or to perform any other contract requirements within the period provided by a "cure notice." The detailed conditions under which a contract may be terminated for default and the procedures for doing this are set forth in FAR Part 49. Once a CO has determined that it is necessary to invoke the Termination for Default clause, the COTR will have no further contact with the contractor unless specifically directed to do so by the CO.

Terminations – Commercial Items

Terminations for commercial items are for convenience or cause. Termination for convenience or cause is governed by FAR 52.212-4. FAR Part 49 does not apply.

G.16.f. Assist with Termination Proceedings

Termination proceedings may involve meetings, discussions, and conference calls between the contractor and the government. The COTR may be asked to assist in preparing for these proceedings by providing documentation supporting a termination decision and by coordinating the settlement document. A settlement document may include the following information:

- ☐ Reasons for termination
- ☐ General principles related to the settlement of any settlement proposal, including contractor obligations under the termination clause
- ☐ Extent of the termination, point at which work is stopped, and the status of any plans, drawings, and data that would have been delivered had the contract been completed
- ☐ Status of any continuing work
- ☐ Obligation of the contractor to terminate subcontracts and general principles to be followed in settling subcontractor settlement proposals
- ☐ Names of subcontractors involved and dates that the termination notices were issued to them
- ☐ Contractor review and settlement of subcontractor settlement proposals and the methods being used

☐ Arrangements for the transfer of title and delivery to the government of any material required by the government

Default Questionnaire

Default questions will assist the COTR in determining the issues that may prompt a contract termination. Once a circumstance has been identified, use the questions to validate the issue. Each checked item will be detailed in a report that the COTR submits to the CO recommending whether or not a contract will be terminated.

Circumstance	Validating Questions
Issues regarding terms and conditions of the contract and applicable laws and regulations	Was there a breach?
	Do the facts support a finding that the contractor has breached the contract?
	Does the breach, on its face, merit the severe remedy of default?
	Has the government met procedural requirements for proceeding with a default termination notice (e.g., issued any required notices)?
	Has the decision to default been made on the merits (i.e., free of outside influence)?
	Has the requiring activity proposed any change in the material requirement for the re-procurement (which would thereby undermine the government case for a default termination)?
Mitigating circumstances	Does the contractor have a good case that it is not at fault, based on such grounds as:
	Impossibility of performance?
	Excusable delay?
	Breach by the government?
	Does the contractor have a good case for contending that default would be arbitrary, capricious, or retaliatory?
Impact on the requirement if the contractor is terminated for default	Have alternatives to termination for default been considered?
	Is there any reasonable probability of meeting the requirement by continuing to work with the contractor? If so, what is the additional time and cost of continuing to work with the contractor?
	Is the deliverable available from other sources and, if yes, what would be the reprocurement lead-time?
	What is the urgency of the need for the deliverable?
	What is the potential for recovering the government's current investment in the contractor (e.g., any government guaranteed loan(s), unliquidated progress payments or advance payments) and reprocurement costs?
	Can the contractor afford to repay or would it go bankrupt?

Circumstance	Validating Questions
Impact on other requirements	Is the contractor essential to other critical work of the government?
	Will the contractor be able to meet other critical government requirements if terminated for default on the instant contract(s)?

H. Termination of COTR Duties

The CO will monitor the COTR's performance during the contract to ensure that the COTR's responsibilities and duties are being carried out. The CO may revoke the COTR appointment at any time. All terminations must be done in writing to the COTR, the COTR's supervisor and the contractor. Before terminating a COTR's appointment for cause, the CO will notify the COTR in writing and consider taking other corrective actions as appropriate. For example, the CO may counsel the COTR or amend the appointment letter to clarify or further limit the COTR's authority.

In cases of gross dereliction or significant ethics violations, the CO may revoke the COTR's authority immediately. In such cases, the COTR must identify all contracts that he or she is managing. The CO must notify the supervisor of the COTR of the incident and other actions to protect the government's interests. The supervisor will notify the COs of other contracts the person may be managing.

If a COTR must request relief from duties, the COTR will notify the CO in sufficient time to permit timely appointment of a successor COTR.

I. COTR Performance Debrief

Step Four of the COTR journey has focused on how to carry out successfully the acquisition process. For the COTR, the acquisition process boils down to this question: how can I best ensure that appropriate needs are discovered, defined, performed and monitored? In other parts of Step Four, various tools have been shown to strengthen the COTR's ability to "stay on top of what is going on!" To ensure that the COTR can walk the walk with all these techniques, tips and responsibilities, a clear sense of "performance stepping stones" needs be in place. That is, COTRs need plan (from the beginning of contract administration) to evaluate smaller facets of the contractor's effort in order to combine them into an initial overall performance picture. Feedback from this picture can then be given to the contractor. This dynamic will continue as larger facets of the effort are evaluated, for a more comprehensive picture to emerge. This "picture" is then further developed into its entirety as the overall performance of the contract is met. The following Figure illustrates this idea:

Evaluation Tools	Partial Performance	Milestone Performance	Full Performance
Effective Communication—are we on the same wavelength? ▪ Post Award Conference ▪ Frequent Interaction ▪ Meetings ▪ In-Process Review ▪ Clarification Sessions ▪ Performance Assessments ▪ Modification Interactions	Scope & Quality Timeliness & Cost Customer Relations	Project Segment(s) Done Match of Technical to Cost Progress Responsiveness Some Deliverables Provided Problem Solving Clarity	Outputs Synergies Viable Relationships Complete Performance Shown Increasing Customer Responsiveness Technical Hand Off Stakeholders' Satisfaction Lessons Learned & Applied Mission Element(s) Met Best Practices Bridge Future Efforts
Project Scrutiny- is the baseline being attained? ▪ Tasking Progress ▪ Deliverables ▪ Compliance ▪ Quality ▪ Cost ▪ Performance Issues			

This monitoring ability sends a clear message to the COTR that the contract or task order file is the blueprint to ensure that surveillance (from the small to the larger performance elements) will continue at higher levels until the complete performance is achieved and well documented.

J. What has gone well and means to improve

J.1. Causes of Past Failures

More important who works than what gets done

Get effort from contractor by describing what is wanted as you go

People working on the project are unclear about what the project is to accomplish

Relating project performance to project description not done

Incomplete, ambiguous and/or conflicting tasks are assigned

Lack of buy-in by users and developers

There are frequent delays while decisions are made

Projects are "fit" to an arbitrary schedule

People involved in the project are ill-informed of the project status

Contractor does effort mostly through government supervision

New, previously unknown requirements are added to the project

When the project is completed, no one is sure if the project is successful.

J.2. Enhancements to Project success

Define requirements in measurable, mission-related terms

Have performance indicators tied to the performance requirements

Have quality assurance schemes to discover match of performance to performance indicators

Have an effective PWS, use incentives where performance is critical to accomplishing the mission and/or have large $ buys

PWS preference is completion rather than term-type

Contract type is fixed price – full, partial, hybrid or redetermined

Best-value selection preferred

Contract must convey a clear, complete flow among performance requirements, performance indicators, quality assurance and performance incentives

Performance evaluation is based on effective performance measurements

STEP FIVE–INCREASING VIABLE **COTR** INFLUENCE

COTRs will actively seek the training they need and seek to be involved in the technical aspects of contract development to ensure that their technical expertise will be used in a timely and effective way. While agencies ultimately control training, COTRs will continually assess their current skills and request new or updated training when appropriate. COTRs are responsible for effectively performing their contracting duties, so they will take an active role in securing training, or at least making sure their supervisors are clearly informed of any training needs.

A. Career model

Training

A COTR has a significant role and responsibility for making sure contracts provide positive results. To effectively perform this role, a COTR needs adequate skills and knowledge. COTRs will also recognize that knowledge required for delegated duties under one contract may be insufficient for another. Continuous skills assessment, and initial and refresher training, are key to successfully performing COTR duties.

A.1.Training Assessment

Each COTR has different skills and knowledge, and delegated COTR duties may vary by contract. The CO and nominated COTR will jointly assess the COTR's knowledge, experience, and skills as related to that needed to effectively perform the delegated duties under the contract. This assessment highlights areas where the designated COTR may need specialized training (in addition to basic or refresher COTR training). The pre-designation interview will result in agreement on a training plan, if needed, for the COTR. Examples of areas for the CO and nominated COTR to review and discuss include:

☐ List of COTR duties

☐ COTR competencies

☐ Type, technical complexity, and size of the contract

Which duties will be delegated to the COTR

Prior training and experience

Physical location of the CO and COTR

The functions and duties (delegated by the CO) and performed by the COTR are described in Steps Two and Three.

The Federal Acquisition Institute has identified fundamental business and technical competencies that a person will have, to effectively perform COTR-related responsibilities (see CONTRACTING OFFICER'S TECHNICAL REPRESENTATIVE (COTR), TRAINING BLUEPRINT). The level of contract monitoring, and skill set needed by a COTR, is influenced by contract type, complexity, and size. Fixed-price contracts for commercial items will not require the same degree of oversight and monitoring as a cost-plus-incentive fee contract for systems development. Also, when the CO and COTR are not co-located, the COTR may need more in-depth knowledge of procurement policy and procedures than when the CO is onsite.

A.2. Training Courses

Training is available through government and commercial sources. The following is a representative list of training courses (but not all inclusive):

Government-sponsored Courses

Agency (e.g., FAA)

(04200) Contract Management for COR/COTRs

(04230) COR/COTR Refresher Training

(04202) Introduction to Source Selection

(04203) Fundamentals of the Federal Acquisition Regulation (FAR)

Defense Acquisition University

CLC 106, COR with a Mission Focus

CLE 003, Technical Review

CLC 004, Market Research

CLC 006, Contract Termination

CLC 007 Contract Source Selection

CLC 010, Proper Use of Non-DoD Contracts

CLC 012, Scheduling

CLC 013, Performance-Based Services

CLC 018, Contractual Incentives

CLM 011, Contracting for the Rest of Us

CLM 013, Work Breakdown Structure

CLM 014, IPT Management & Leadership

CLM 016, COR Course

CLM 024, Contracting Overview

Federal Acquisition Institute

CON 100, Shaping Smart Business Arrangements

CON 120, Mission Focused Contracting

CON 214, Business Decisions for Contracting

CON 215, Intermediate Contracting for Mission Support

CON 216, Legal Considerations in Contracting

CON 217, Cost Analysis and Negotiation Technique

CON 218, Advance Contracting for Mission Support

CON 353, Advanced Business Solutions

USDA Graduate School

Comprehensive COTR Workshop (ACQI7523D)

Contracting Basics for COTRs (ACQI7503D)

COTR Refresher (ACQI7513D)

Basic Contract Administration (ACQI7500D)

Contracting Basics for Administrative Personnel (ACQI7502D)

Introduction to Government Contracting (ACQI7501D)

Acquisition Planning (ACQI7505D)

Government Contract Law (ACQI8505D)

7 Steps to Performance-Based Acquisition and Performance-Based Management (ACQI9299D)

Department of Interior University

Contracting Officer's Representative Course (CORs/COTRs) Basic Certification

Commercially Available Courses

Government Training Inc. provides worldwide training and consulting to government agencies and contractors that support government in areas of business and financial management, acquisition and contracting, physical and cyber security, and grant writing. Our management team and instructors are seasoned executives with demonstrated experience in areas of federal, state, local and DoD needs and mandates. The following is a sample of professional development courses available from Government Training Inc. For details, go to www.GovernmentTrainingInc.com.

Advanced Contract Administration (3-day course)

Basic Contract Administration (4-day course)

COR COTR - Advanced (3-day course)

COR COTR - Refresher (3-day course)

COR COTR (5-day course)

Cost Estimating (3-day course)

Earned Value Management - Workshop for EVM (4½-day course)

Federal Appropriations Law - GAO - (Redbook) Managers Update (1-day course)

GAO's Principles of Federal Appropriations Law (4-day course)

Government Contract Law - For non-Lawyers (3-day course)

Intro to FAR (3-day course)

Market Research (2-day course)

Negotiating Techniques (3-day course)

Performance Accountability (2-day course)

Performance-based Contracting (3-day course)

Procurement Ethics (2-day course)

Project Management (3-day course)

Purchase Card Buys (2-day course)

R&D Contracting (3-day course)

Source Selection (3-day course)

Strategic Planning (3-day course)

Management Concepts Incorporated

Contracting Officer's Representative Course 1070

COR/COTR Refresher 1071

Contract Administration I 1022

Contract Administration II 1213

ESI International

The COTR Training Program

COTR Management of IT Service Contracts

COTR Refresher

Administration of Commercial Contracts

Advanced Contract Administration

Northwest Procurement Institute

COR/COTR Certification Course 1026

COR/COTR Inspector Workshop - Level I 1027

COR/COTR Refresher Seminar 1028

COR/COTR Workshop - Level II 1029

COR/COTR Seminar - Level III 1030

B. Continuous learning and professional development

The Office of Federal Procurement Policy has issued certification guidance for the federal COTR community (see Attachment Thirteen, http://www.governmenttraininginc. com/The-COTR-Handbook.asp). The information given in this section is based on the FAC-COTR guidance. Continuous learning points (CLP) are awarded for successful completion of continuous learning activities. Guidance follows on how training, professional activities, and education can be used to meet the CLP requirements for refresher training. All activities must be job-related.

B.1. Training

Awareness training - Periodically agencies conduct briefing sessions to acquaint the workforce with new or changed policy. Generally, no testing or assessment of knowledge gained is required.

Learning Modules and Training Courses - These may be formal or informal offerings from a recognized training organization, including in-house training course/sessions, which include some form of testing/assessment for knowledge gained.

Performing Self-Directed Study - An individual can keep current or enhance his or her capabilities through a self-directed study program agreed to by the supervisor.

Teaching - Employees are encouraged to share their knowledge and insights with others through teaching of courses or learning modules.

Mentoring - Helping others to learn and become more productive workers or managers benefits the agency and the individuals involved.

B.2. Professional Activities

Participating in Organization Management - Membership alone in a professional organization will not be considered as fulfilling continuous learning requirements, but participation in the organization leadership will. This includes holding elected/appointed positions, committee leadership roles, or running an activity for an organization that you are permitted to join under current ethics law and regulation. The employee must first ensure that participating in the management of an organization is allowed by the agency.

Attending/Speaking/Presenting at Professional Seminars/Symposia/Conferences - Employees can receive points for attending professional seminars or conferences that are job related. However, the supervisor needs to determine that the individual learned something meaningful from the experience. Because significant effort is involved in preparing and delivering presentations, credit will be given for each hour invested in the preparation and presentation.

Publishing - Writing articles related to acquisition for publication generally meets the criteria for continuous learning. Points will be awarded only in the year published. Compliance with agency publication policy is required.

Participating in Workshops - Points will be awarded for workshops with planned learning outcomes.

B.3. Education

Formal training - Continuing Education Units (CEUs) as a guide for assigning points for formal training programs that award CEUs. CEUs can be converted to points at 10 CLP points per CEU.

Formal academic programs - For formal academic programs offered by educational institutions, each semester hour is equal to one CEU. A three-hour credit course would be worth three CEUs and 30 CLP points, assuming that it is applicable to the acquisition function.

C. Certification Responsibilities

1. Office of Senior Procurement Executive (OSPE) is responsible for issuing written department-wide policy and procedures that include internal controls for certifications, initial and continuous learning requirements, approval processes, and other necessary support for operating administrations to implement this program.

2. Operating Administration Chief Acquisition Officers (OACAOs) are responsible for identifying COTRs within their organizations. OACAOs are also responsible for funding, implementing and administering this program within their organization, including written guidance detailing the COTR nomination, appointment, and termination process and, if necessary, any supplemental written guidance detailing internal approvals and selection of any specific training curriculum. OACAOs shall ensure the agency COTR database contains accurate and current information relative to the training, certification, and appointment of all COTRs.

3. Supervisors of COTRs are responsible for assessing and approving achievement of competencies under the FAC-COTR program. Supervisors shall, in conjunction with the employee, develop and update a career development plan (such as an Individual

Development Plan (IDP)) that shows completion of essential and departmental/agency-specific COTR training, and continuing learning requirements. Supervisors shall review and validate data entered by employees into the agency COTR database; and ensure the fulfillment of the continuous learning requirements are met for their employees.

4. Contracting Officers (COs) are responsible for validating that training and certification requirements have been met prior to appointing an individual as a COTR.

5. Contracting Officer's Technical Representatives (COTRs) are responsible for meeting the standards, including, entering their training data into the agency COTR database, updating

their existing COTR records in a timely manner and keeping these records current to reflect their certification status and continuous learning points.

6. Acquisition Career Manager (ACM) is responsible for reviewing and approving all applications for certification, monitoring continuous learning requirements and COTR database records, and providing acquisition career guidance.

C.1. Certification Policy

1. Certification will consist of competency-based core and assignment-specific training to achieve certification, and ongoing continuous learning to maintain certification.

2. All individuals appointed as a COTR to a contract after November 26, 2007, must be certified no later than six months from their date of appointment and maintain their skills currency through continuous learning.

3. Individuals who have been properly appointed by a CO and hold a COTR delegation (appointment) letter on an active contract on or prior to November 26, 2007, may be considered to have met the FAC-COTR requirements, provided the individual shows evidence of completion of COTR training based on previous agency COTR Training Standards or another federal agency training program that was previously determined by FAI to be in alignment with the FAC-COTR program, and submits the necessary documents to obtain certification.

4. Individuals who have served in the COTR role and participated in another federal agency's COTR training previous to the FAC-COTR program may seek recognition for fulfillment of the FAC-COTR requirements and demonstrate their proficiency by completing a fulfillment request form.

5. Individuals who hold a Federal Acquisition Certification in Contracting (FAC-C) Level I or Federal Acquisition Certification for Program/Project Managers (FAC-P/PM) Mid-Level/ Journeyman are considered to have met the FAC-COTR requirements but must still submit the necessary documents to obtain certification. (It will be noted that someone having their FAC-COTR does NOT automatically make them either FAC-C Level I or FAC-P/PM Mid-Level/Journeyman certified).

C.2. Certification training requirements

COTRs must have a minimum of 40 hours of training to achieve certification. The training can be obtained through the Federal Acquisition Institute (FAI), the Defense Acquisition University (DAU), commercially available sources, colleges or universities, or OA-specific courses. Twenty-two of the required 40 hours of training must cover the essential

COTR competencies listed in this section. The remaining 18 hours of the required 40 hours of training will consist of department-wide or OA specific courses, electives, and/or those identified by the COTR's supervisor in consultation with the CO, as necessary, for managing a particular contract. The training must be comprehensive and specific to COTR duties. A minimum of eight hours of the required 18 hours must include training on performance-based acquisition (PBA) or earned value management (EVM). Examples of additional training topics include service contracts, construction contracts, time and materials contracts, green purchasing, socioeconomic issues, etc.

C.3. Certification Maintenance Requirements

Certification is subject to renewal every two years. To maintain certification, a COTR must complete a minimum of 40 additional CLPs every two years in acquisition or COTR-related training, preferably through a refresher COTR training course.

A COTR will not repeat a course until after a minimum of four years has elapsed. Any acquisition-related bureau, federal, or commercial training course for which a certificate of training is issued is acceptable. Acceptable training methods include videotape, CD/DVD, classroom, and online courses.

C.4. Continuous Learning Points

The following is a summary chart of recommended points:

Creditable Activities	Point Credit (See Note)
Academic Courses	
Quarter Hour	10 per Quarter Hour
Semester Hour	10 per Semester Hour
Continuing Education Unit (CEU)	10 per CEU
Equivalency Exams	Same points as awarded for the course
Training Courses/Modules	
Defense Acquisition University (DAU) Courses/Modules	10 per CEU (see DAU catalog) or:
• Awareness Briefing/Training – no testing/assessment associated • Continuous Learning Modules – testing/assessment associated	.5 point per hour of instruction 1 point per hour of instruction
Other Functional Training	1 point per hour of instruction

Creditable Activities	Point Credit (See Note)
Equivalency Exams	Same points as awarded for the course
Professional Activities	
Professional Exam/License/Certificate	10-30 points
Teaching/Lecturing	2 points per hour; maximum of 20 points per year
Symposia/Conference Presentations	2 points per hour; maximum of 20 points per year
Workshop Participation	1 point per hour; maximum of 8 points per day and 20 points per year
Symposia/Conference Attendance	.5 point per hour; maximum of 4 points per day and 20 points per year
Publications	10 to 40 points

Note: All activities may earn points only in the year accomplished, awarded or published.

D. Broader application across organizational activities

Attachment Ten (http://www.governmenttraininginc.com/The-COTR-Handbook.asp) demonstrates the need to have COTR duties be a meaningful element in the performance evaluation of the COTR. Attachment Eleven (http://www.governmenttraininginc.com/The-COTR-Handbook.asp) sets forth a rating system to strengthen COTR career development. These two attachments stimulate the incorporation of COTR duties performed as an integral part of long-term government employee development. Having the experience of representing the technical community in effectively carrying out the acquisition process to have certain needs be met better can be a major factor toward successful career growth.

E. What has gone well and means to improve

In a recent report by the Merit Systems Protection Board, it was found that COTRs, agencies, and government-wide policymakers can all take steps to improve the ability of COTRs to do their jobs effectively. While COTR management is fundamentally an agency responsibility, there are actions that COTRs themselves can take to improve their own ability to manage contracts better. The bottom line here is a more proactive stance to ensure that COTRs are given comprehensive opportunities to perform professional duties successfully.

E.1. COTR Self Reliance

There are actions that COTRs can take to improve their ability to perform their contract duties effectively. First, COTRs should actively seek the training they need and seek to be involved in the technical aspects of contract development to ensure that their technical expertise will be used in a timely and effective way. They should continually assess their current skills and request new or updated training when appropriate. COTRs are responsible for effectively performing their contracting duties, so they need to take an active role in securing training, or at least making sure their supervisors are clearly informed of any training needs. When COTRs know of potential procurement activities, they should seek to be involved in the technical aspects throughout the contract lifecycle. It makes sense that a COTR can more effectively, and perhaps more efficiently, oversee a contract if he or she is involved in establishing the technical aspects of the contract.

E.2. Managing COTRs Better

Managing COTRs is a fundamental part of a successful contracting function. An agency can make any number of changes in the way it uses contracting regulations, in the way it structures contracts, and even in what it purchases with contracts. However, successful contract outcomes will always rely in large part on the federal employees involved in contracting work. Failure to consider COTR management as a critical component of the agency's contracting function will inevitably limit the agency's overall success in contracting. Agencies need to do better at complying with the regulatory requirements for managing COTRs and at managing COTRs day-to-day in the performance of their contracting work. Some of the specific recommendations are straightforward; others may be more challenging to implement. Some recommendations may require developing new policies and all recommendations require more consistent implementation and better oversight of policies. Several are as follows:

1. Formal delegation is a straightforward, meaningful action that agencies should implement on more than a pro forma basis.

2. Provide the right training to COTRs in the right way.

3. Strategically manage COTRs as a critical workforce. COTRs are critical to an agency's mission, especially if the agency relies significantly on contracting to accomplish its mission. To accomplish this, agencies need to establish effective mechanisms to identify and track COTRs and their competencies. Once COTRs are identified and located, agencies should compare their existing competencies with those the agency needs them to have, and hire or train COTRs to meet those needs.

4. Manage COTRs better on a day-to-day basis as they do their contracting work. Doing so means to improve the degree to which COTRs are selected and assigned based on established criteria.

5. Involve COTRs early in the contracting process. When COTRs are involved early, even as early as in the determination of a need to purchase a product or service, they can ensure that the contract is clear and accurate, especially with regard to the technical requirements. A well-developed contract is easier to oversee and more frequently yields deliverables that meet the needs of the government.

6. Involve COTRs in all the technical tasks of the contract. When COTRs more frequently perform all types of contracting tasks, both pre- and post-award, they reported better contract outcomes.

7. Ensure that COTRs have adequate time to perform their COTR work. This is because COTRs who believed they have enough time to perform their contracting work also reported better contract outcomes.

8. Rate COTRs on the performance of the contracting work. When agencies do rate COTRs on the performance of their contracting work, contract outcomes are better. However, to ensure adequate accountability, agencies must also do a better job at clearly conveying to COTRs what their responsibilities and authorities are for their contracting work.

9. Consider the other federal employees who affect the COTRs' work. The competence and ethical behavior of the other federal employees with whom COTRs work on contracting, as well as the support these other federal employees provide to COTRs, can affect how well COTRs perform their contracting work. COTRs who rated their supervisors, senior agency managers, COs, and other agency employees with whom they work on contracting issues as being competent, ethical, and supportive of the COTRs' work, also reported better contract outcomes. Agencies need to ensure they have the right people, with the right skills, to perform all parts of the contracting process.

Two issues involving the management of COTRs are worthy of attention by government-wide policymakers and practitioner groups to take advantage of economies of scale, help improve agencies' ability to manage COTRs, and help maintain the COTR workforce government-wide.

Establish a government-wide method to identify and track COTRs. Procurement policymakers have established a government-wide database for COTRs. However, it would be helpful to agencies and other policy makers to be able to identify COTRs within existing HR

databases. In this way, COTR data could be readily considered by agencies along with data for other critical occupational groups in the agency's strategic human capital planning activities.

Recognize the strategic value of the COTR workforce. However, given the enormous financial ramifications of the work performed by COTRs, specific guidance on managing COTRs has been issued by OFPP (see Attachment Thirteen, http://www.governmenttraininginc.com/The-COTR-Handbook.asp). The intent of this guidance is to send a clear message to agency HR and procurement staff that COTRs are critical to effective contract management.

Overall, contract success depends on all the involved participants described above doing everything they can to carry out their duties effectively and efficiently. While COTRs, agencies, or policymakers can produce benefits by acting on the recommendations within their control, the greatest improvements will require all parties to work together to improve the ability of COTRs to effectively perform their contracting duties.

E.3. Implications

E.3.a. Composite summary of lessons learned

The CO relies on the advice and support of many specialists from the technical, financial, legal, safety, security, small business and other disciplines that can make up the acquisition team. In a contract for services, the COTR is one of the most important and serves as the "eyes and ears" of the CO.

There are three central facets of a COTR's role: (1) a technical information conduit, (2) a contracting and regulatory liaison, and (3) a business partnership manager. The changing nature of acquisition work places significant importance on COTR activities. It is essential that all COTRs understand their responsibilities and are provided with appropriate support, training experiences, and developmental tools to effectively perform these responsibilities.

When COTRs are well-prepared and managed well, and thus can better perform their contracting-related work, all outcomes (quality, timeliness, completeness and cost) may be improved because they are related to each other. The reverse is also true. When COTRs are not able to perform their contracting work effectively, then all contract outcomes are likely to be affected in a negative way.

E.3.b. Ongoing COTR challenges and ways to meet them

It is imperative that the COTRs involved in the technical aspects of the contract have the expertise, authority, and managerial support to effectively perform their contracting duties on behalf of the government. COTRs who are formally delegated the authority to perform

contract work are more likely to be appointed as COTRs early in the contracting process, perform a variety of pre- and post-award contract tasks more frequently, and report more contract training. Formal delegation may actually work to improve contract outcomes through increasing these day-to-day activities.

Several COTR management issues are related to improved contract outcomes. When COTRs are formally delegated their authority to perform contracting work by the CO, they report better contract outcomes. In addition, when COTRs have sufficient (initial and repeated) training in contracting, technical, and general competencies presented in the right way, contract outcomes are better. While agencies ultimately control training, COTRs will continually assess their current skills and request new or updated training when appropriate. COTRs are responsible for effectively performing their contracting duties, so they will take an active role in securing training, or at least making sure their supervisors are clearly informed of any training needs.

When COTRs know of potential procurement activities, they will seek to be involved in the technical aspects of the contract beginning with contract development. Their involvement in pre-award technical activities is critical because a well-developed contract lays a foundation for more positive contracting outcomes. COTRs provide the technical expertise to ensure that the SOW's technical requirements are complete and accurate, to establish sound technical review criteria, and to appropriately establish the scope within which all parties to the contract must work. It makes sense that a COTR can more effectively and, perhaps more efficiently, oversee a contract if he or she is involved in establishing the technical aspects of the contract. And, as our data demonstrate, COTR involvement in the pre-award technical aspects of the contract is related to more positive contract outcomes.

E.3.c. Ongoing organizational challenges and ways to fulfill them

Managing COTRs is a fundamental part of a successful contracting function. An agency can make any number of changes in the way it uses contracting regulations, in the way it structures contracts, and even in what it purchases with contracts. However, successful contract outcomes will always rely in large part on the federal employees involved in contracting work. Failure to consider COTR management as a critical component of the agency's contracting function will inevitably limit the agency's overall success in contracting. Agencies need to do better at complying with the regulatory requirements for managing COTRs and at managing COTRs day-to-day in the performance of their contracting work.

Ensuring that the government meets the public's interests in achieving successful contract outcomes requires that agencies have enough federal employees with the right

skills and competencies to design and oversee contracts. Well-formulated contracting rules and procedures and superior COs alone are not sufficient to ensure that contracts meet the government's technical and programmatic needs. Agencies need to be able to compare what they need and what they have, and develop plans to alleviate any shortcomings in COTR numbers and competencies, particularly since one-third of COTRs will soon be eligible to retire.

Agencies must overcome the fundamental problem of identifying and locating their COTRs if they are to effectively manage them as a critical workforce. Agencies need to fulfill the regulatory aspects of managing COTRs to include formal delegation of authority, improved COTR training, and strategic management of the COTR workforce. Agencies also need to improve the day-to-day management of COTRs. These day-to-day issues include improving COTR selection and assignment, ensuring COTRs begin early in the contracting process, ensuring COTRs perform critical pre-award technical contracting tasks, ensuring COTRs have enough time to do their contracting work, rating COTRs on the performance of their contracting work, and considering the other federal employees who affect the COTRs' contracting work. Fulfilling the regulatory requirements for managing COTRs and managing COTRs more effectively day-to-day are significantly related to more positive contract outcomes. Agencies cannot take less expensive contracts lightly and assume they will more easily achieve the desired outcomes. It is important for agencies to develop good contracts and manage them well, no matter what the overall cost of the contract.

Changing the type of contract – for example, shifting to less-complex pricing arrangements – will not yield much improvement alone in contract outcomes. Improving contract outcomes also involves having the COTR exercise "leadership" to ensure and sustain that the right performance is occurring at the right time to have the contractor provide the expected outputs and outcomes.

Formal delegation is consistently related to more positive contract outcomes. Therefore, it is important that agencies view formal delegation of authority as more than a pro-forma requirement. Formal delegation of authority is required, and is one of the more definitive and straightforward steps an agency can take to promote the effectiveness and efficiency of the COTR workforce.

Increasing the amount of ongoing training in selected groups of topics could be an effective and efficient approach to COTR career development. Agencies will select the topics by assessing the competencies of their COTRs to ensure that training is provided in the most appropriate topic areas. Agencies can do more to ensure that COTRs are trained to perform their contracting work effectively and incentivized to do additional professional development.

Agencies must ensure that COTRs are trained, and that training is kept current to maximize the effect on positive contract outcomes.

E.3.d. Bridging these challenges through best practices

COTRs, agencies, and government-wide policymakers can all take steps to improve the ability of COTRs to do their jobs effectively.

E.3.d.i. Oversight

Well-developed and well-managed contracts need appropriate and transparent rules and procedures, plus a federal contracting workforce that can effectively apply them. In recent years, the government has modernized contracting rules and procedures to better support its ever-increasing use of technology and the shift to knowledge-based work, as well as to balance the need for both flexibility and accountability. Considerable effort has also been made to improve agencies' management of their COs, who carry out the business aspects of contracting. However, from a business perspective, even the best-managed contract is not successful if its deliverables fail to meet technical and program requirements. Despite this imperative, almost no work has been done to assess agencies' management of COTRs – the employees who provide the technical expertise necessary to clearly convey the government's technical requirements; to oversee the technical work of the contractor; and to ensure that the deliverables meet the technical requirements of the government. With the new Federal Acquisition Certification requirements (for both COTRs and program and project managers) this shortcoming will, of necessity, need to be corrected.

E.3.d.ii. Flexibility

Factors such as how an agency is organized, how much contracting it does, and how complex the items are that are being purchased, affect the complexity of the agency's contracting activities. Agencies have considerable flexibility in adjusting their contracting function to best suit their organization and specific contracting needs.

Small agencies that do little contracting may find it most effective and efficient to centralize the procurement function in one person within the office of administration. This one CO would then conduct procurement activities as requested by program managers throughout the agency.

Large agencies, or those that make many complex and costly purchases, may have a multi-person procurement office within their office of administration. Large agencies also may find it more effective and efficient to decentralize the procurement function along major program or bureau designations. Large agencies may also use "integrated project teams" (IPTs) composed of a number of professionals from the procurement, program, technical, finance, supply, and accounting fields who share responsibility for developing and managing a particular contract.

In either case, agencies can seek assistance from other agencies' contracting and technical staff to help better manage the contracting workload. Two examples are the National Business Center at the Department of Interior (www.nbc.gov) and GSA (www.gsaadvantage.gov). Also, inter-agency purchasing can help to obtain timely support and technical guidance for needs currently being fulfilled by other agencies.

E.3.d.iii. Management Outcomes

Historically, the COTR function was considered a small part of "other duties as assigned" to most technical staff. But, the need and impact of having a COTR function continues to increase. Today, it is viewed as an equivalent professional-development activity to any other career-enhancing situation. To continue to provide the right organizational message, opportunities and accomplishment feedback to the COTR community, agency acquisition management strategies need to be better focused to improved contract results. To that end, COTRs need to build a continuing improvement function as the "bridge" from one contracting situation to the other. This means doing an "after-action review" of the just-completed procurement effort to assess what went well, what can be done better and apply both of these findings to strengthening future buys. In turn, this information needs to be made available to all COTR colleagues through a "best practices database." COTRs about to engage in new procurement efforts can then use this database as one of the key information sources to carrying out the next acquisition activity.

Reference information (see www.acquisition.gov for additional documents and links)

RULES AND REGULATIONS THAT APPLY TO FEDERAL ACQUISITIONS

Title	Code of Federal Regulations (CFRs)	Coverage
Office of Federal Procurement Policy (OFPP) Policy Letters	N/A	Establishes government policies for acquiring supplies and services
The Federal Acquisition Regulation (FAR)	48 CFR Ch. I	Establishes government-wide rules and regulations that apply generally to the acquisition of supplies and services
FAR Supplements	48 CFR Chs. 2-53	Establishes regulations that apply generally to the acquisition of supplies and services within the issuing federal department or agency

RULES AND REGULATIONS THAT APPLY TO FEDERAL ACQUISITIONS

Title	Code of Federal Regulations (CFRs)	Coverage
Labor	29 CFR, 41 CFR Ch. 50	Establishes rules for socioeconomic objectives and related programs under its cognizance, such as the Fair Labor Standards Act
Small Business Administration (SBA)	13 CFR	Establishes rules for socioeconomic objectives and the related programs under its cognizance, such as the small business set-aside program
OMB Circular No. A-130	N/A	Management of Federal Information Resources

Attachment One

Glossary of Acquisition and Contract Terms

Acceptance

The act of an authorized representative of the government by which the government, for itself or as agent of another, assumes ownership of existing identified supplies or approves specific services rendered as partial or complete performance of a contract.

Acquisition

The acquiring by contract with appropriated funds of supplies or services (including construction) by and for the use of the federal government through purchase, lease, or barter, whether the supplies or services are already in existence or must be created, developed, demonstrated, and evaluated.

Administrative Contracting Officer (ACO)

A government contracting officer who handles the business administration of the contract, often at a location other than the one that made the contract.

Allocation

Funds made available for departmental subdivisions from the department allocation: a control point.

Allotment

Authorization by an agency head to an agency subdivision to incur obligations within a specified amount.

Apportionment

Statutory authorization to spend from VA for specified purposes.

Alternative Dispute Resolution (ADR)

Any procedure or combination of procedures voluntarily used to resolve issues in controversy without the need to resort to litigation. ADR procedures may include assisted settlement negotiations, conciliation, facilitation, mediation and fact-finding, mini-trials, and arbitration.

Best and Final Offer (BAFO)

An advanced step in the source selection process which permits an offeror to submit revised technical and cost proposals, after clarification and discussion of the offeror's original proposal(s)

Best Practices

Techniques that agencies may use to help detect and avoid problems in the acquisition, management, and administration of contracts; Best practices are practical techniques gained from practical experience that may be used to improve the procurement process.

Bid

A prospective contractor's (bidder's) reply to a sealed bid solicitation document (IFB); Needs only government acceptance to constitute a binding contract; Sealed Bid as identified under Title VII – Competition in Contract Act of 1984.

Bidders Conference

In sealed bid acquisitions, a meeting of prospective bidders arranged by the CO during the solicitation period to help solicited firms fully understand the government's requirement and to give them an opportunity to ask questions.

Bidders List (Solicitation Mailing List)

List of sources maintained by the procuring office from which bids (sealed bidding) or proposals or quotations may be solicited.

Bilateral Modification

Contract modifications accomplished by mutual action of the involved parties; bilateral modifications are used to make negotiated equitable adjustments resulting from change orders and to reflect other agreements of the parties modifying the terms of contracts.

Blanket Purchase Agreement (BPA)

A negotiated agreement between a contractor and the government, under which individual "calls" may be placed for a specified period of time and within a stipulated amount.

Breach of Contract

A breach occurs when the government or the contractor fails to fulfill the terms and conditions of the contract and there is no relief available under the terms of the contract or the contractor has committed fraud or a gross mistake amounting to fraud.

Budget

The federal administrative package presented to Congress each year by the president as the nation's basic financial planning document.

Change Order

Unilateral direction to a contractor to modify a contractual requirement within the scope of the contract, pursuant to the Changes clause contained in the contract.

Claim

A written demand by one of the contracting parties seeking payment of money for a certain amount, adjustment or interpretation of contract terms, or other relief arising under or relating to the contract; A claim can be "under a contract," meaning that it is directly connected to that contract, or "relating to a contract," meaning that it is indirectly associated with that contract.

Closeout

Administrative closeout of a contract after receiving evidence of its physical completion; when completed, the closeout procedures ensure that all administrative tasks were accomplished.

Commerce Business Daily (CBD)

Publication synopsizing proposed government acquisitions, sales, and contract awards. Also publishes information on subcontracting opportunities and advance notices of acquisitions.

Commitment

A firm administrative reservation of funds authorizing subsidiary activities to start action leading to an acquisition obligation.

Competitive Proposal

Technical and Cost Proposals for negotiated acquisitions as cited in Title VII – Competition in Contracting Act of 1984.

Competitive Range

In competitive negotiations, the group of firms, which have the potential to receive the contract award(s).

Comptroller General

Head of the General Accounting Office appointed for a 15-year term by the president (and confirmed by the Senate).

Constructive Change

A constructive change occurs when the CO, or a duly authorized representative, changes the contract without following the required legal procedures to formally modify a contract. A constructive change can result from either a specific action or a failure to act.

Contracts

All types of agreements and orders for obtaining supplies or services. Includes awards and notices of award; contracts of a fixed-price, cost, cost-plus-a-fee, or the issuance of job orders, task orders or task letters; letter contracts, purchase orders and supplemental agreements, to name a few.

Contract Financing Payment

A disbursement of monies to a contractor under a contract clause or other authorization prior to acceptance of supplies or services by the government; contract financing payments include: Advance payments; delivery payments; partial payments; progress payments based on percentage or stage of completion; payments under fixed-price construction contracts; payments under fixed price Architect-Engineer contracts; and interim payments on cost-type contracts. Contract financing payments do not include invoice payments or payments for partial deliveries. No interest penalty is paid to the contractor as a result of delayed contract financing payments.

Contracting

Sometimes referred to as procurement; Purchasing, renting, leasing or otherwise obtaining supplies or services. Includes description (but not determination) of supplies and services required, solicitation of sources, preparation and award of contracts, and all phases of contract administration.

Contract Modification

This describes any written change in the terms of the contract.

Contract Type

A reference to the pricing terms of the agreement between a buyer and a seller; may refer to the special nature of other important terms in the agreement.

Cost-reimbursement Contracts

In general, a category of contracts whose use is based on payment by the government to a contractor of allowable costs as prescribed by the contract. Normally, only "best efforts" of the

contractor are involved. Includes (i) cost, (ii) cost sharing, (iii) cost-plus-fixed-fee, (iv) cost-plus-incentive-fee, and (v) cost-plus-award-fee contracts.

Cost Overrun

The amount by which a contractor exceeds (i) the estimated cost, and/or (ii) the final limitation of his contract.

Data

All recorded information to be delivered under a contract. Technical data excludes management and financial data.

Delay

Failure to perform the service or provide the product during the performance or delivery period established in the contract. Delays can be either excusable or non-excusable.

Determination and Findings (D&F)

Written justification by a CO for such things as: (i) entering into contracts by negotiation, (ii) making advance payments in negotiated acquisitions, (iii) determining the type of contract to use.

Economic Price Adjustment Provision

Contractual provision for resetting the contract price when a contingency, such as a change in cost of labor or materials occurs: commonly used in gasoline or heating oil contracts.

Excusable Delays

Excusable delays are beyond the control and without the fault or negligence of a contractor or its subcontractors at any tier. A delay is excusable when the contractor can prove the delay is caused by government performance. When government actions cause the contractor to stop performing, the contractor may be excused from complying with the schedule.

Federal Acquisition Regulation (FAR)

The primary regulation for use by all federal executive agencies in the acquisition of supplies and services with appropriated funds.

Fee

An amount, in addition to allowable costs, paid to contractors having CPFF, CPAF, or CPIF contracts. In CPFF contracts, the fee is a fixed percentage (stated in dollar amount) of the initially estimated cost of the acquisition.

Fixed-price Contracts

In general, a category of contracts whose use is based on the establishment of a firm price to complete the required work; Includes (i) firm fixed-price, (ii) fixed-price with escalation, (iii) fixed-price redeterminable, and (iv) fixed-price with incentive provisions contracts.

Government Property

Refers to all property owned by, leased to, or otherwise acquired by the government under the terms of the contract.

Indefinite Delivery/Indefinite Quantity

Used when the precise quantity of items or specific time of delivery desired is not know. Usually will specify a maximum and/or minimum quantity; Such acquisition is effected via (i) a definite quantity contract, (ii) a requirement contract, or (iii) an indefinite quantity contract. May be established through either sealed bid or negotiated procedures.

Inspection

The act of examining and testing supplies or services including, when appropriate, raw materials, components, and intermediate assemblies to determine whether they conform to contract requirements.

Invitation for Bid (IFB)

A solicitation document used in sealed bidding acquisitions.

Joint Consolidated List for Debarred, Ineligible, and Suspended Contractors

A list of contractors who are partially or wholly prevented from award of government contracts, for various reasons.

Letter Contract

An interim type of contractual agreement, sometimes called a "Letter of Intent," authorizing the commencement of manufacturing of supplies or performance of services. Used in negotiated acquisitions only when a definitized fixed-price or cost-reimbursement contract cannot be written until a later date.

Material

Anything incorporated into, or consumed in, the manufacture of an end item; Includes raw and processed material, parts, components, assemblies and usable tools.

Modifications

Any formal revision of the terms of a contract, either within or outside the scope of the agreement: includes Change orders.

Negotiation

The method of acquisition used when one or more of the basic conditions incident to sealed bidding is absent and/or when there is justification under one or more of the seven exceptions provided by the Competition in Contracting Act of 1984.

Negotiation Authority

Authority to negotiate a contract under one of the seven statutory exceptions granted by Congress, rather than the sealed bid method of acquisition.

Nonconformance

This occurs when the contractor presents a deliverable to the government that does not conform to contract requirements. A nonconformance is evaluated to determine if it is a major (substantive) discrepancy or a minor one. Minor nonconformities may be accepted as is, when the savings realized by the contractor do not exceed the cost to the government for processing a formal modification.

Non-excusable Delays

When a contractor cannot justify a delay as being beyond their control; contractors are responsible for meeting contract delivery or performance schedule requirements and for all costs incurred in making up for the "lost time" associated with other than an excusable delay.

Obligation

A monetary liability of the government limited in amount of the legal liability of the government at the time of recording; must be supported by documentary evidence of the transaction involved.

Offer/Proposal/Quotation

A prospective contractor's response to the solicitation form (RFP/RFQ) used for a negotiated acquisition.

Office of Management and Budget

Basic financial control agency in the executive branch; Reports directly to the president.

Office of Small and Disadvantaged Business Utilization (OSDBU)

VA's program office with responsibility for advocating small business concerns; Serves as liaison office with SBA on certificates of competency.

Option

A contractual clause permitting an increase in the quantity of supplies beyond that originally stipulated or an extension in the time for which services on a time basis may be required.

Partial Payment

A method of payment based on acceptance of a particular part of contract performance.

Past-performance Information

Relevant information for future source selection decisions regarding contractor actions under previously awarded contracts.

Performance-based Payments

Contract financing payments that are not payment for accepted items and are not subject to the interest penalty provisions of prompt payment; these payments are fully recoverable in the same manner as progress payments, in the event the contractor defaults.

Performance Monitoring

Activities that a CO and other government personnel use to ensure supplies and/or services acquired under contracts conform to prescribed quality, quantity, and other requirements. Monitoring activities include, but are not limited to, inspection and acceptance, as well as quality assurance techniques.

Post-award Orientation

A planned, structured discussion between government and contractor that focuses on understanding the technical aspects of the contract, identifying and resolving oversights, preventing problems, averting misunderstandings, deciding how to solve problems that may occur later, and reaching agreement on common issues.

Pre-award Phase

That period of time that covers actions taken once the requirement has been identified and before the procurement is awarded to a contractor(s). The pre-award phase includes the pre-solicitation phase.

Pre-award Survey

Study of a prospective contractor's financial, organizational and operational capability, and managerial status, made prior to contract award, to determine his responsibility and eligibility for government acquisition.

Pre-solicitation Conference

A meeting held with potential contractors prior to a formal conference solicitation to discuss technical and other problems connected with a proposed acquisition. The conference is also used to elicit the interest of prospective contractors in pursuing the task.

Price and Fee Ceiling Price

The negotiated monetary limit – in a fixed-price-type contract – to the amount that the government is obligated to pay; Costs incurred beyond this point must be absorbed by the contractor.

Progress Payments

Payments made to the prime contractor during the life of a fixed-price-type contract on the basis of percentage of the total incurred cost or total direct labor and material cost. These are very common in construction contracts.

Progressing

The monitoring of contract performance by personnel of the government agency or of the prime contractor.

Prompt Payment

When the government pays the contractor prior to the invoice payment date; the prompt payment discount is an invoice payment reduction voluntarily offered to the government by the contractor for prompt payment and is made before the due date stated on the invoice.

Property

Personal property, and includes materials, special tooling, special test equipment, and agency-particular property.

Property Administrator

An authorized representative of the CO assigned to administer contract requirements and obligations relating to government property.

Property Control System

A contractor's method to establish, record, identify, and mark government property used while working under a government contract.

Protest

A formal action by an interested party, which challenges the government's ability to progress with a solicitation or contract performance until the challenger's issues are resolved.

Purchase Order

A contractual acquisition document used primarily to purchase supplies and non-personal services when the aggregate amount involved in any one transaction is relatively small (i.e., not exceeding $25,000).

Purchase Request

Document that describes the required supplies or services so that an acquisition can be initiated; some activities actually refer to the document by this title; others use different titles, such as Purchase Directive, etc. Requests must be placed on forms established by government acquisition regulations.

Qualified Products List

A list of products that are pre-tested in advance of actual acquisition to determine which suppliers can comply properly with specification requirements.

Quality Assurance

The function to determine whether a contractor has fulfilled contract obligations pertaining to quality and quantity, including inspections performed by the government.

Request for Proposal

A formal solicitation form; Acceptance by the government is legally binding upon the offeror.

Request for Quotation

An informal solicitation form commonly used in small purchase procedures. Acceptance is not legally binding upon the offeror.

Request for Technical Proposal

Solicitation document used in Step One of Two-Step Sealed Bidding; normally in letter form, it asks only for technical information. Price and cost breakdowns are solicited only during Step Two.

Requiring Activity

Any activity originating a request for supplies or services.

Sealed Bid

See Bid.

Small Business Administration

A federal agency created to foster and protect the interests of small business concerns.

Solicitation-award phase

The solicitation-award phase is that period of time covering actions taken once the CO has issued a solicitation and before award is made.

Statement of Work

Although varying widely in precise definition, the term generally covers that portion of a contract that describes the actual work to be done by means of specifications or other minimum requirements, quantities, performance dates, and a statement of requisite quality.

Stop Work Order

A written or oral order to stop work under a contract; if an oral stop work order is given to the contractor, it is only binding when confirmed in writing by the CO and signed by the contractor.

Subcontract

A contract between a buyer, usually the prime contractor, and a seller in which a significant part of the supplies or services being obtained is for eventual use in a government contract; The term frequently implies a substantial dollar value and/or non-standard specifications.

Supplemental Agreement

Bilateral written amendment to a contract by which the government and the contractor settle price and/or performance adjustments to the basic contract.

Technical Analysis

An analysis prepared by the COTR focusing on the technical aspects of a contractor's response to a government request. The technical analysis is used by the CO for making decisions to change the contract.

Technical Evaluation

Analysis of activities and functions that cause costs or other changes to occur within a contract; The analysis is a means for determining the impact of any delivery delays on the requirement, value of proposed consideration other than price or acceptability of a value, acceptability of a value-engineering proposal, or acceptability of substitute material. The technical evaluation indicates if the government will be harmed and include documentation supporting any modification request.

Termination for Convenience

Termination for convenience occurs when the government requires the contractor to discontinue performance because completion of the work is no longer in the government's best interest. The government has the right to terminate without cause and limit contractor recovery to costs incurred, profit on work done, and cost of preparing a termination settlement proposal. Recovery of anticipated profit is precluded. Termination for convenience will be considered when the requirement is no longer needed, the quantity needed has been reduced, or when there has been a radical change in the requirement beyond the contractor's expertise.

Termination for Default (or Cause)

Termination for default (or cause) occurs when the contractor fails to perform in accordance with the contract. The government will terminate a contract either for default or cause, when it is determined that to do so would be in its best interest. The word "cause" relates to a termination action and is normally used in the commercial marketplace. The word "default" is traditionally used in government contracting. A contract is terminated for default (or cause) when there is no other alternative for obtaining performance, given contractor problems and deficiencies, and the government has a sustainable case for default.

Time and Materials/Labor Hour Contract

Negotiated contracts based on specified fixed hourly rates to complete a given task; Used only in situations where it is not possible at the outset to estimate the extent or duration of the work involved or to anticipate cost with any substantial accuracy; least desirable contract type for the government.

Termination

The canceling of all or part of a prime contract or a subcontract prior to its completion through performance; It may be for the convenience of the government, or default of the contractor due to non-performance.

Unilateral Modification

Unilateral modifications are changes to a contract signed only by the government CO. This type of modification is used to make administrative changes that are minor in nature and do not materially affect contract performance, issue change orders that are authorized by the Changes clause, make changes authorized by other contract clauses, such as stop-work, termination, or option clauses, or exercise of an option.

Unsolicited Proposal

Innovative ideas, either written or oral, made to the government by organizations or individuals acting in their own behalf. Such proposals have no relation to a particular solicitation used by the government as a basis for acquisition.

Value Engineering

An incentive plan used to encourage cost reduction and cost avoidance by providing contractors with profit incentives for developing changes that will reduce overall cost while maintaining accomplishment of the required function of the item or service being acquired.

Attachments 2-11 are at the reference section of the web site at www.GovernmentTrainingInc. com.